THIRD EDITION

Kubernetes: Up and Running
Dive into the Future of Infrastructure

Brendan Burns, Joe Beda, Kelsey Hightower,
and Lachlan Evenson

Beijing · Boston · Farnham · Sebastopol · Tokyo

Kubernetes: Up and Running

by Brendan Burns, Joe Beda, Kelsey Hightower, and Lachlan Evenson

Printed in the United States of America.

Published by O'Reilly Media, Inc., 1005 Gravenstein Highway North, Sebastopol, CA 95472.

O'Reilly books may be purchased for educational, business, or sales promotional use. Online editions are also available for most titles (*http://oreilly.com*). For more information, contact our corporate/institutional sales department: 800-998-9938 or *corporate@oreilly.com*.

Acquisition Editor: John Devins
Development Editor: Sarah Gray
Production Editor: Katherine Tozer
Copyeditor: Piper Editorial Consulting, LLC
Proofreader: Penelope Perkins

Indexer: Ellen Troutman-Zaig
Interior Designer: David Futato
Cover Designer: Karen Montgomery
Illustrator: Kate Dullea

September 2017: First Edition
August 2019: Second Edition
August 2022: Third Edition

Revision History for the Third Edition
2022-08-02: First Release

See *http://oreilly.com/catalog/errata.csp?isbn=9781098110208* for release details.

978-1-098-11020-8

[LSI]

Table of Contents

Preface

Kubernetes would like to thank every sysadmin who has woken up at 3 a.m. to restart a process. Every developer who pushed code to production only to find that it didn't run like it did on their laptop. Every systems architect who mistakenly pointed a load test at the production server because of a leftover hostname that they hadn't updated. It was the pain, the weird hours, and the weird errors that inspired the development of Kubernetes. In a single sentence: Kubernetes intends to radically simplify the task of building, deploying, and maintaining distributed systems. It has been inspired by decades of real-world experience building reliable systems, and it has been designed from the ground up to make that experience if not euphoric, at least pleasant. We hope you enjoy the book!

Who Should Read This Book

Whether you are new to distributed systems or have been deploying cloud native systems for years, containers and Kubernetes can help you achieve new levels of velocity, agility, reliability, and efficiency. This book describes the Kubernetes cluster orchestrator and how its tools and APIs can be used to improve the development, delivery, security, and maintenance of distributed applications. Though no previous experience with Kubernetes is assumed, to make maximal use of the book, you should be comfortable building and deploying server-based applications. Familiarity with concepts like load balancers and network storage will be useful, though not required. Likewise, experience with Linux, Linux containers, and Docker, though not essential, will help you make the most of this book.

Why We Wrote This Book

We have been involved with Kubernetes since its very beginnings. It has been truly remarkable to watch it transform from a curiosity largely used in experiments to a crucial production-grade infrastructure that powers large-scale production applications in varied fields, from machine learning to online services. As this transition occurred, it became increasingly clear that a book that captured both how to use the core concepts in Kubernetes and the motivations behind the development of those concepts would be an important contribution to the state of cloud native application development. We hope that in reading this book, you not only learn how to build reliable, scalable applications on top of Kubernetes but also receive insight into the core challenges of distributed systems that led to its development.

Why We Updated This Book

The Kubernetes ecosystem has continued to grow and evolve since the first and second editions of this book. There have been many Kubernetes releases, and many more tools and patterns for using Kubernetes have become de facto standards. In the third edition, we focused on the addition of topics that have grown in interest in the Kubernetes ecosystem including security, accessing Kubernetes from programming languages, as well as multicluster application deployments. We also updated all of the existing chapters to reflect the changes and evolution in Kubernetes since the first and second editions. We fully expect to revise this book again in a few years (and look forward to doing so) as Kubernetes continues to evolve.

A Word on Cloud Native Applications Today

From the first programming languages, to object-oriented programming, to the development of virtualization and cloud infrastructure, the history of computer science is a history of the development of abstractions that hide complexity and empower you to build ever more sophisticated applications. Despite this, the development of reliable, scalable applications is still dramatically more challenging than it ought to be. In recent years, containers and container orchestration APIs like Kubernetes have proven to be an important abstraction that radically simplifies the development of reliable, scalable distributed systems. Containers and orchestrators enable developers to build and deploy applications with a speed, agility, and reliability that would have seemed like science fiction only a few years ago.

Navigating This Book

This book is organized as follows. Chapter 1 outlines the high-level benefits of Kubernetes without diving too deeply into the details. If you are new to Kubernetes, this is a great place to start to understand why you should read the rest of the book.

Chapter 2 provides a detailed introduction to containers and containerized application development. If you've never really played around with Docker before, this chapter will be a useful introduction. If you are already a Docker expert, it will likely be mostly review.

Chapter 3 covers how to deploy Kubernetes. While most of this book focuses on how to *use* Kubernetes, you need to get a cluster up and running before you start using it. Although running a cluster for production is outside the scope of this book, this chapter presents a couple of easy ways to create a cluster so that you can understand how to use Kubernetes. Chapter 4 covers a selection of common commands used to interact with a Kubernetes cluster.

Starting with Chapter 5, we dive into the details of deploying an application using Kubernetes. We cover Pods (Chapter 5), labels and annotations (Chapter 6), services (Chapter 7), Ingress (Chapter 8), and ReplicaSets (Chapter 9). These form the core basics of what you need to deploy your service in Kubernetes. We then cover deployments (Chapter 10), which tie together the life cycle of a complete application.

After those chapters, we cover some more specialized objects in Kubernetes: DaemonSets (Chapter 11), Jobs (Chapter 12), and ConfigMaps and Secrets (Chapter 13). While these chapters are essential for many production applications, if you are just learning Kubernetes, you can skip them and return to them later, after you gain more experience and expertise.

Next we introduce role-based access control (Chapter 14) and cover service meshes (Chapter 15) and integrating storage (Chapter 16) into Kubernetes. We discuss extending Kubernetes (Chapter 17) and accessing Kubernetes from programming languages (Chapter 18). We then focus on securing Pods (Chapter 19) along with Kubernetes policy and governance (Chapter 20).

Finally, we conclude with some examples of how to develop and deploy multicluster applications (Chapter 21) and a discussion of how to organize your applications in source control (Chapter 22).

Online Resources

You will want to install Docker (*https://docker.com*). You likely will also want to familiarize yourself with the Docker documentation if you have not already done so.

Likewise, you will want to install the `kubectl` command-line tool (*https://kubernetes.io*). You may also want to join the Kubernetes Slack channel (*http://slack.kubernetes.io*), where you will find a large community of users who are willing to talk and answer questions at nearly any hour of the day.

Finally, as you grow more advanced, you may want to engage with the open source Kubernetes repository on GitHub (*https://github.com/kubernetes/kubernetes*).

Conventions Used in This Book

The following typographical conventions are used in this book:

Italic
> Indicates new terms, URLs, email addresses, filenames, and file extensions.

`Constant width`
> Used for program listings, as well as within paragraphs to refer to program elements such as variable or function names, databases, data types, environment variables, statements, and keywords.

`Constant width bold`
> Shows commands or other text that should be typed literally by the user.

`Constant width italic`
> Shows text that should be replaced with user-supplied values or by values determined by context.

 This icon signifies a tip, suggestion, or general note.

 This icon indicates a warning or caution.

Using Code Examples

Supplemental material (code examples, exercises, etc.) is available for download at *https://github.com/kubernetes-up-and-running/examples*.

This book is here to help you get your job done. In general, if example code is offered with this book, you may use it in your programs and documentation. You do not need to contact us for permission unless you're reproducing a significant portion of the code. For example, writing a program that uses several chunks of code from this book does not require permission. Selling or distributing a CD-ROM of examples from O'Reilly books does require permission. Answering a question by citing this book and quoting example code does not require permission. Incorporating a significant amount of example code from this book into your product's documentation does require permission.

We appreciate, but do not require, attribution. An attribution usually includes the title, author, publisher, and ISBN. For example: "*Kubernetes: Up and Running*, 3rd edition, by Brendan Burns, Joe Beda, Kelsey Hightower, and Lachlan Evenson (O'Reilly). Copyright 2019 Brendan Burns, Joe Beda, Kelsey Hightower, and Lachlan Evenson, 978-1-098-11020-8."

If you feel your use of code examples falls outside fair use or the permission given above, feel free to contact us at *permissions@oreilly.com*.

O'Reilly Online Learning

 For almost 40 years, *O'Reilly Media* has provided technology and business training, knowledge, and insight to help companies succeed.

Our unique network of experts and innovators share their knowledge and expertise through books, articles, conferences, and our online learning platform. O'Reilly's online learning platform gives you on-demand access to live training courses, in-depth learning paths, interactive coding environments, and a vast collection of text and video from O'Reilly and 200+ other publishers. For more information, please visit *http://oreilly.com*.

How to Contact Us

Please address comments and questions concerning this book to the publisher:

O'Reilly Media, Inc.
1005 Gravenstein Highway North
Sebastopol, CA 95472
800-998-9938 (in the United States or Canada)
707-829-0515 (international or local)
707-829-0104 (fax)

We have a web page for this book, where we list errata, examples, and any additional information. You can access this page at *https://oreil.ly/kubernetesUR3*.

Email *bookquestions@oreilly.com* to comment or ask technical questions about this book.

For more information about our books, courses, conferences, and news, see our website at *http://www.oreilly.com*.

Find us on LinkedIn: *https://linkedin.com/company/oreilly-media*.

Follow us on Twitter: *http://twitter.com/oreillymedia*.

Watch us on YouTube: *http://www.youtube.com/oreillymedia*.

Acknowledgments

We would like to acknowledge everyone who helped us develop this book. This includes our editors, Virginia Wilson and Sarah Grey, and all of the great folks at O'Reilly, as well as the technical reviewers who provided tremendous feedback that significantly improved the book. Finally, we would like to thank all of our first edition and second edition readers who took the time to report errata that were found and fixed in this third edition. Thank you all! We're very grateful.

## CHAPTER 1

Introduction

Kubernetes is an open source orchestrator for deploying containerized applications. It was originally developed by Google, inspired by a decade of experience deploying scalable, reliable systems in containers via application-oriented APIs.[1]

Since its introduction in 2014, Kubernetes has grown to be one of the largest and most popular open source projects in the world. It has become the standard API for building cloud native applications, present in nearly every public cloud. Kubernetes is a proven infrastructure for distributed systems that is suitable for cloud native developers of all scales, from a cluster of Raspberry Pi computers to a datacenter full of the latest machines. It provides the software necessary to successfully build and deploy reliable, scalable distributed systems.

You may be wondering what we mean when we say "reliable, scalable distributed systems." More and more services are delivered over the network via APIs. These APIs are often delivered by a *distributed system*, the various pieces that implement the API running on different machines, connected via the network and coordinating their actions via network communication. Because we increasingly rely on these APIs for all aspects of our daily lives (e.g., finding directions to the nearest hospital), these systems must be highly *reliable*. They cannot fail, even if a part of the system crashes or otherwise stops working. Likewise, they must maintain *availability* even during software rollouts or other maintenance events. Finally, because more and more of the world is coming online and using such services, they must be highly *scalable* so that they can grow their capacity to keep up with ever-increasing usage without radical redesign of the distributed system that implements the services. In many

---

1 Brendan Burns et al., "Borg, Omega, and Kubernetes: Lessons Learned from Three Container-Management Systems over a Decade," *ACM Queue* 14 (2016): 70–93, available at *https://oreil.ly/ltE1B*.

cases this also means growing (and shrinking) the capacity automatically so that your application can be maximally efficient.

Depending on when and why you have come to hold this book in your hands, you may have varying degrees of experience with containers, distributed systems, and Kubernetes. You may be planning on building your application on top of public cloud infrastructure, in private data centers, or in some hybrid environment. Regardless of your experience, this book should enable you to make the most of Kubernetes.

There are many reasons people come to use containers and container APIs like Kubernetes, but we believe they can all be traced back to one of these benefits:

- Development velocity
- Scaling (of both software and teams)
- Abstracting your infrastructure
- Efficiency
- Cloud native ecosystem

In the following sections, we describe how Kubernetes can help provide each of these features.

Velocity

Velocity is the key component in nearly all software development today. The software industry has evolved from shipping products as boxed CDs or DVDs to software that is delivered over the network via web-based services that are updated hourly. This changing landscape means that the difference between you and your competitors is often the speed with which you can develop and deploy new components and features, or the speed with which you can respond to innovations developed by others.

It is important to note, however, that velocity is not defined in terms of simply raw speed. While your users are always looking for iterative improvements, they are more interested in a highly reliable service. Once upon a time, it was OK for a service to be down for maintenance at midnight every night. But today, all users expect constant uptime, even if the software they are running is changing constantly.

Consequently, velocity is measured not in terms of the raw number of features you can ship per hour or day, but rather in terms of the number of things you can ship while maintaining a highly available service.

In this way, containers and Kubernetes can provide the tools that you need to move quickly, while staying available. The core concepts that enable this are:

- Immutability
- Declarative configuration
- Online self-healing systems
- Shared reusable libraries and tools

These ideas all interrelate to radically improve the speed with which you can reliably deploy new software.

The Value of Immutability

Containers and Kubernetes encourage developers to build distributed systems that adhere to the principles of immutable infrastructure. With *immutable* infrastructure, once an artifact is created in the system, it does not change via user modifications.

Traditionally, computers and software systems have been treated as *mutable* infrastructure. With mutable infrastructure, changes are applied as incremental updates to an existing system. These updates can occur all at once, or spread out across a long period of time. A system upgrade via the `apt-get update` tool is a good example of an update to a mutable system. Running `apt` sequentially downloads any updated binaries, copies them on top of older binaries, and makes incremental updates to configuration files. With a mutable system, the current state of the infrastructure is not represented as a single artifact, but rather as an accumulation of incremental updates and changes over time. On many systems, these incremental updates come not just from system upgrades, but operator modifications as well. Furthermore, in any system run by a large team, it is highly likely that these changes will have been performed by many different people and, in many cases, will not have been recorded anywhere.

In contrast, in an immutable system, rather than a series of incremental updates and changes, an entirely new, complete image is built, where the update simply replaces the entire image with the newer image in a single operation. There are no incremental changes. As you can imagine, this is a significant shift from the more traditional world of configuration management.

To make this more concrete in the world of containers, consider two different ways to upgrade your software:

- You can log in to a container, run a command to download your new software, kill the old server, and start the new one.
- You can build a new container image, push it to a container registry, kill the existing container, and start a new one.

At first blush, these two approaches might seem largely indistinguishable. So what is it about the act of building a new container that improves reliability?

The key differentiation is the artifact that you create, and the record of how you created it. These records make it easy to understand exactly the differences in some new version and, if something goes wrong, to determine what has changed and how to fix it.

Additionally, building a new image rather than modifying an existing one means the old image is still around, and can quickly be used for a rollback if an error occurs. In contrast, once you copy your new binary over an existing binary, such a rollback is nearly impossible.

Immutable container images are at the core of everything that you will build in Kubernetes. It is possible to imperatively change running containers, but this is an antipattern to be used only in extreme cases where there are no other options (e.g., if it is the only way to temporarily repair a mission-critical production system). And even then, the changes must also be recorded through a declarative configuration update at some later time, after the fire is out.

Declarative Configuration

Immutability extends beyond containers running in your cluster to the way you describe your application to Kubernetes. Everything in Kubernetes is a *declarative configuration object* that represents the desired state of the system. It is the job of Kubernetes to ensure that the actual state of the world matches this desired state.

Much like mutable versus immutable infrastructure, declarative configuration is an alternative to *imperative* configuration, where the state of the world is defined by the execution of a series of instructions rather than a declaration of the desired state of the world. While imperative commands define actions, declarative configurations define state.

To understand these two approaches, consider the task of producing three replicas of a piece of software. With an imperative approach, the configuration would say "run A, run B, and run C." The corresponding declarative configuration would be "replicas equals three."

Because it describes the state of the world, declarative configuration does not have to be executed to be understood. Its impact is concretely declared. Since the effects of declarative configuration can be understood before they are executed, declarative configuration is far less error-prone. Further, the traditional tools of software development, such as source control, code review, and unit testing, can be used in declarative configuration in ways that are impossible for imperative instructions. The idea of storing declarative configuration in source control is often referred to as "infrastructure as code."

Lately the idea of GitOps has begun to formalize the practice of infrastructure as code with source control as the source of truth. When you adopt GitOps, changes to production are made entirely via pushes to a Git repository, which are then reflected into your cluster via automation. Indeed, your production Kubernetes cluster is viewed as effectively a read-only environment. Additionally, GitOps is being increasingly integrated into cloud-provided Kubernetes services as the easiest way to declaratively manage your cloud native infrastructure.

The combination of declarative state stored in a version control system and the ability of Kubernetes to make reality match this declarative state makes rollback of a change trivially easy. It is simply restating the previous declarative state of the system. This is usually impossible with imperative systems, because although the imperative instructions describe how to get you from point A to point B, they rarely include the reverse instructions that can get you back.

Self-Healing Systems

Kubernetes is an online, self-healing system. When it receives a desired state configuration, it does not simply take a set of actions to make the current state match the desired state a single time. It *continuously* takes actions to ensure that the current state matches the desired state. This means that not only will Kubernetes initialize your system, but it will guard it against any failures or perturbations that might destabilize the system and affect reliability.

A more traditional operator repair involves a manual series of mitigation steps, or human intervention, performed in response to some sort of alert. Imperative repair like this is more expensive (since it generally requires an on-call operator to be available to enact the repair). It is also generally slower, since a human must often wake up and log in to respond. Furthermore, it is less reliable because the imperative series of repair operations suffers from all of the problems of imperative management described in the previous section. Self-healing systems like Kubernetes both reduce the burden on operators and improve the overall reliability of the system by performing reliable repairs more quickly.

As a concrete example of this self-healing behavior, if you assert a desired state of three replicas to Kubernetes, it does not just create three replicas—it continuously ensures that there are exactly three replicas. If you manually create a fourth replica, Kubernetes will destroy one to bring the number back to three. If you manually destroy a replica, Kubernetes will create one to again return you to the desired state.

Online self-healing systems improve developer velocity because the time and energy you might otherwise have spent on operations and maintenance can instead be spent on developing and testing new features.

In a more advanced form of self-healing, there has been significant recent work in the *operator* paradigm for Kubernetes. With operators, more advanced logic needed to maintain, scale, and heal a specific piece of software (MySQL, for example) is encoded into an operator application that runs as a container in the cluster. The code in the operator is responsible for more targeted and advanced health detection and healing than can be achieved via Kubernetes's generic self-healing. Often this is packaged up as "operators," which are discussed in Chapter 17.

Scaling Your Service and Your Teams

As your product grows, it's inevitable that you will need to scale both your software and the teams that develop it. Fortunately, Kubernetes can help with both of these goals. Kubernetes achieves scalability by favoring *decoupled* architectures.

Decoupling

In a decoupled architecture, each component is separated from other components by defined APIs and service load balancers. APIs and load balancers isolate each piece of the system from the others. APIs provide a buffer between implementer and consumer, and load balancers provide a buffer between running instances of each service.

Decoupling components via load balancers makes it easy to scale the programs that make up your service, because increasing the size (and therefore the capacity) of the program can be done without adjusting or reconfiguring any of the other layers of your service.

Decoupling servers via APIs makes it easier to scale the development teams because each team can focus on a single, smaller *microservice* with a comprehensible surface area. Crisp APIs between microservices limit the amount of cross-team communication overhead required to build and deploy software. This communication overhead is often the major restricting factor when scaling teams.

Easy Scaling for Applications and Clusters

Concretely, when you need to scale your service, the immutable, declarative nature of Kubernetes makes this scaling trivial to implement. Because your containers are immutable, and the number of replicas is merely a number in a declarative config, scaling your service upward is simply a matter of changing a number in a configuration file, asserting this new declarative state to Kubernetes, and letting it take care of the rest. Alternatively, you can set up autoscaling and let Kubernetes do it for you.

Of course, that sort of scaling assumes that there are resources available in your cluster to consume. Sometimes you actually need to scale up the cluster itself. Again, Kubernetes makes this task easier. Because many machines in a cluster are entirely identical to other machines in that set and the applications themselves are decoupled from the details of the machine by containers, adding additional resources to the cluster is simply a matter of imaging a new machine of the same class and joining it into the cluster. This can be accomplished via a few simple commands or via a prebaked machine image.

One of the challenges of scaling machine resources is predicting their use. If you are running on physical infrastructure, the time to obtain a new machine is measured in days or weeks. On both physical and cloud infrastructures, predicting future costs is difficult because it is hard to predict the growth and scaling needs of specific applications.

Kubernetes can simplify forecasting future compute costs. To understand why this is true, consider scaling up three teams: A, B, and C. Historically you have seen that each team's growth is highly variable and thus hard to predict. If you are provisioning individual machines for each service, you have no choice but to forecast based on the maximum expected growth for each service, since machines dedicated to one team cannot be used for another team. If, instead, you use Kubernetes to decouple the teams from the specific machines they are using, you can forecast growth based on the aggregate growth of all three services. Combining three variable growth rates into a single growth rate reduces statistical noise and produces a more reliable forecast of expected growth. Furthermore, decoupling the teams from specific machines means that teams can share fractional parts of one another's machines, reducing even further the overheads associated with forecasting growth of computing resources.

Finally, Kubernetes makes it possible to achieve automatic scaling (both up and down) of resources. Especially in a cloud environment where new machines can be created via APIs, combining Kubernetes with autoscaling for both the applications and the clusters themselves means that you can always rightsize your costs for the current load.

Scaling Development Teams with Microservices

As noted in a variety of research, the ideal team size is the "two-pizza team," or roughly six to eight people. This group size often results in good knowledge sharing, fast decision making, and a common sense of purpose. Larger teams tend to suffer from issues of hierarchy, poor visibility, and infighting, which hinder agility and success.

However, many projects require significantly more resources to be successful and achieve their goals. Consequently, there is a tension between the ideal team size for agility and the necessary team size for the product's end goals.

The common solution to this tension has been the development of decoupled, service-oriented teams that each build a single microservice. Each small team is responsible for the design and delivery of a service that is consumed by other small teams. The aggregation of all of these services ultimately provides the implementation of the overall product's surface area.

Kubernetes provides numerous abstractions and APIs that make it easier to build these decoupled microservice architectures:

- *Pods*, or groups of containers, can group together container images developed by different teams into a single deployable unit.
- Kubernetes *services* provide load balancing, naming, and discovery to isolate one microservice from another.
- *Namespaces* provide isolation and access control, so that each microservice can control the degree to which other services interact with it.
- *Ingress* objects provide an easy-to-use frontend that can combine multiple microservices into a single externalized API surface area.

Finally, decoupling the application container image and machine means that different microservices can colocate on the same machine without interfering with one another, reducing the overhead and cost of microservice architectures. The health-checking and rollout features of Kubernetes guarantee a consistent approach to application rollout and reliability, which ensures that a proliferation of microservice teams does not also result in a proliferation of different approaches to service production life cycle and operations.

Separation of Concerns for Consistency and Scaling

In addition to the consistency that Kubernetes brings to operations, the decoupling and separation of concerns produced by the Kubernetes stack lead to significantly greater consistency for the lower levels of your infrastructure. This enables you to scale infrastructure operations to manage many machines with a single small, focused team. We have talked at length about the decoupling of application container and machine/operating system (OS), but an important aspect of this decoupling is that the container orchestration API becomes a crisp contract that separates the responsibilities of the application operator from the cluster orchestration operator. We call this the "not my monkey, not my circus" line. The application developer relies on the service-level agreement (SLA) delivered by the container orchestration API, without worrying about the details of how this SLA is achieved. Likewise, the container orchestration API reliability engineer focuses on delivering the orchestration API's SLA without worrying about the applications that are running on top of it.

Decoupling concerns means that a small team running a Kubernetes cluster can be responsible for supporting hundreds or even thousands of teams running applications within that cluster (Figure 1-1). Likewise, a small team can be responsible for dozens (or more) of clusters running around the world. It's important to note that the same decoupling of containers and OS enables the OS reliability engineers to focus on the SLA of the individual machine's OS. This becomes another line of separate responsibility, with the Kubernetes operators relying on the OS SLA, and the OS operators worrying solely about delivering that SLA. Again, this enables you to scale a small team of OS experts to a fleet of thousands of machines.

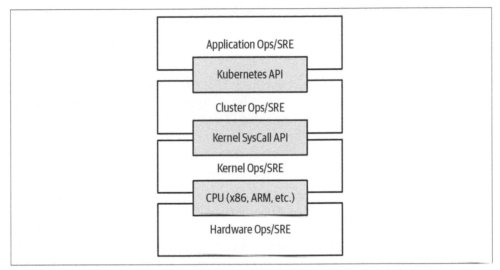

Figure 1-1. An illustration of how different operations teams are decoupled using APIs

Of course, devoting even a small team to managing an OS is beyond the scope of many organizations. In these environments, a managed Kubernetes-as-a-Service (KaaS) provided by a public cloud provider is a great option. As Kubernetes has become increasingly ubiquitous, KaaS has become increasingly available as well, to the point where it is now offered on nearly every public cloud. Of course, using KaaS has some limitations, since the operator makes decisions for you about how the Kubernetes clusters are built and configured. For example, many KaaS platforms disable alpha features because they can destabilize the managed cluster.

In addition to a fully managed Kubernetes service, there is a thriving ecosystem of companies and projects that help to install and manage Kubernetes. There is a full spectrum of solutions between doing it "the hard way" and a fully managed service.

Consequently, whether to use KaaS or manage it yourself (or something in between) is a decision each user needs to make based on the skills and demands of their situation. Often for small organizations, KaaS provides an easy-to-use solution that enables them to focus their time and energy on building the software to support their work rather than managing a cluster. For larger organizations that can afford a dedicated team for managing its Kubernetes cluster, managing it that way may make sense since it enables greater flexibility in terms of cluster capabilities and operations.

Abstracting Your Infrastructure

The goal of the public cloud is to provide easy-to-use, self-service infrastructure for developers to consume. However, too often cloud APIs are oriented around mirroring the infrastructure that IT expects (e.g., "virtual machines"), not the concepts (e.g., "applications") that developers want to consume. Additionally, in many cases the cloud comes with particular details in implementation or services that are specific to the cloud provider. Consuming these APIs directly makes it difficult to run your application in multiple environments, or spread between cloud and physical environments.

The move to application-oriented container APIs like Kubernetes has two concrete benefits. First, as we described previously, it separates developers from specific machines. This makes the machine-oriented IT role easier, since machines can simply be added in aggregate to scale the cluster, and in the context of the cloud it also enables a high degree of portability since developers are consuming a higher-level API that is implemented in terms of the specific cloud infrastructure APIs.

When your developers build their applications in terms of container images and deploy them in terms of portable Kubernetes APIs, transferring your application between environments, or even running in hybrid environments, is simply a matter of sending the declarative config to a new cluster. Kubernetes has a number of plug-ins that can abstract you from a particular cloud. For example, Kubernetes services know how to create load balancers on all major public clouds as well as several different private and physical infrastructures. Likewise, Kubernetes PersistentVolumes and PersistentVolumeClaims can be used to abstract your applications away from specific storage implementations. Of course, to achieve this portability, you need to avoid cloud-managed services (e.g., Amazon's DynamoDB, Azure's Cosmos DB, or Google's Cloud Spanner), which means that you will be forced to deploy and manage open source storage solutions like Cassandra, MySQL, or MongoDB.

Putting it all together, building on top of Kubernetes application-oriented abstractions ensures that the effort you put into building, deploying, and managing your application is truly portable across a wide variety of environments.

Efficiency

In addition to the developer and IT management benefits that containers and Kubernetes provide, there is also a concrete economic benefit to the abstraction. Because developers no longer think in terms of machines, their applications can be colocated on the same machines without impacting the applications themselves. This means that tasks from multiple users can be packed tightly onto fewer machines.

Efficiency can be measured by the ratio of the useful work performed by a machine or process to the total amount of energy spent doing so. When it comes to deploying and managing applications, many of the available tools and processes (e.g., bash scripts, `apt` updates, or imperative configuration management) are somewhat inefficient. When discussing efficiency, it's often helpful to think of both the monetary cost of running a server and the human cost required to manage it.

Running a server incurs a cost based on power usage, cooling requirements, datacenter space, and raw compute power. Once a server is racked and powered on (or clicked and spun up), the meter literally starts running. Any idle CPU time is money wasted. Thus, it becomes part of the system administrator's responsibilities to keep utilization at acceptable levels, which requires ongoing management. This is where containers and the Kubernetes workflow come in. Kubernetes provides tools that automate the distribution of applications across a cluster of machines, ensuring higher levels of utilization than are possible with traditional tooling.

A further increase in efficiency comes from the fact that a developer's test environment can be quickly and cheaply created as a set of containers running in a personal view of a shared Kubernetes cluster (using a feature called *namespaces*). In the past, turning up a test cluster for a developer might have meant turning up three machines. With Kubernetes, it is simple to have all developers share a single test cluster, aggregating their usage onto a much smaller set of machines. Reducing the overall number of machines used in turn drives up the efficiency of each system: since more of the resources (CPU, RAM, etc.) on each individual machine are used, the overall cost of each container becomes much lower.

Reducing the cost of development instances in your stack enables development practices that might previously have been cost-prohibitive. For example, with your application deployed via Kubernetes, it becomes conceivable to deploy and test every single commit contributed by every developer throughout your entire stack.

When the cost of each deployment is measured in terms of a small number of containers, rather than multiple complete virtual machines (VMs), the cost you incur for such testing is dramatically lower. Returning to the original value of Kubernetes, this increased testing also increases velocity, since you have strong signals as to the reliability of your code as well as the granularity of detail required to quickly identify where a problem may have been introduced.

Finally, as mentioned in previous sections, the use of automatic scaling to add resources when needed, but remove them when they are not, can also be used to drive the overall efficiency of your applications while maintaining their required performance characteristics.

Cloud Native Ecosystem

Kubernetes was designed from the ground up to be an extensible environment and a broad and welcoming community. These design goals and its ubiquity in so many compute environments have led to a vibrant and large ecosystem of tools and services that have grown up around Kubernetes. Following the lead of Kubernetes (and Docker and Linux before it), most of these projects are also open source. This means that a developer beginning to build does not have to start from scratch. In the years since it was released, tools for nearly every task, from machine learning to continuous development and serverless programming models have been built for Kubernetes. Indeed, in many cases the challenge isn't finding a potential solution, but rather deciding which of the many solutions is best suited to the task. The wealth of tools in the cloud native ecosystem has itself become a strong reason for many people to adopt Kubernetes. When you leverage the cloud native ecosystem, you can use community-built and supported projects for nearly every part of your system, allowing you to focus on the development of the core business logic and services that are uniquely yours.

As with any open source ecosystem, the primary challenge is the variety of possible solutions and the fact that there is often a lack of end-to-end integration. One possible way to navigate this complexity is the technical guidance of the Cloud Native Computing Foundation (CNCF). The CNCF acts as a industry-neutral home for cloud native projects' code and intellectual property. It has three levels of project maturity to help guide your adoption of cloud native projects. The majority of projects in the CNCF are in the *sandbox* stage. Sandbox indicates that a project is still in early development, and adoption is not recommended unless you are an early adopter and/or interested in contributing to the development of the project. The next stage in maturity is *incubating*. Incubating projects are ones that have proven their utility and stability via adoption and production usage; however, they are still developing and growing their communities. While there are hundreds of sandbox projects, there are barely more than 20 incubating projects. The final stage of CNCF projects is *graduated*. These projects are fully mature and widely adopted. There are only a few graduated projects, including Kubernetes itself.

Another way to navigate the cloud native ecosystem is via integration with Kubernetes-as-a-Service. At this point, most of the KaaS offerings also have additional services via open source projects from the cloud native ecosystem. Because these services are integrated into cloud-supported products, you can be assured that the projects are mature and production ready.

Summary

Kubernetes was built to radically change the way that applications are built and deployed in the cloud. Fundamentally, it was designed to give developers more velocity, efficiency, and agility. At this point, many of the internet services and applications that you use every day are running on top of Kubernetes. You are probably already a Kubernetes user, you just didn't know it! We hope this chapter has given you an idea of why you should deploy your applications using Kubernetes. Now that you are convinced of that, the following chapters will teach you *how* to deploy your applications.

## CHAPTER 2

Creating and Running Containers

Kubernetes is a platform for creating, deploying, and managing distributed applications. These applications come in many different shapes and sizes, but ultimately, they are all comprised of one or more programs that run on individual machines. These programs accept input, manipulate data, and then return the results. Before we can even consider building a distributed system, we must first consider how to build the *application container images* that contain these programs and make up the pieces of our distributed system.

Application programs are typically comprised of a language runtime, libraries, and your source code. In many cases, your application relies on external shared libraries such as libc and libssl. These external libraries are generally shipped as shared components in the OS that you have installed on a particular machine.

This dependency on shared libraries causes problems when an application developed on a programmer's laptop has a dependency on a shared library that isn't available when the program is rolled out to the production OS. Even when the development and production environments share the exact same version of the OS, problems can occur when developers forget to include dependent asset files inside a package that they deploy to production.

The traditional methods of running multiple programs on a single machine require that all of these programs share the same versions of shared libraries on the system. If the different programs are developed by different teams or organizations, these shared dependencies add needless complexity and coupling between these teams.

A program can only execute successfully if it can be reliably deployed onto the machine where it should run. Too often the state of the art for deployment involves running imperative scripts, which inevitably have twisty and byzantine failure cases.

This makes the task of rolling out a new version of all or parts of a distributed system a labor-intensive and difficult task.

In Chapter 1, we argued strongly for the value of immutable images and infrastructure. This immutability is exactly what the container image provides. As we will see, it easily solves all the problems of dependency management and encapsulation just described.

When working with applications, it's often helpful to package them in a way that makes sharing them with others easy. Docker, the default tool most people use for containers, makes it easy to package an executable and push it to a remote registry where it can later be pulled by others. At the time of writing, container registries are available in all of the major public clouds, and services to build images in the cloud are also available in many of them. You can also run your own registry using open source or commercial systems. These registries make it easy for users to manage and deploy private images, while image-builder services provide easy integration with continuous delivery systems.

For this chapter, and the remainder of the book, we are going to work with a simple example application that we built to help show this workflow in action. You can find the application on GitHub (*https://oreil.ly/unTLs*).

Container images bundle a program and its dependencies into a single artifact under a root filesystem. The most popular container image format is the Docker image format, which has been standardized by the Open Container Initiative to the OCI image format. Kubernetes supports both Docker- and OCI-compatible images via Docker and other runtimes. Docker images also include additional metadata used by a container runtime to start a running application instance based on the contents of the container image.

This chapter covers the following topics:

- How to package an application using the Docker image format
- How to start an application using the Docker container runtime

Container Images

For nearly everyone, their first interaction with any container technology is with a container image. A *container image* is a binary package that encapsulates all of the files necessary to run a program inside of an OS container. Depending on how you first experiment with containers, you will either build a container image from your local filesystem or download a preexisting image from a *container registry*. In either case, once the container image is present on your computer, you can run that image to produce a running application inside an OS container.

The most popular and widespread container image format is the Docker image format, which was developed by the Docker open source project for packaging, distributing, and running containers using the docker command. Subsequently, work has begun by Docker, Inc., and others to standardize the container image format via the Open Container Initiative (OCI) project. While the OCI standard achieved a 1.0 release milestone in mid-2017, adoption of these standards is proceeding slowly. The Docker image format continues to be the de facto standard and is made up of a series of filesystem layers. Each layer adds, removes, or modifies files from the preceding layer in the filesystem. This is an example of an *overlay* filesystem. The overlay system is used both when packaging up the image and when the image is actually being used. During runtime, there are a variety of different concrete implementations of such filesystems, including aufs, overlay, and overlay2.

Container Layering

The phrases "Docker image format" and "container images" may be a bit confusing. The image isn't a single file but rather a specification for a manifest file that points to other files. The manifest and associated files are often treated by users as a unit. The level of indirection allows for more efficient storage and transmittal. Associated with this format is an API for uploading and downloading images to an image registry.

Container images are constructed with a series of filesystem layers, where each layer inherits and modifies the layers that came before it. To help explain this in detail, let's build some containers. Note that for correctness, the ordering of the layers should be bottom up, but for ease of understanding, we take the opposite approach:

```
.
└─ container A: a base operating system only, such as Debian
   └─ container B: build upon #A, by adding Ruby v2.1.10
   └─ container C: build upon #A, by adding Golang v1.6
```

At this point we have three containers: A, B, and C. B and C are *forked* from A and share nothing besides the base container's files. Taking it further, we can build on top of B by adding Ruby on Rails (version 4.2.6). We may also want to support a legacy application that requires an older version of Ruby on Rails (e.g., version 3.2.x). We can build a container image to support that application based on B also, planning to someday migrate the app to version 4:

```
. (continuing from above)
└─ container B: build upon #A, by adding Ruby v2.1.10
   └─ container D: build upon #B, by adding Rails v4.2.6
   └─ container E: build upon #B, by adding Rails v3.2.x
```

Conceptually, each container image layer builds upon a previous one. Each parent reference is a pointer. While the example here is a simple set of containers, other real-world containers can be part of a larger extensive directed acyclic graph.

Container images are typically combined with a container configuration file, which provides instructions on how to set up the container environment and execute an application entry point. The container configuration often includes information on how to set up networking, namespace isolation, resource constraints (cgroups), and what `syscall` restrictions should be placed on a running container instance. The container root filesystem and configuration file are typically bundled using the Docker image format.

Containers fall into two main categories:

- System containers
- Application containers

System containers seek to mimic virtual machines and often run a full boot process. They often include a set of system services typically found in a VM, such as `ssh`, `cron`, and `syslog`. When Docker was new, these types of containers were much more common. Over time, they have come to be seen as poor practice and application containers have gained favor.

Application containers differ from system containers in that they commonly run a single program. While running a single program per container might seem like an unnecessary constraint, it provides the perfect level of granularity for composing scalable applications and is a design philosophy that is leveraged heavily by Pods. We will examine how Pods work in detail in Chapter 5.

Building Application Images with Docker

In general, container orchestration systems like Kubernetes are focused on building and deploying distributed systems made up of application containers. Consequently, we will focus on application containers for the remainder of this chapter.

Dockerfiles

A Dockerfile can be used to automate the creation of a Docker container image.

Let's start by building an application image for a simple Node.js program. This example would be very similar for many other dynamic languages, like Python or Ruby.

The simplest of npm/Node/Express apps has two files: *package.json* (Example 2-1) and *server.js* (Example 2-2). Put these in a directory and then run `npm install express --save` to establish a dependency on Express and install it.

Example 2-1. package.json

```json
{
  "name": "simple-node",
  "version": "1.0.0",
  "description": "A sample simple application for Kubernetes Up & Running",
  "main": "server.js",
  "scripts": {
    "start": "node server.js"
  },
  "author": ""
}
```

Example 2-2. server.js

```js
var express = require('express');

var app = express();
app.get('/', function (req, res) {
  res.send('Hello World!');
});
app.listen(3000, function () {
  console.log('Listening on port 3000!');
  console.log('  http://localhost:3000');
});
```

To package this up as a Docker image, create two additional files: *.dockerignore* (Example 2-3) and the Dockerfile (Example 2-4). The Dockerfile is a recipe for how to build the container image, while *.dockerignore* defines the set of files that should be ignored when copying files into the image. A full description of the syntax of the Dockerfile is available on the Docker website (*https://dockr.ly/2XUanvl*).

Example 2-3. .dockerignore

```
node_modules
```

Example 2-4. Dockerfile

```dockerfile
# Start from a Node.js 16 (LTS) image ❶
FROM node:16

# Specify the directory inside the image in which all commands will run ❷
WORKDIR /usr/src/app

# Copy package files and install dependencies ❸
COPY package*.json ./
RUN npm install
RUN npm install express
```

```
# Copy all of the app files into the image ❹
COPY . .

# The default command to run when starting the container ❺
CMD [ "npm", "start" ]
```

❶ Every Dockerfile builds on other container images. This line specifies that we are starting from the node:16 image on the Docker Hub. This is a preconfigured image with Node.js 16.

❷ This line sets the work directory in the container image for all following commands.

❸ These three lines initialize the dependencies for Node.js. First, we copy the package files into the image. This will include *package.json* and *package-lock.json*. The RUN command then runs the correct command *in the container* to install the necessary dependencies.

❹ Now we copy the rest of the program files into the image. This will include everything except *node_modules*, as that is excluded via the *.dockerignore* file.

❺ Finally, we specify the command that should be run when the container is run.

Run the following command to create the simple-node Docker image:

```
$ docker build -t simple-node .
```

When you want to run this image, you can do it with the following command. Navigate to *http://localhost:3000* to access the program running in the container:

```
$ docker run --rm -p 3000:3000 simple-node
```

At this point, our simple-node image lives in the local Docker registry where the image was built and is only accessible to a single machine. The true power of Docker comes from the ability to share images across thousands of machines and the broader Docker community.

Optimizing Image Sizes

There are several gotchas people encounter when they begin to experiment with container images that lead to overly large images. The first thing to remember is that files that are removed by subsequent layers in the system are actually still present in the images; they're just inaccessible. Consider the following situation:

```
.
└─ layer A: contains a large file named 'BigFile'
    └─ layer B: removes 'BigFile'
        └─ layer C: builds on B by adding a static binary
```

You might think that *BigFile* is no longer present in this image. After all, when you run the image, it is no longer accessible. But in fact it is still present in layer A, which means that whenever you push or pull the image, *BigFile* is still transmitted through the network, even if you can no longer access it.

Another pitfall revolves around image caching and building. Remember that each layer is an independent delta from the layer below it. Every time you change a layer, it changes every layer that comes after it. Changing the preceding layers means that they need to be rebuilt, repushed, and repulled to deploy your image to development.

To understand this more fully, consider two images:

```
.
└─ layer A: contains a base OS
    └─ layer B: adds source code server.js
        └─ layer C: installs the 'node' package
```

versus:

```
.
└─ layer A: contains a base OS
    └─ layer B: installs the 'node' package
        └─ layer C: adds source code server.js
```

It seems obvious that both of these images will behave identically, and indeed the first time they are pulled, they do. However, consider what happens when *server.js* changes. In the second case, it is only that change that needs to be pulled or pushed, but in the first case, both *server.js* and the layer providing the node package need to be pulled and pushed, since the node layer is dependent on the *server.js* layer. In general, you want to order your layers from least likely to change to most likely to change in order to optimize the image size for pushing and pulling. This is why, in Example 2-4, we copy the *package*.json* files and install dependencies before copying the rest of the program files. A developer is going to update and change the program files much more often than the dependencies.

Image Security

When it comes to security, there are no shortcuts. When building images that will ultimately run in a production Kubernetes cluster, be sure to follow best practices for packaging and distributing applications. For example, don't build containers with passwords baked in—and this includes not just in the final layer, but any layers in the image. One of the counterintuitive problems introduced by container layers is that deleting a file in one layer doesn't delete that file from preceding layers. It still takes up space, and it can be accessed by anyone with the right tools—an enterprising attacker can simply create an image that only consists of the layers that contain the password.

Secrets and images should *never* be mixed. If you do so, you will be hacked, and you will bring shame to your entire company or department. We all want to be on TV someday, but there are better ways to go about that.

Additionally, because container images are narrowly focused on running individual applications, a best practice is to minimize the files within the container image. Every additional library in an image provides a potential vector for vulnerabilities to appear in your application. Depending on the language, you can achieve very small images with a very tight set of dependencies. This smaller set ensures that your image isn't exposed to vulnerabilities in libraries it would never use.

Multistage Image Builds

One of the most common ways to accidentally build large images is to do the actual program compilation as part of the construction of the application container image. Compiling code as part of the image build feels natural, and it is the easiest way to build a container image from your program. The trouble with doing this is that it leaves all of the unnecessary development tools, which are usually quite large, lying around inside your image and slowing down your deployments.

To resolve this problem, Docker introduced *multistage builds*. With multistage builds, rather than producing a single image, a Docker file can actually produce multiple images. Each image is considered a stage. Artifacts can be copied from preceding stages to the current stage.

To illustrate this concretely, we will look at how to build our example application, kuard. This is a somewhat complicated application that involves a React.js frontend (with its own build process) that then gets embedded into a Go program. The Go program runs a backend API server that the *React.js* frontend interacts with.

A simple Dockerfile might look like this:

```
FROM golang:1.17-alpine

# Install Node and NPM
RUN apk update && apk upgrade && apk add --no-cache git nodejs bash npm

# Get dependencies for Go part of build
RUN go get -u github.com/jteeuwen/go-bindata/...
RUN go get github.com/tools/godep
RUN go get github.com/kubernetes-up-and-running/kuard

WORKDIR /go/src/github.com/kubernetes-up-and-running/kuard

# Copy all sources in
COPY . .

# This is a set of variables that the build script expects
```

```
ENV VERBOSE=0
ENV PKG=github.com/kubernetes-up-and-running/kuard
ENV ARCH=amd64
ENV VERSION=test

# Do the build. This script is part of incoming sources.
RUN build/build.sh

CMD [ "/go/bin/kuard" ]
```

This Dockerfile produces a container image containing a static executable, but it also contains all of the Go development tools and the tools to build the *React.js* frontend and the source code for the application, neither of which are needed by the final application. The image, across all layers, adds up to over 500 MB.

To see how we would do this with multistage builds, examine the following multistage Dockerfile:

```
# STAGE 1: Build
FROM golang:1.17-alpine AS build

# Install Node and NPM
RUN apk update && apk upgrade && apk add --no-cache git nodejs bash npm

# Get dependencies for Go part of build
RUN go get -u github.com/jteeuwen/go-bindata/...
RUN go get github.com/tools/godep

WORKDIR /go/src/github.com/kubernetes-up-and-running/kuard

# Copy all sources in
COPY . .

# This is a set of variables that the build script expects
ENV VERBOSE=0
ENV PKG=github.com/kubernetes-up-and-running/kuard
ENV ARCH=amd64
ENV VERSION=test

# Do the build. Script is part of incoming sources.
RUN build/build.sh

# STAGE 2: Deployment
FROM alpine

USER nobody:nobody
COPY --from=build /go/bin/kuard /kuard

CMD [ "/kuard" ]
```

This Dockerfile produces two images. The first is the *build* image, which contains the Go compiler, *React.js* toolchain, and source code for the program. The second is the *deployment* image, which simply contains the compiled binary. Building a container image using multistage builds can reduce your final container image size by hundreds of megabytes and thus dramatically speed up your deployment times, since generally, deployment latency is gated on network performance. The final image produced from this Dockerfile is somewhere around 20 MB.

These scripts are present in the kuard repository on GitHub (*https://oreil.ly/6c9MX*) and you can build and run this image with the following commands:

```
# Note: if you are running on Windows you may need to fix line-endings using:
# --config core.autocrlf=input
$ git clone https://github.com/kubernetes-up-and-running/kuard
$ cd kuard
$ docker build -t kuard .
$ docker run --rm -p 8080:8080 kuard
```

Storing Images in a Remote Registry

What good is a container image if it's only available on a single machine?

Kubernetes relies on the fact that images described in a Pod manifest are available across every machine in the cluster. One option for getting this image to all machines in the cluster would be to export the kuard image and import it on each of them. We can't think of anything more tedious than managing Docker images this way. The process of manually importing and exporting Docker images has human error written all over it. Just say no!

The standard within the Docker community is to store Docker images in a remote registry. There are tons of options when it comes to Docker registries, and what you choose will be largely based on your needs in terms of security and collaboration features.

Generally speaking, the first choice you need to make regarding a registry is whether to use a private or a public registry. Public registries allow anyone to download images stored in the registry, while private registries require authentication to download images. In choosing public versus private, it's helpful to consider your use case.

Public registries are great for sharing images with the world because they allow for easy, unauthenticated use of the container images. You can easily distribute your software as a container image and have confidence that users everywhere will have the exact same experience.

In contrast, a private registry is best for storing applications that are private to your service and that you don't want the world to use. Additionally, private registries often provide better availability and security guarantees because they are specific to you and your images rather than serving the world.

Regardless, to push an image, you need to authenticate to the registry. You can generally do this with the `docker login` command, though there are some differences for certain registries. In the examples in this book we are pushing to the Google Cloud Platform registry, called the Google Container Registry (GCR); other clouds, including Azure and Amazon Web Services (AWS), also have hosted container registries. For new users hosting publicly readable images, the Docker Hub (*https://hub.docker.com*) is a great place to start.

Once you are logged in, you can tag the `kuard` image by prepending the target Docker registry. You can also append an identifier that is usually used for the version or variant of that image, separated by a colon (`:`):

```
$ docker tag kuard gcr.io/kuar-demo/kuard-amd64:blue
```

Then you can push the `kuard` image:

```
$ docker push gcr.io/kuar-demo/kuard-amd64:blue
```

Now that the `kuard` image is available on a remote registry, it's time to deploy it using Docker. When we pushed the image to GCR, it was marked as public, so it will be available everywhere without authentication.

The Container Runtime Interface

Kubernetes provides an API for describing an application deployment, but relies on a container runtime to set up an application container using the container-specific APIs native to the target OS. On a Linux system that means configuring cgroups and namespaces. The interface to this container runtime is defined by the Container Runtime Interface (CRI) standard. The CRI API is implemented by a number of different programs, including the `containerd-cri` built by Docker and the `cri-o` implementation contributed by Red Hat. When you install the Docker tooling, the `containerd` runtime is also installed and used by the Docker daemon.

Starting with release 1.25 of Kubernetes, only container runtimes that support the CRI will work with Kubernetes. Fortunately, managed Kubernetes providers have made this transition nearly automatic for users of managed Kubernetes.

Running Containers with Docker

In Kubernetes, containers are usually launched by a daemon on each node called the *kubelet*; however, it's easier to get started with containers using the Docker command-line tool. The Docker CLI tool can be used to deploy containers. To deploy a container from the `gcr.io/kuar-demo/kuard-amd64:blue` image, run the following command:

```
$ docker run -d --name kuard \
  --publish 8080:8080 \
  gcr.io/kuar-demo/kuard-amd64:blue
```

This command starts the kuard container and maps ports 8080 on your local machine to 8080 in the container. The --publish option can be shortened to -p. This forwarding is necessary because each container gets its own IP address, so listening on *localhost* inside the container doesn't cause you to listen on your machine. Without the port forwarding, connections will be inaccessible to your machine. The -d option specifies that this should run in the background (daemon), while --name kuard gives the container a friendly name.

Exploring the kuard Application

kuard exposes a simple web interface, which you can load by pointing your browser at *http://localhost:3000* or via the command line:

```
$ curl http://localhost:8080
```

kuard also exposes a number of interesting functions that we will explore later on in this book.

Limiting Resource Usage

Docker enables applications to use fewer resources by exposing the underlying cgroup technology provided by the Linux kernel. These capabilities are likewise used by Kubernetes to limit the resources each Pod uses.

Limiting memory resources

One of the key benefits to running applications within a container is the ability to restrict resource utilization. This allows multiple applications to coexist on the same hardware and ensures fair usage.

To limit kuard to 200 MB of memory and 1 GB of swap space, use the --memory and --memory-swap flags with the docker run command.

Stop and remove the current kuard container:

```
$ docker stop kuard
$ docker rm kuard
```

Then start another kuard container using the appropriate flags to limit memory usage:

```
$ docker run -d --name kuard \
  --publish 8080:8080 \
  --memory 200m \
  --memory-swap 1G \
  gcr.io/kuar-demo/kuard-amd64:blue
```

If the program in the container uses too much memory, it will be terminated.

Limiting CPU resources

Another critical resource on a machine is the CPU. Restrict CPU utilization using the `--cpu-shares` flag with the `docker run` command:

```
$ docker run -d --name kuard \
  --publish 8080:8080 \
  --memory 200m \
  --memory-swap 1G \
  --cpu-shares 1024 \
  gcr.io/kuar-demo/kuard-amd64:blue
```

Cleanup

Once you are done building an image, you can delete it with the `docker rmi` command:

```
docker rmi <tag-name>
```

or:

```
docker rmi <image-id>
```

Images can either be deleted via their tag name (e.g., `gcr.io/kuar-demo/kuard-amd64:blue`) or via their image ID. As with all ID values in the `docker` tool, the image ID can be shortened as long as it remains unique. Generally only three or four characters of the ID are necessary.

It's important to note that unless you explicitly delete an image, it will live on your system forever, *even* if you build a new image with an identical name. Building this new image simply moves the tag to the new image; it doesn't delete or replace the old image.

Consequently, as you iterate while you are creating a new image, you will often create many, many different images that take up unnecessary space on your computer. To see the images currently on your machine, you can use the `docker images` command. You can then delete tags you are no longer using.

Docker provides a tool called `docker system prune` for doing general cleanup. This will remove all stopped containers, all untagged images, and all unused image layers cached as part of the build process. Use it carefully.

A slightly more sophisticated approach is to set up a `cron` job to run an image garbage collector. For example, you can easily run `docker system prune` as a recurring `cron` job, once per day or once per hour, depending on how many images you are creating.

Summary

Application containers provide a clean abstraction for applications, and when packaged in the Docker image format, applications become easy to build, deploy, and distribute. Containers also provide isolation between applications running on the same machine, which helps avoid dependency conflicts.

In future chapters, we'll see how the ability to mount external directories means we can run not only stateless applications in a container, but also applications like MySQL and others that generate lots of data.

## CHAPTER 3

Deploying a Kubernetes Cluster

Now that you have successfully built an application container, the next step is to learn how to transform it into a complete, reliable, scalable distributed system. To do that, you need a working Kubernetes cluster. At this point, there are cloud-based Kubernetes services in most public clouds that make it easy to create a cluster with a few command-line instructions. We highly recommend this approach if you are just getting started with Kubernetes. Even if you are ultimately planning on running Kubernetes on bare metal, it's a good way to quickly get started with Kubernetes, learn about Kubernetes itself, and then learn how to install it on physical machines. Furthermore, managing a Kubernetes cluster is a complicated task in itself, and, for most people, it makes sense to defer this management to the cloud—especially when the management service is free in most clouds.

Of course, using a cloud-based solution requires paying for those cloud-based resources as well as having an active network connection to the cloud. For these reasons, local development can be more attractive, and in that case, the minikube tool provides an easy-to-use way to get a local Kubernetes cluster up and running in a VM on your local laptop or desktop. Though this is a nice option, minikube only creates a single-node cluster, which doesn't quite demonstrate all of the aspects of a complete Kubernetes cluster. For that reason, we recommend people start with a cloud-based solution, unless it really doesn't work for their situation. A more recent alternative is to run a Docker-in-Docker cluster, which can spin up a multinode cluster on a single machine. This project is still in beta, though, so keep in mind that you may encounter unexpected issues.

If you truly insist on starting on bare metal, see the Appendix at the end of this book for instructions for building a cluster from a collection of Raspberry Pi single-board computers. These instructions use the kubeadm tool and can be adapted to other machines beyond Raspberry Pis.

Installing Kubernetes on a Public Cloud Provider

This chapter covers installing Kubernetes on the three major cloud providers: the Google Cloud Platform, Microsoft Azure, and Amazon Web Services.

If you choose to use a cloud provider to manage Kubernetes, you need to install only one of these options; once you have a cluster configured and ready to go, you can skip to "The Kubernetes Client" on page 33, unless you would prefer to install Kubernetes elsewhere.

Installing Kubernetes with Google Kubernetes Engine

The Google Cloud Platform (GCP) offers a hosted Kubernetes-as-a-Service called Google Kubernetes Engine (GKE). To get started with GKE, you need a Google Cloud Platform account with billing enabled and the gcloud tool (*https://oreil.ly/uuUQD*) installed.

Once you have gcloud installed, set a default zone:

```
$ gcloud config set compute/zone us-west1-a
```

Then you can create a cluster:

```
$ gcloud container clusters create kuar-cluster --num-nodes=3
```

This will take a few minutes. When the cluster is ready, you can get credentials for the cluster using:

```
$ gcloud container clusters get-credentials kuar-cluster
```

If you run into trouble, you can find the complete instructions for creating a GKE cluster in the Google Cloud Platform documentation (*https://oreil.ly/HMwnD*).

Installing Kubernetes with Azure Kubernetes Service

Microsoft Azure offers a hosted Kubernetes-as-a-Service as part of the Azure Container Service. The easiest way to get started with Azure Container Service is to use the built-in Azure Cloud Shell in the Azure portal. You can activate the shell by clicking the shell icon in the upper-right toolbar:

The shell has the az tool automatically installed and configured to work with your Azure environment.

Alternatively, you can install the az CLI (*https://oreil.ly/xpLCa*) on your local machine.

When you have the shell up and working, you can run:

```
$ az group create --name=kuar --location=westus
```

Once the resource group is created, you can create a cluster using:

```
$ az aks create --resource-group=kuar --name=kuar-cluster
```

This will take a few minutes. Once the cluster is created, you can get credentials for the cluster with:

```
$ az aks get-credentials --resource-group=kuar --name=kuar-cluster
```

If you don't already have the kubectl tool installed, you can install it using:

```
$ az aks install-cli
```

You can find complete instructions for installing Kubernetes on Azure in the Azure documentation (*https://oreil.ly/hsLWA*).

Installing Kubernetes on Amazon Web Services

Amazon offers a managed Kubernetes service called Elastic Kubernetes Service (EKS). The easiest way to create an EKS cluster is via the open source eksctl command-line tool (*https://eksctl.io*).

Once you have eksctl installed and in your path, you can run the following command to create a cluster:

```
$ eksctl create cluster
```

For more details on installation options (such as node size and more), view the help using this command:

```
$ eksctl create cluster --help
```

The cluster installation includes the right configuration for the kubectl command-line tool. If you don't already have kubectl installed, follow the instructions in the documentation (*https://oreil.ly/rorrD*).

Installing Kubernetes Locally Using minikube

If you need a local development experience, or you don't want to pay for cloud resources, you can install a simple single-node cluster using minikube. Alternatively, if you have already installed Docker Desktop, it comes bundled with a single-machine installation of Kubernetes.

While minikube (or Docker Desktop) is a good simulation of a Kubernetes cluster, it's really intended for local development, learning, and experimentation. Because it only runs in a VM on a single node, it doesn't provide the reliability of a distributed Kubernetes cluster. In addition, certain features described in this book require integration with a cloud provider. These features are either not available or work in a limited way with minikube.

 You need to have a hypervisor installed on your machine to use minikube. For Linux and macOS, this is generally VirtualBox (*https://virtualbox.org*). On Windows, the Hyper-V hypervisor is the default option. Make sure you install the hypervisor before using minikube.

You can find the minikube tool on GitHub (*https://oreil.ly/iHcuV*). There are binaries for Linux, macOS, and Windows that you can download. Once you have the minikube tool installed, you can create a local cluster using:

```
$ minikube start
```

This will create a local VM, provision Kubernetes, and create a local kubectl configuration that points to that cluster. As mentioned previously, this cluster only has a single node, so while it is useful, it has some differences with most production deployments of Kubernetes.

When you are done with your cluster, you can stop the VM with:

```
$ minikube stop
```

If you want to remove the cluster, you can run:

```
$ minikube delete
```

Running Kubernetes in Docker

A different approach to running a Kubernetes cluster, which has been developed more recently, uses Docker containers to simulate multiple Kubernetes nodes instead of running everything in a virtual machine. The kind project (*https://kind.sigs.k8s.io*) provides a great experience for launching and managing test clusters in Docker. (*kind* stands for Kubernetes IN Docker.) kind is still a work in progress (pre 1.0), but is widely used by those building Kubernetes for fast and easy testing.

Installation instructions for your platform can be found at the kind site (*https://oreil.ly/EOgJn*). Once you get it installed, creating a cluster is as easy as:

```
$ kind create cluster --wait 5m
$ export KUBECONFIG="$(kind get kubeconfig-path)"
$ kubectl cluster-info
$ kind delete cluster
```

The Kubernetes Client

The official Kubernetes client is kubectl: a command-line tool for interacting with the Kubernetes API. kubectl can be used to manage most Kubernetes objects, such as Pods, ReplicaSets, and Services. kubectl can also be used to explore and verify the overall health of the cluster.

We'll use the kubectl tool to explore the cluster you just created.

Checking Cluster Status

The first thing you can do is check the version of the cluster that you are running:

```
$ kubectl version
```

This will display two different versions: the version of the local kubectl tool, as well as the version of the Kubernetes API server.

Don't worry if these versions are different. The Kubernetes tools are backward- and forward-compatible with different versions of the Kubernetes API as long as you stay within two minor versions for both the tools and the cluster and don't try to use newer features on an older cluster. Kubernetes follows the semantic versioning specification, where the minor version is the middle number (e.g., the 18 in 1.18.2). However, you will want to make sure that you are within the supported version skew, which is three versions. If you are not, you may run into problems.

Now that we've established that you can communicate with your Kubernetes cluster, we'll explore the cluster in more depth.

First, you can get a simple diagnostic for the cluster. This is a good way to verify that your cluster is generally healthy:

```
$ kubectl get componentstatuses
```

The output should look like this:

```
NAME                  STATUS    MESSAGE              ERROR
scheduler             Healthy   ok
controller-manager    Healthy   ok
etcd-0                Healthy   {"health": "true"}
```

As Kubernetes changes and improves over time, the output of the kubectl command sometimes changes. Don't worry if the output doesn't look exactly identical to what is shown in the examples in this book.

You can see here the components that make up the Kubernetes cluster. The `controller-manager` is responsible for running various controllers that regulate behavior in the cluster; for example, ensuring that all of the replicas of a service are available and healthy. The `scheduler` is responsible for placing different Pods onto different nodes in the cluster. Finally, the `etcd` server is the storage for the cluster where all of the API objects are stored.

Listing Kubernetes Nodes

Next, you can list out all of the nodes in your cluster:

```
$ kubectl get nodes
NAME    STATUS   ROLES                  AGE   VERSION
kube0   Ready    control-plane,master   45d   v1.22.4
kube1   Ready    <none>                 45d   v1.22.4
kube2   Ready    <none>                 45d   v1.22.4
kube3   Ready    <none>                 45d   v1.22.4
```

You can see this is a four-node cluster that's been up for 45 days. In Kubernetes, nodes are separated into `control-plane` nodes that contain containers like the API server, scheduler, etc., which manage the cluster, and `worker` nodes where your containers will run. Kubernetes won't generally schedule work onto `control-plane` nodes to ensure that user workloads don't harm the overall operation of the cluster.

You can use the `kubectl describe` command to get more information about a specific node, such as kube1:

```
$ kubectl describe nodes kube1
```

First, you see basic information about the node:

```
Name:           kube1
Role:
Labels:         beta.kubernetes.io/arch=arm
                beta.kubernetes.io/os=linux
                kubernetes.io/hostname=node-1
```

You can see that this node is running the Linux OS on an ARM processor.

Next, you see information about the operation of `kube1` itself (dates have been removed from this output for concision):

```
Conditions:
  Type                Status   ...   Reason                       Message
  -----               ------   ...   ------                       -------
  NetworkUnavailable  False    ...   FlannelIsUp                  Flannel...
  MemoryPressure      False    ...   KubeletHasSufficientMemory   kubelet...
  DiskPressure        False    ...   KubeletHasNoDiskPressure     kubelet...
  PIDPressure         False    ...   KubeletHasSufficientPID      kubelet...
  Ready               True     ...   KubeletReady                 kubelet...
```

These statuses show that the node has sufficient disk and memory space and is reporting that it is healthy to the Kubernetes master. Next, there is information about the capacity of the machine:

```
Capacity:
  alpha.kubernetes.io/nvidia-gpu:      0
  cpu:                                 4
  memory:                              882636Ki
  pods:                                110
Allocatable:
  alpha.kubernetes.io/nvidia-gpu:      0
  cpu:                                 4
  memory:                              882636Ki
  pods:                                110
```

Then there is information about the software on the node, including the version of Docker that is running, the versions of Kubernetes and the Linux kernel, and more:

```
System Info:
  Machine ID:                 44d8f5dd42304af6acde62d233194cc6
  System UUID:                c8ab697e-fc7e-28a2-7621-94c691120fb9
  Boot ID:                    e78d015d-81c2-4876-ba96-106a82da263e
  Kernel Version:             4.19.0-18-amd64
  OS Image:                   Debian GNU/Linux 10 (buster)
  Operating System:           linux
  Architecture:               amd64
  Container Runtime Version:  containerd://1.4.12
  Kubelet Version:            v1.22.4
  Kube-Proxy Version:         v1.22.4
PodCIDR:                      10.244.1.0/24
PodCIDRs:                     10.244.1.0/24
```

Finally, there is information about the Pods that are currently running on this node:

```
Non-terminated Pods:         (3 in total)
  Namespace   Name        CPU Requests CPU Limits Memory Requests Memory Limits
  ---------   ----        ------------ ---------- --------------- -------------
  kube-system kube-dns... 260m (6%)    0 (0%)     140Mi (16%)     220Mi (25%)
  kube-system kube-fla... 0 (0%)       0 (0%)     0 (0%)          0 (0%)
  kube-system kube-pro... 0 (0%)       0 (0%)     0 (0%)          0 (0%)
Allocated resources:
  (Total limits may be over 100 percent, i.e., overcommitted.
  CPU Requests  CPU Limits     Memory Requests Memory Limits
  ------------  ----------     --------------- -------------
  260m (6%)     0 (0%)         140Mi (16%)     220Mi (25%)
No events.
```

From this output, you can see the Pods on the node (e.g., the kube-dns Pod that supplies DNS services for the cluster), the CPU and memory that each Pod is requesting from the node, as well as the total resources requested. It's worth noting here that Kubernetes tracks both the *requests* and the upper *limits* for resources for each Pod that runs on a machine. The difference between requests and limits is described in detail in Chapter 5, but in a nutshell, resources requested by a Pod are guaranteed to be present on the node, while a Pod's limit is the maximum amount of a given resource that a Pod can consume. A Pod's limit can be higher than its request, in which case the extra resources are supplied on a best-effort basis. They are not guaranteed to be present on the node.

Cluster Components

One of the interesting aspects of Kubernetes is that many of the components that make up the Kubernetes cluster are actually deployed using Kubernetes itself. We'll take a look at a few of these. These components use a number of the concepts that we'll introduce in later chapters. All of these components run in the kube-system namespace.[1]

Kubernetes Proxy

The Kubernetes proxy is responsible for routing network traffic to load-balanced services in the Kubernetes cluster. To do its job, the proxy must be present on every node in the cluster. Kubernetes has an API object named DaemonSet, which you will learn about in Chapter 11, that is used in many clusters to accomplish this. If your cluster runs the Kubernetes proxy with a DaemonSet, you can see the proxies by running:

```
$ kubectl get daemonSets --namespace=kube-system kube-proxy
NAME          DESIRED   CURRENT   READY   UP-TO-DATE   AVAILABLE   NODE SELECTOR
kube-proxy    5         5         5       5            5           ...   45d
```

Depending on how your cluster is set up, the DaemonSet for the kube-proxy may be named something else, or it's possible that it won't use a DaemonSet at all. Regardless, the kube-proxy container should be running on all nodes in a cluster.

Kubernetes DNS

Kubernetes also runs a DNS server, which provides naming and discovery for the services that are defined in the cluster. This DNS server also runs as a replicated service on the cluster. Depending on the size of your cluster, you may see one or more DNS servers running in your cluster. The DNS service is run as a Kubernetes deployment, which manages these replicas (this may also be named coredns or some other variant):

---

1 As you'll learn in the next chapter, a namespace in Kubernetes is an entity for organizing Kubernetes resources. You can think of it like a folder in a filesystem.

```
$ kubectl get deployments --namespace=kube-system core-dns
NAME       DESIRED   CURRENT   UP-TO-DATE   AVAILABLE   AGE
core-dns   1         1         1            1           45d
```

There is also a Kubernetes service that performs load balancing for the DNS server:

```
$ kubectl get services --namespace=kube-system core-dns
NAME       CLUSTER-IP    EXTERNAL-IP   PORT(S)        AGE
core-dns   10.96.0.10    <none>        53/UDP,53/TCP  45d
```

This shows that the DNS service for the cluster has the address 10.96.0.10. If you log in to a container in the cluster, you'll see that this has been populated into the */etc/resolv.conf* file for the container.

Kubernetes UI

If you want to visualize your cluster in a graphical user interface, most of the cloud providers integrate such a visualization into the GUI for their cloud. If your cloud provider doesn't provide such a UI, or you prefer an in-cluster GUI, there is a community supported GUI that you can install. See the documentation (*https://oreil.ly/wKfEx*) on how to install the dashboard for these clusters. You can also use extensions for development environments like Visual Studio Code to see the state of your cluster at a glance.

Summary

Hopefully at this point you have a Kubernetes cluster (or three) up and running and you've used a few commands to explore the cluster you have created. Next, we'll spend some more time exploring the CLI to that Kubernetes cluster and teach you how to master the kubectl tool. Throughout the rest of the book, you'll be using kubectl and your test cluster to explore the various objects in the Kubernetes API.

## CHAPTER 4

Common kubectl Commands

The kubectl command-line utility is a powerful tool, and in the following chapters, you will use it to create objects and interact with the Kubernetes API. Before that, however, it makes sense to go over the basic kubectl commands that apply to all Kubernetes objects.

Namespaces

Kubernetes uses *namespaces* to organize objects in the cluster. You can think of each namespace as a folder that holds a set of objects. By default, the kubectl command-line tool interacts with the default namespace. If you want to use a different namespace, you can pass kubectl the --namespace flag. For example, kubectl --namespace=mystuff references objects in the mystuff namespace. You can also use the shorthand -n flag if you're feeling concise. If you want to interact with all namespaces—for example, to list all Pods in your cluster—you can pass the --all-namespaces flag.

Contexts

If you want to change the default namespace more permanently, you can use a *context*. This gets recorded in a kubectl configuration file, usually located at *$HOME/.kube/config*. This configuration file also stores how to both find and authenticate to your cluster. For example, you can create a context with a different default namespace for your kubectl commands using:

```
$ kubectl config set-context my-context --namespace=mystuff
```

This creates a new context, but it doesn't actually start using it yet. To use this newly created context, you can run:

```
$ kubectl config use-context my-context
```

Contexts can also be used to manage different clusters or different users for authenticating to those clusters using the --users or --clusters flags with the set-context command.

Viewing Kubernetes API Objects

Everything contained in Kubernetes is represented by a RESTful resource. Throughout this book, we refer to these resources as *Kubernetes objects*. Each Kubernetes object exists at a unique HTTP path; for example, *https://your-k8s.com/api/v1/namespaces/default/pods/my-pod* leads to the representation of a Pod in the default namespace named my-pod. The kubectl command makes HTTP requests to these URLs to access the Kubernetes objects that reside at these paths.

The most basic command for viewing Kubernetes objects via kubectl is get. If you run kubectl get <resource-name>, you will get a listing of all resources in the current namespace. If you want to get a specific resource, you can use kubectl get <resource-name> <obj-name>.

By default, kubectl uses a human-readable printer for viewing the responses from the API server, but this human-readable printer removes many of the details of the objects to fit each object on one terminal line. One way to get slightly more information is to add the -o wide flag, which gives more details, on a longer line. If you want to view the complete object, you can also view the objects as raw JSON or YAML using the -o json or -o yaml flags, respectively.

A common option for manipulating the output of kubectl is to remove the headers, which is often useful when combining kubectl with Unix pipes (e.g., kubectl ... | awk ...). If you specify the --no-headers flag, kubectl will skip the headers at the top of the human-readable table.

Another common task is extracting specific fields from the object. kubectl uses the JSONPath query language to select fields in the returned object. The complete details of JSONPath are beyond the scope of this chapter, but as an example, this command will extract and print the IP address of the specified Pod:

```
$ kubectl get pods my-pod -o jsonpath --template={.status.podIP}
```

You can also view multiple objects of different types by using a comma separated list of types, for example:

```
$ kubectl get pods,services
```

This will display all Pods and services for a given namespace.

If you are interested in more detailed information about a particular object, use the describe command:

```
$ kubectl describe <resource-name> <obj-name>
```

This will provide a rich multiline human-readable description of the object as well as any other relevant, related objects and events in the Kubernetes cluster.

If you would like to see a list of supported fields for each supported type of Kubernetes object, you can use the explain command:

```
$ kubectl explain pods
```

Sometimes you want to continually observe the state of a particular Kubernetes resource to see changes to the resource when they occur. For example, you might be waiting for your application to restart. The --watch flag enables this. You can add this flag to any kubectl get command to continuously monitor the state of a particular resource.

Creating, Updating, and Destroying Kubernetes Objects

Objects in the Kubernetes API are represented as JSON or YAML files. These files are either returned by the server in response to a query or posted to the server as part of an API request. You can use these YAML or JSON files to create, update, or delete objects on the Kubernetes server.

Let's assume that you have a simple object stored in *obj.yaml*. You can use kubectl to create this object in Kubernetes by running:

```
$ kubectl apply -f obj.yaml
```

Notice that you don't need to specify the resource type of the object; it's obtained from the object file itself.

Similarly, after you make changes to the object, you can use the apply command again to update the object:

```
$ kubectl apply -f obj.yaml
```

The apply tool will only modify objects that are different from the current objects in the cluster. If the objects you are creating already exist in the cluster, it will simply exit successfully without making any changes. This makes it useful for loops where you want to ensure the state of the cluster matches the state of the filesystem. You can repeatedly use apply to reconcile state.

If you want to see what the `apply` command will do without actually making the changes, you can use the `--dry-run` flag to print the objects to the terminal without actually sending them to the server.

 If you feel like making interactive edits instead of editing a local file, you can instead use the `edit` command, which will download the latest object state and then launch an editor that contains the definition:

```
$ kubectl edit <resource-name> <obj-name>
```

After you save the file, it will be automatically uploaded back to the Kubernetes cluster.

The `apply` command also records the history of previous configurations in an annotation within the object. You can manipulate these records with the `edit-last-applied`, `set-last-applied`, and `view-last-applied` commands. For example:

```
$ kubectl apply -f myobj.yaml view-last-applied
```

will show you the last state that was applied to the object.

When you want to delete an object, you can simply run:

```
$ kubectl delete -f obj.yaml
```

It is important to note that kubectl will not prompt you to confirm the deletion. Once you issue the command, the object *will* be deleted.

Likewise, you can delete an object using the resource type and name:

```
$ kubectl delete <resource-name> <obj-name>
```

Labeling and Annotating Objects

Labels and annotations are tags for your objects. We'll discuss the differences in Chapter 6, but for now, you can update the labels and annotations on any Kubernetes object using the `label` and `annotate` commands. For example, to add the `color=red` label to a Pod named `bar`, you can run:

```
$ kubectl label pods bar color=red
```

The syntax for annotations is identical.

By default, `label` and `annotate` will not let you overwrite an existing label. To do this, you need to add the `--overwrite` flag.

If you want to remove a label, you can use the `<label-name>-` syntax:

```
$ kubectl label pods bar color-
```

This will remove the color label from the Pod named bar.

Debugging Commands

kubectl also makes a number of commands available for debugging your containers. You can use the following to see the logs for a running container:

```
$ kubectl logs <pod-name>
```

If you have multiple containers in your Pod, you can choose the container to view using the -c flag.

By default, kubectl logs lists the current logs and exits. If you instead want to continuously stream the logs back to the terminal without exiting, you can add the -f (follow) command-line flag.

You can also use the exec command to execute a command in a running container:

```
$ kubectl exec -it <pod-name> -- bash
```

This will provide you with an interactive shell inside the running container so that you can perform more debugging.

If you don't have bash or some other terminal available within your container, you can always attach to the running process:

```
$ kubectl attach -it <pod-name>
```

The attach command is similar to kubectl logs but will allow you to send input to the running process, assuming that process is set up to read from standard input.

You can also copy files to and from a container using the cp command:

```
$ kubectl cp <pod-name>:</path/to/remote/file> </path/to/local/file>
```

This will copy a file from a running container to your local machine. You can also specify directories, or reverse the syntax to copy a file from your local machine back out to the container.

If you want to access your Pod via the network, you can use the port-forward command to forward network traffic from the local machine to the Pod. This enables you to securely tunnel network traffic through to containers that might not be exposed anywhere on the public network. For example, the following command:

```
$ kubectl port-forward <pod-name> 8080:80
```

opens up a connection that forwards traffic from the local machine on port 8080 to the remote container on port 80.

You can also use the `port-forward` command with services by specifying `services/<service-name>` instead of `<pod-name>`, but note that if you do port-forward to a service, the requests will only ever be forwarded to a single Pod in that service. They will not go through the service load balancer.

If you want to view Kubernetes events, you can use the `kubectl get events` command to see a list of the latest 10 events on all objects in a given namespace:

```
$ kubectl get events
```

You can also stream events as they happen by adding `--watch` to the `kubectl get events` command. You may also wish to include `-A` to see events in all namespaces.

Finally, if you are interested in how your cluster is using resources, you can use the `top` command to see the list of resources in use by either nodes or Pods. This command:

```
$ kubectl top nodes
```

will display the total CPU and memory in use by the nodes in terms of both absolute units (e.g., cores) and percentage of available resources (e.g., total number of cores). Similarly, this command:

```
$ kubectl top pods
```

will show all Pods and their resource usage. By default it only displays Pods in the current namespace, but you can add the `--all-namespaces` flag to see resource usage by all Pods in the cluster.

These `top` commands only work if a metrics server is running in your cluster. Metrics servers are present in nearly every managed Kubernetes environment and many unmanaged environments as well. But if these commands fail, it may be because you need to install a metrics server.

Cluster Management

The `kubectl` tool can also be used to manage the cluster itself. The most common action that people take to manage their cluster is to cordon and drain a particular node. When you *cordon* a node, you prevent future Pods from being scheduled onto that machine. When you *drain* a node, you remove any Pods that are currently running on that machine. A good example use case for these commands would be removing a physical machine for repairs or upgrades. In that scenario, you can use `kubectl cordon` followed by `kubectl drain` to safely remove the machine from the cluster. Once the machine is repaired, you can use `kubectl uncordon` to re-enable Pods scheduling onto the node. There is no `undrain` command; Pods will naturally get scheduled onto the empty node as they are created. For something quick affecting a node (e.g., a machine reboot), it is generally unnecessary to cordon or drain; it's only necessary if the machine will be out of service long enough that you want the Pods to move to a different machine.

Command Autocompletion

kubectl supports integration with your shell to enable tab completion for both commands and resources. Depending on your environment, you may need to install the bash-completion package before you activate command autocompletion. You can do this using the appropriate package manager:

```
# macOS
$ brew install bash-completion

# CentOS/Red Hat
$ yum install bash-completion

# Debian/Ubuntu
$ apt-get install bash-completion
```

When installing on macOS, make sure to follow the instructions from brew about how to activate tab completion using your *${HOME}/.bash_profile*.

Once bash-completion is installed, you can temporarily activate it for your terminal using:

```
$ source <(kubectl completion bash)
```

To make this automatic for every terminal, add it to your *${HOME}/.bashrc* file:

```
$ echo "source <(kubectl completion bash)" >> ${HOME}/.bashrc
```

If you use zsh, you can find similar instructions online (*https://oreil.ly/aYujA*).

Alternative Ways of Viewing Your Cluster

In addition to kubectl, there are other tools for interacting with your Kubernetes cluster. For example, there are plug-ins for several editors that integrate Kubernetes and the editor environment, including:

- Visual Studio Code (*http://bit.ly/32ijGV1*)
- IntelliJ (*http://bit.ly/2Gen1eG*)
- Eclipse (*http://bit.ly/2XHi6gP*)

If you are using a managed Kubernetes service, most of them also feature a graphical interface to Kubernetes integrated into their web-based user experience. Managed

Kubernetes in the public cloud also integrates with sophisticated monitoring tools that can help you gain insights into how your applications are running.

There are also several open source graphical interfaces for Kubernetes including Rancher Dashboard (*https://oreil.ly/mliob*) and the Headlamp project (*https://oreil.ly/lDvbs*).

Summary

kubectl is a powerful tool for managing your applications in your Kubernetes cluster. This chapter has illustrated many of the common uses for the tool, but kubectl has a great deal of built-in help available. You can start viewing this help with:

```
$ kubectl help
```

or:

```
$ kubectl help <command-name>
```

CHAPTER 5
Pods

In earlier chapters, we discussed how you might go about containerizing your application, but in real-world deployments of containerized applications, you will often want to colocate multiple applications into a single atomic unit, scheduled onto a single machine.

A canonical example of such a deployment is illustrated in Figure 5-1, which consists of a container serving web requests and a container synchronizing the filesystem with a remote Git repository.

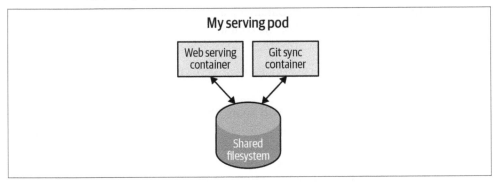

Figure 5-1. An example Pod with two containers and a shared filesystem

At first, it might seem tempting to wrap both the web server and the Git synchronizer into a single container. After closer inspection, however, the reasons for the separation become clear. First, the two containers have significantly different requirements in terms of resource usage. Take, for example, memory: because the web server is serving user requests, we want to ensure that it is always available and responsive. On the other hand, the Git synchronizer isn't really user-facing and has a "best effort" quality of service.

Suppose that our Git synchronizer has a memory leak. We need to ensure that the Git synchronizer cannot use up memory that we want to use for our web server, since this can affect performance or even crash the server.

This sort of resource isolation is exactly the sort of thing that containers are designed to accomplish. By separating the two applications into two separate containers, we can ensure reliable web server operation.

Of course, the two containers are quite symbiotic; it makes no sense to schedule the web server on one machine and the Git synchronizer on another. Consequently, Kubernetes groups multiple containers into a single atomic unit called a *Pod*. (The name goes with the whale theme of Docker containers, since a pod is also a group of whales.)

Though the grouping of multiple containers into a single Pod seemed controversial or confusing when it was first introduced in Kubernetes, it has subsequently been adopted by a variety of different applications to deploy their infrastructure. For example, several service mesh implementations use a second *sidecar* container to inject network management into an application's Pod.

Pods in Kubernetes

A Pod is a collection of application containers and volumes running in the same execution environment. Pods, not containers, are the smallest deployable artifact in a Kubernetes cluster. This means all of the containers in a Pod always land on the same machine.

Each container within a Pod runs in its own cgroup, but they share a number of Linux namespaces.

Applications running in the same Pod share the same IP address and port space (network namespace), have the same hostname (UTS namespace), and can communicate using native interprocess communication channels over System V IPC or POSIX message queues (IPC namespace). However, applications in different Pods are isolated from each other; they have different IP addresses, hostnames, and more. Containers in different Pods running on the same node might as well be on different servers.

Thinking with Pods

One of the most common questions people ask when adopting Kubernetes is "What should I put in a Pod?"

Sometimes people see Pods and think, "Aha! A WordPress container and a MySQL database container join together to make a WordPress instance. They should be in the same Pod." However, this kind of Pod is actually an example of an antipattern for Pod construction. There are two reasons for this. First, WordPress and its database are not truly symbiotic. If the WordPress container and the database container land on different machines, they still can work together quite effectively, since they communicate over a network connection. Secondly, you don't necessarily want to scale WordPress and the database as a unit. WordPress itself is mostly stateless, so you may want to scale your WordPress frontends in response to frontend load by creating more WordPress Pods. Scaling a MySQL database is much trickier, and you would be much more likely to increase the resources dedicated to a single MySQL Pod. If you group the WordPress and MySQL containers together in a single Pod, you are forced to use the same scaling strategy for both containers, which doesn't fit well.

In general, the right question to ask yourself when designing Pods is "Will these containers work correctly if they land on different machines?" If the answer is no, a Pod is the correct grouping for the containers. If the answer is yes, using multiple Pods is probably the correct solution. In the example at the beginning of this chapter, the two containers interact via a local filesystem. It would be impossible for them to operate correctly if the containers were scheduled on different machines.

In the remaining sections of this chapter, we will describe how to create, introspect, manage, and delete Pods in Kubernetes.

The Pod Manifest

Pods are described in a Pod *manifest*, which is just a text-file representation of the Kubernetes API object. Kubernetes strongly believes in *declarative configuration*, which means that you write down the desired state of the world in a configuration file and then submit that configuration to a service that takes actions to ensure the desired state becomes the actual state.

 Declarative configuration is different from *imperative configuration*, where you simply take a series of actions (for example, `apt-get install foo`) to modify the state of a system. Years of production experience have taught us that maintaining a written record of the system's desired state leads to a more manageable, reliable system. Declarative configuration has numerous advantages, such as enabling code review for configurations and documenting the current state of the system for distributed teams. Additionally, it is the basis for all of the self-healing behaviors in Kubernetes that keep applications running without user action.

The Kubernetes API server accepts and processes Pod manifests before storing them in persistent storage (etcd). The scheduler also uses the Kubernetes API to find Pods that haven't been scheduled to a node. It then places the Pods onto nodes depending on the resources and other constraints expressed in the Pod manifests. The scheduler can place multiple Pods on the same machine as long as there are sufficient resources. However, scheduling multiple replicas of the same application onto the same machine is worse for reliability, since the machine is a single failure domain. Consequently, the Kubernetes scheduler tries to ensure that Pods from the same application are distributed onto different machines for reliability in the presence of such failures. Once scheduled to a node, Pods don't move and must be explicitly destroyed and rescheduled.

Multiple instances of a Pod can be deployed by repeating the workflow described here. However, ReplicaSets (Chapter 9) are better suited for running multiple instances of a Pod. (It turns out they're also better at running a single Pod, but we'll get into that later.)

Creating a Pod

The simplest way to create a Pod is via the imperative `kubectl run` command. For example, to run our same kuard server, use:

```
$ kubectl run kuard --generator=run-pod/v1 \
    --image=gcr.io/kuar-demo/kuard-amd64:blue
```

You can see the status of this Pod by running:

```
$ kubectl get pods
```

You may initially see the container as `Pending`, but eventually you will see it transition to `Running`, which means that the Pod and its containers have been successfully created.

For now, you can delete this Pod by running:

```
$ kubectl delete pods/kuard
```

We will now move on to writing a complete Pod manifest by hand.

Creating a Pod Manifest

You can write Pod manifests using YAML or JSON, but YAML is generally preferred because it is slightly more human-editable and supports comments. Pod manifests (and other Kubernetes API objects) should really be treated in the same way as source code, and things like comments help explain the Pod to new team members.

Pod manifests include a couple of key fields and attributes: namely, a `metadata` section for describing the Pod and its labels, a `spec` section for describing volumes, and a list of containers that will run in the Pod.

In Chapter 2, we deployed kuard using the following Docker command:

```
$ docker run -d --name kuard \
  --publish 8080:8080 \
  gcr.io/kuar-demo/kuard-amd64:blue
```

You can achieve a similar result by instead writing Example 5-1 to a file named *kuard-pod.yaml* and then using `kubectl` commands to load that manifest to Kubernetes.

Example 5-1. kuard-pod.yaml

```
apiVersion: v1
kind: Pod
metadata:
  name: kuard
spec:
  containers:
    - image: gcr.io/kuar-demo/kuard-amd64:blue
      name: kuard
      ports:
        - containerPort: 8080
          name: http
          protocol: TCP
```

Though it may initially seem more cumbersome to manage your application in this manner, this written record of desired state is the best practice in the long run, especially for large teams with many applications.

Running Pods

In the previous section, we created a Pod manifest that can be used to start a Pod running kuard. Use the `kubectl apply` command to launch a single instance of kuard:

```
$ kubectl apply -f kuard-pod.yaml
```

The Pod manifest will be submitted to the Kubernetes API server. The Kubernetes system will then schedule that Pod to run on a healthy node in the cluster, where the `kubelet` daemon will monitor it. Don't worry if you don't understand all the moving parts of Kubernetes right now; we'll get into more details throughout the book.

Listing Pods

Now that we have a Pod running, let's go find out some more about it. Using the kubectl command-line tool, we can list all Pods running in the cluster. For now, this should only be the single Pod that we created in the previous step:

```
$ kubectl get pods
NAME     READY    STATUS    RESTARTS   AGE
kuard    1/1      Running   0          44s
```

You can see the name of the Pod (kuard) that we gave it in the previous YAML file. In addition to the number of ready containers (1/1), the output also shows the status, the number of times the Pod was restarted, and the age of the Pod.

If you ran this command immediately after the Pod was created, you might see:

```
NAME     READY    STATUS    RESTARTS   AGE
kuard    0/1      Pending   0          1s
```

The Pending state indicates that the Pod has been submitted but hasn't been scheduled yet. If a more significant error occurs, such as an attempt to create a Pod with a container image that doesn't exist, it will also be listed in the status field.

By default, the kubectl command-line tool is concise in the information it reports, but you can get more information via command-line flags. Adding -o wide to any kubectl command will print out slightly more information (while still keeping the information to a single line). Adding -o json or -o yaml will print out the complete objects in JSON or YAML, respectively. If you ever want to see an exhaustive, verbose logging of what kubectl is doing, you can add the --v=10 flag for comprehensive logging at the expense of readability.

Pod Details

Sometimes, the single-line view is insufficient because it is too terse. Additionally, Kubernetes maintains numerous events about Pods that are present in the event stream, not attached to the Pod object.

To find out more information about a Pod (or any Kubernetes object), you can use the kubectl describe command. For example, to describe the Pod we previously created, you can run:

```
$ kubectl describe pods kuard
```

This outputs a bunch of information about the Pod in different sections. At the top is basic information about the Pod:

```
Name:          kuard
Namespace:     default
Node:          node1/10.0.15.185
Start Time:    Sun, 02 Jul 2017 15:00:38 -0700
Labels:        <none>
Annotations:   <none>
Status:        Running
IP:            192.168.199.238
Controllers:   <none>
```

Then there is information about the containers running in the Pod:

```
Containers:
  kuard:
    Container ID:  docker://055095...
    Image:         gcr.io/kuar-demo/kuard-amd64:blue
    Image ID:      docker-pullable://gcr.io/kuar-demo/kuard-amd64@sha256:a580...
    Port:          8080/TCP
    State:         Running
      Started:     Sun, 02 Jul 2017 15:00:41 -0700
    Ready:         True
    Restart Count: 0
    Environment:   <none>
    Mounts:
      /var/run/secrets/kubernetes.io/serviceaccount from default-token-cg5f5 (ro)
```

Finally, there are events related to the Pod, such as when it was scheduled, when its image was pulled, and if/when it had to be restarted because of failing health checks:

```
Events:
  Seen  From                SubObjectPath           Type     Reason     Message
  ----  ----                -------------           ------   ------     -------
  50s   default-scheduler                           Normal   Scheduled  Success...
  49s   kubelet, node1      spec.containers{kuard}  Normal   Pulling    pulling...
  47s   kubelet, node1      spec.containers{kuard}  Normal   Pulled     Success...
  47s   kubelet, node1      spec.containers{kuard}  Normal   Created    Created...
  47s   kubelet, node1      spec.containers{kuard}  Normal   Started    Started...
```

Deleting a Pod

When it is time to delete a Pod, you can delete it either by name:

```
$ kubectl delete pods/kuard
```

or you can use the same file that you used to create it:

```
$ kubectl delete -f kuard-pod.yaml
```

When a Pod is deleted, it is *not* immediately killed. Instead, if you run kubectl get pods, you will see that the Pod is in the Terminating state. All Pods have a termination *grace period*. By default, this is 30 seconds. When a Pod is transitioned to Terminating, it no longer receives new requests. In a serving scenario, the grace period is important for reliability because it allows the Pod to finish any active requests that it may be in the middle of processing before it is terminated.

 When you delete a Pod, any data stored in the containers associated with that Pod will be deleted as well. If you want to persist data across multiple instances of a Pod, you need to use Persistent Volumes, described at the end of this chapter.

Accessing Your Pod

Now that your Pod is running, you're going to want to access it for a variety of reasons. You may want to load the web service that is running in the Pod. You may want to view its logs to debug a problem that you are seeing, or even execute other commands inside the Pod to help debug. The following sections detail various ways you can interact with the code and data running inside your Pod.

Getting More Information with Logs

When your application needs debugging, it's helpful to be able to dig deeper than `describe` to understand what the application is doing. Kubernetes provides two commands for debugging running containers. The `kubectl logs` command downloads the current logs from the running instance:

```
$ kubectl logs kuard
```

Adding the `-f` flag will cause the logs to stream continuously.

The `kubectl logs` command always tries to get logs from the currently running container. Adding the `--previous` flag will get logs from a previous instance of the container. This is useful, for example, if your containers are continuously restarting due to a problem at container startup.

 While using `kubectl logs` is useful for occasional debugging of containers in production environments, it's generally useful to use a log aggregation service. There are several open source log aggregation tools, like Fluentd and Elasticsearch, as well as numerous cloud logging providers. These log aggregation services provide greater capacity for storing a longer duration of logs as well as rich log searching and filtering capabilities. Many also provide the ability to aggregate logs from multiple Pods into a single view.

Running Commands in Your Container with exec

Sometimes logs are insufficient, and to truly determine what's going on, you need to execute commands in the context of the container itself. To do this, you can use:

```
$ kubectl exec kuard -- date
```

You can also get an interactive session by adding the `-it` flag:

```
$ kubectl exec -it kuard -- ash
```

Copying Files to and from Containers

In the previous chapter, we showed how to use the `kubectl cp` command to access files in a Pod. Generally speaking, copying files into a container is an antipattern. You really should treat the contents of a container as immutable. But occasionally it's the most immediate way to stop the bleeding and restore your service to health, since it is quicker than building, pushing, and rolling out a new image. Once you stop the bleeding, however, it is critically important that you immediately go and do the image build and rollout, or you are guaranteed to forget the local change that you made to your container and overwrite it in the subsequent regularly scheduled rollout.

Health Checks

When you run your application as a container in Kubernetes, it is automatically kept alive for you using a *process health check*. This health check simply ensures that the main process of your application is always running. If it isn't, Kubernetes restarts it.

However, in most cases, a simple process check is insufficient. For example, if your process has deadlocked and is unable to serve requests, a process health check will still believe that your application is healthy since its process is still running.

To address this, Kubernetes introduced health checks for application *liveness*. Liveness health checks run application-specific logic, like loading a web page, to verify that the application is not just still running, but is functioning properly. Since these liveness health checks are application-specific, you have to define them in your Pod manifest.

Liveness Probe

Once the kuard process is up and running, we need a way to confirm that it is actually healthy and shouldn't be restarted. Liveness probes are defined per container, which means each container inside a Pod is health checked separately. In Example 5-2, we add a liveness probe to our kuard container, which runs an HTTP request against the /healthy path on our container.

Example 5-2. kuard-pod-health.yaml

```yaml
apiVersion: v1
kind: Pod
metadata:
  name: kuard
spec:
  containers:
    - image: gcr.io/kuar-demo/kuard-amd64:blue
      name: kuard
      livenessProbe:
        httpGet:
          path: /healthy
          port: 8080
        initialDelaySeconds: 5
        timeoutSeconds: 1
        periodSeconds: 10
        failureThreshold: 3
      ports:
        - containerPort: 8080
          name: http
          protocol: TCP
```

The preceding Pod manifest uses an `httpGet` probe to perform an HTTP GET request against the /healthy endpoint on port 8080 of the kuard container. The probe sets an `initialDelaySeconds` of 5, and thus will not be called until 5 seconds after all the containers in the Pod are created. The probe must respond within the 1-second timeout, and the HTTP status code must be equal to or greater than 200 and less than 400 to be considered successful. Kubernetes will call the probe every 10 seconds. If more than three consecutive probes fail, the container will fail and restart.

You can see this in action by looking at the kuard status page. Create a Pod using this manifest and then port-forward to that Pod:

```
$ kubectl apply -f kuard-pod-health.yaml
$ kubectl port-forward kuard 8080:8080
```

Point your browser to *http://localhost:8080*. Click the "Liveness Probe" tab. You should see a table that lists all of the probes that this instance of kuard has received. If you click the "Fail" link on that page, kuard will start to fail health checks. Wait long enough, and Kubernetes will restart the container. At that point, the display will reset and start over again. Details of the restart can be found by running the command `kubectl describe pods kuard`. The "Events" section will have text similar to the following:

```
Killing container with id docker://2ac946...:pod "kuard_default(9ee84...)"
container "kuard" is unhealthy, it will be killed and re-created.
```

While the default response to a failed liveness check is to restart the Pod, the actual behavior is governed by the Pod's restartPolicy. There are three options for the restart policy: Always (the default), OnFailure (restart only on liveness failure or nonzero process exit code), or Never.

Readiness Probe

Of course, liveness isn't the only kind of health check we want to perform. Kubernetes makes a distinction between *liveness* and *readiness*. Liveness determines if an application is running properly. Containers that fail liveness checks are restarted. Readiness describes when a container is ready to serve user requests. Containers that fail readiness checks are removed from service load balancers. Readiness probes are configured similarly to liveness probes. We explore Kubernetes services in detail in Chapter 7.

Combining the readiness and liveness probes helps ensure only healthy containers are running within the cluster.

Startup Probe

Startup probes have recently been introduced to Kubernetes as an alternative way of managing slow-starting containers. When a Pod is started, the startup probe is run before any other probing of the Pod is started. The startup probe proceeds until it either times out (in which case the Pod is restarted) or it succeeds, at which time the liveness probe takes over. Startup probes enable you to poll slowly for a slow-starting container while also enabling a responsive liveness check once the slow-starting container has initialized.

Advanced Probe Configuration

Probes in Kubernetes have a number of advanced options, including how long to wait after Pod startup to start probing, how many failures should be considered a true failure, and how many successes are necessary to reset the failure count. All of these configurations receive default values when left unspecified, but they may be necessary for more advanced use cases such as applications that are inherently flaky or take a long time to start up.

Other Types of Health Checks

In addition to HTTP checks, Kubernetes also supports tcpSocket health checks that open a TCP socket; if the connection succeeds, the probe succeeds. This style of probe is useful for non-HTTP applications, such as databases or other non–HTTP-based APIs.

Finally, Kubernetes allows exec probes. These execute a script or program in the context of the container. Following typical convention, if this script returns a zero exit code, the probe succeeds; otherwise, it fails. exec scripts are often useful for custom application validation logic that doesn't fit neatly into an HTTP call.

Resource Management

Most people move into containers and orchestrators like Kubernetes because of the radical improvements in image packaging and reliable deployment they provide. In addition to application-oriented primitives that simplify distributed system development, equally important is that they allow you to increase the overall utilization of the compute nodes that make up the cluster. The basic cost of operating a machine, either virtual or physical, is basically constant regardless of whether it is idle or fully loaded. Consequently, ensuring that these machines are maximally active increases the efficiency of every dollar spent on infrastructure.

Generally speaking, we measure this efficiency with the utilization metric. *Utilization* is defined as the amount of a resource actively being used divided by the amount of a resource that has been purchased. For example, if you purchase a one-core machine, and your application uses one-tenth of a core, then your utilization is 10%. With scheduling systems like Kubernetes managing resource packing, you can drive your utilization to greater than 50%. To achieve this, you have to tell Kubernetes about the resources your application requires so that Kubernetes can find the optimal packing of containers onto machines.

Kubernetes allows users to specify two different resource metrics. Resource *requests* specify the minimum amount of a resource required to run the application. Resource *limits* specify the maximum amount of a resource that an application can consume. Let's look at these in greater detail in the following sections.

Kubernetes recognizes a large number of different notations for specifying resources, from literals ("12345") to millicores ("100m"). Of important note is the distinction between MB/GB/PB and MiB/GiB/PiB. The former is the familiar power of two units (e.g., 1 MB == 1,024 KB) while the latter is power of 10 units (1MiB == 1000KiB).

A common source of errors is specifying milliunits via a lowercase *m* versus megaunits via an uppercase *M*. Concretely, "400m" is 0.4 MB, not 400Mb, a significant difference!

Resource Requests: Minimum Required Resources

When a Pod requests the resources required to run its containers, Kubernetes guarantees that these resources are available to the Pod. The most commonly requested resources are CPU and memory, but Kubernetes supports other resource types as well, such as GPUs. For example, to request that the kuard container land on a machine with half a CPU free and get 128 MB of memory allocated to it, we define the Pod as shown in Example 5-3.

Example 5-3. kuard-pod-resreq.yaml

```
apiVersion: v1
kind: Pod
metadata:
  name: kuard
spec:
  containers:
    - image: gcr.io/kuar-demo/kuard-amd64:blue
      name: kuard
      resources:
        requests:
          cpu: "500m"
          memory: "128Mi"
      ports:
        - containerPort: 8080
          name: http
          protocol: TCP
```

 Resources are requested per container, not per Pod. The total resources requested by the Pod is the sum of all resources requested by all containers in the Pod because the different containers often have very different CPU requirements. For example, if a Pod contains a web server and data synchronizer, the web server is user-facing and likely needs a great deal of CPU, while the data synchronizer can make do with very little.

Requests are used when scheduling Pods to nodes. The Kubernetes scheduler will ensure that the sum of all requests of all Pods on a node does not exceed the capacity of the node. Therefore, a Pod is guaranteed to have at least the requested resources when running on the node. Importantly, "request" specifies a minimum. It does not specify a maximum cap on the resources a Pod may use. To explore what this means, let's look at an example.

Imagine a container whose code attempts to use all available CPU cores. Suppose that we create a Pod with this container that requests 0.5 CPU. Kubernetes schedules this Pod onto a machine with a total of 2 CPU cores. As long as it is the only Pod on the machine, it will consume all 2.0 of the available cores, despite only requesting 0.5 CPU.

If a second Pod with the same container and the same request of 0.5 CPU lands on the machine, then each Pod will receive 1.0 cores. If a third, identical Pod is scheduled, each Pod will receive 0.66 cores. Finally, if a fourth identical Pod is scheduled, each Pod will receive the 0.5 core it requested, and the node will be at capacity.

CPU requests are implemented using the `cpu-shares` functionality in the Linux kernel.

Memory requests are handled similarly to CPU, but there is an important difference. If a container is over its memory request, the OS can't just remove memory from the process, because it's been allocated. Consequently, when the system runs out of memory, the `kubelet` terminates containers whose memory usage is greater than their requested memory. These containers are automatically restarted, but with less available memory on the machine for the container to consume.

Since resource requests guarantee resource availability to a Pod, they are critical to ensuring that containers have sufficient resources in high-load situations.

Capping Resource Usage with Limits

In addition to setting the resources required by a Pod, which establishes the minimum resources available to it, you can also set a maximum on a its resource usage via resource *limits*.

In our previous example, we created a kuard Pod that requested a minimum of 0.5 of a core and 128 MB of memory. In the Pod manifest in Example 5-4, we extend this configuration to add a limit of 1.0 CPU and 256 MB of memory.

Example 5-4. kuard-pod-reslim.yaml

```
apiVersion: v1
kind: Pod
metadata:
  name: kuard
spec:
  containers:
    - image: gcr.io/kuar-demo/kuard-amd64:blue
      name: kuard
      resources:
        requests:
          cpu: "500m"
```

```
        memory: "128Mi"
      limits:
        cpu: "1000m"
        memory: "256Mi"
    ports:
      - containerPort: 8080
        name: http
        protocol: TCP
```

When you establish limits on a container, the kernel is configured to ensure that consumption cannot exceed these limits. A container with a CPU limit of 0.5 cores will only ever get 0.5 cores, even if the CPU is otherwise idle. A container with a memory limit of 256 MB will not be allowed additional memory; for example, `malloc` will fail if its memory usage exceeds 256 MB.

Persisting Data with Volumes

When a Pod is deleted or a container restarts, any and all data in the container's filesystem is also deleted. This is often a good thing, since you don't want to leave around cruft that happened to be written by your stateless web application. In other cases, having access to persistent disk storage is an important part of a healthy application. Kubernetes models such persistent storage.

Using Volumes with Pods

To add a volume to a Pod manifest, there are two new stanzas to add to our configuration. The first is a new `spec.volumes` section. This array defines all of the volumes that may be accessed by containers in the Pod manifest. It's important to note that not all containers are required to mount all volumes defined in the Pod. The second addition is the `volumeMounts` array in the container definition. This array defines the volumes that are mounted into a particular container and the path where each volume should be mounted. Note that two different containers in a Pod can mount the same volume at different mount paths.

The manifest in Example 5-5 defines a single new volume named `kuard-data`, which the kuard container mounts to the `/data` path.

Example 5-5. kuard-pod-vol.yaml

```
apiVersion: v1
kind: Pod
metadata:
  name: kuard
spec:
  volumes:
    - name: "kuard-data"
```

```
    hostPath:
      path: "/var/lib/kuard"
  containers:
    - image: gcr.io/kuar-demo/kuard-amd64:blue
      name: kuard
      volumeMounts:
        - mountPath: "/data"
          name: "kuard-data"
      ports:
        - containerPort: 8080
          name: http
          protocol: TCP
```

Different Ways of Using Volumes with Pods

There are a variety of ways you can use data in your application. The following are some of these ways and the recommended patterns for Kubernetes:

Communication/synchronization

In the first example of a Pod, we saw how two containers used a shared volume to serve a site while keeping it synchronized to a remote Git location (Figure 5-1). To achieve this, the Pod uses an `emptyDir` volume. Such a volume is scoped to the Pod's lifespan, but it can be shared between two containers, forming the basis for communication between our Git sync and web serving containers.

Cache

An application may use a volume that is valuable for performance, but not required for correct operation of the application. For example, perhaps the application keeps prerendered thumbnails of larger images. Of course, they can be reconstructed from the original images, but that makes serving the thumbnails more expensive. You want such a cache to survive a container restart due to a health-check failure, and thus `emptyDir` works well for the cache use case as well.

Persistent data

Sometimes you will use a volume for truly persistent data—data that is independent of the lifespan of a particular Pod, and should move between nodes in the cluster if a node fails or a Pod moves to a different machine. To achieve this, Kubernetes supports a wide variety of remote network storage volumes, including widely supported protocols like NFS and iSCSI as well as cloud provider network storage like Amazon Elastic Block Store, Azure File and Azure Disk, and Google's Persistent Disk.

Mounting the host filesystem

Other applications don't actually need a persistent volume, but they do need some access to the underlying host filesystem. For example, they may need access to the */dev* filesystem to perform raw block-level access to a device on the system. For these cases, Kubernetes supports the `hostPath` volume, which can mount arbitrary locations on the worker node into the container. Example 5-5 uses the hostPath volume type. The volume created is */var/lib/kuard* on the host.

Here is an example of using an NFS server:

```
...
# Rest of pod definition above here
volumes:
    - name: "kuard-data"
      nfs:
        server: my.nfs.server.local
        path: "/exports"
```

Persistent volumes are a deep topic. Chapter 16 has a more in-depth examination of the subject.

Putting It All Together

Many applications are stateful, and as such we must preserve any data and ensure access to the underlying storage volume regardless of what machine the application runs on. As we saw earlier, this can be achieved using a persistent volume backed by network-attached storage. We also want to ensure that a healthy instance of the application is running at all times, which means we want to make sure the container running kuard is ready before we expose it to clients.

Through a combination of persistent volumes, readiness and liveness probes, and resource restrictions, Kubernetes provides everything needed to run stateful applications reliably. Example 5-6 pulls this all together into one manifest.

Example 5-6. kuard-pod-full.yaml

```
apiVersion: v1
kind: Pod
metadata:
  name: kuard
spec:
  volumes:
    - name: "kuard-data"
      nfs:
        server: my.nfs.server.local
        path: "/exports"
  containers:
    - image: gcr.io/kuar-demo/kuard-amd64:blue
      name: kuard
      ports:
        - containerPort: 8080
          name: http
          protocol: TCP
      resources:
```

```
    requests:
      cpu: "500m"
      memory: "128Mi"
    limits:
      cpu: "1000m"
      memory: "256Mi"
  volumeMounts:
    - mountPath: "/data"
      name: "kuard-data"
  livenessProbe:
    httpGet:
      path: /healthy
      port: 8080
    initialDelaySeconds: 5
    timeoutSeconds: 1
    periodSeconds: 10
    failureThreshold: 3
  readinessProbe:
    httpGet:
      path: /ready
      port: 8080
    initialDelaySeconds: 30
    timeoutSeconds: 1
    periodSeconds: 10
    failureThreshold: 3
```

The definition of the Pod has grown over the course of this chapter. Each new capability added to your application also adds a new section to its definition.

Summary

Pods represent the atomic unit of work in a Kubernetes cluster. They are comprised of one or more containers working together symbiotically. To create one, you write a Pod manifest and submit it to the Kubernetes API server by using the command-line tool or (less frequently) by making HTTP and JSON calls to the server directly.

Once you've submitted the manifest to the API server, the Kubernetes scheduler finds a machine where the Pod can fit and schedules the Pod to that machine. After it's scheduled, the kubelet daemon on that machine is responsible for creating the containers that correspond to the Pod, as well as performing any health checks defined in the Pod manifest.

Once a Pod is scheduled to a node, no rescheduling occurs if that node fails. Additionally, to create multiple replicas of the same Pod, you have to create and name them manually. In Chapter 9, we introduce the ReplicaSet object and show how you can automate the creation of multiple identical Pods and ensure that they are re-created in the event of a node machine failure.

## CHAPTER 6

Labels and Annotations

Kubernetes was made to grow with you as your application scales in both size and complexity. Labels and annotations are fundamental concepts in Kubernetes that let you work in sets of things that map to how *you* think about your application. You can organize, mark, and cross-index all of your resources to represent the groups that make the most sense for your application.

Labels are key/value pairs that can be attached to Kubernetes objects such as Pods and ReplicaSets. They can be arbitrary and are useful for attaching identifying information to Kubernetes objects. Labels provide the foundation for grouping objects.

Annotations, on the other hand, provide a storage mechanism that resembles labels: key/value pairs designed to hold nonidentifying information that tools and libraries can leverage. Unlike labels, annotations are not meant for querying, filtering, or otherwise differentiating Pods from each other.

Labels

Labels provide identifying metadata for objects. These are fundamental qualities of the object that will be used for grouping, viewing, and operating. The motivations for labels grew out of Google's experience in running large and complex applications. A couple of lessons emerged from this experience:

- Production abhors a singleton. When deploying software, users often start with a single instance. However, as the application matures, these singletons often multiply and become sets of objects. With this in mind, Kubernetes uses labels to deal with sets of objects instead of single instances.

- Any hierarchy imposed by the system will fall short for many users. In addition, user groupings and hierarchies change over time. For instance, a user may start out with the idea that all apps are made up of many services. However, over time, a service may be shared across multiple apps. Kubernetes labels are flexible enough to adapt to these situations and more.

See the great site reliability book *Site Reliability Engineering* by Betsy Beyer et al. (O'Reilly) for deeper background on how Google approaches production systems.

Labels have simple syntax. They are key/value pairs, where both the key and value are represented by strings. Label keys can be broken down into two parts: an optional prefix and a name, separated by a slash. The prefix, if specified, must be a DNS subdomain with a 253-character limit. The key name is required and have a maximum length of 63 characters. Names must also start and end with an alphanumeric character and permit the use of dashes (-), underscores (_), and dots (.) between characters.

Label values are strings with a maximum length of 63 characters. The contents of the label values follow the same rules as label keys. Table 6-1 shows some valid label keys and values.

Table 6-1. Label examples

Key	Value
acme.com/app-version	1.0.0
appVersion	1.0.0
app.version	1.0.0
kubernetes.io/cluster-service	true

When domain names are used in labels and annotations, they are expected to be aligned to that particular entity in some way. For example, a project might define a canonical set of labels used to identify the various stages of application deployment such as staging, canary, and production. Or a cloud provider might define provider-specific annotations that extend Kubernetes objects to activate features specific to their service.

Applying Labels

Here we create a few deployments (a way to create an array of Pods) with some interesting labels. We'll take two apps (called `alpaca` and `bandicoot`) and have two environments and two versions for each.

First, create the `alpaca-prod` deployment and set the `ver`, `app`, and `env` labels:

```
$ kubectl run alpaca-prod \
  --image=gcr.io/kuar-demo/kuard-amd64:blue \
  --replicas=2 \
  --labels="ver=1,app=alpaca,env=prod"
```

Next, create the `alpaca-test` deployment and set the `ver`, `app`, and `env` labels with the appropriate values:

```
$ kubectl run alpaca-test \
  --image=gcr.io/kuar-demo/kuard-amd64:green \
  --replicas=1 \
  --labels="ver=2,app=alpaca,env=test"
```

Finally, create two deployments for `bandicoot`. Here we name the environments `prod` and `staging`:

```
$ kubectl run bandicoot-prod \
  --image=gcr.io/kuar-demo/kuard-amd64:green \
  --replicas=2 \
  --labels="ver=2,app=bandicoot,env=prod"
$ kubectl run bandicoot-staging \
  --image=gcr.io/kuar-demo/kuard-amd64:green \
  --replicas=1 \
  --labels="ver=2,app=bandicoot,env=staging"
```

At this point, you should have four deployments—`alpaca-prod`, `alpaca-test`, `bandicoot-prod`, and `bandicoot-staging`:

```
$ kubectl get deployments --show-labels

NAME                ... LABELS
alpaca-prod         ... app=alpaca,env=prod,ver=1
alpaca-test         ... app=alpaca,env=test,ver=2
bandicoot-prod      ... app=bandicoot,env=prod,ver=2
bandicoot-staging   ... app=bandicoot,env=staging,ver=2
```

We can visualize this as a Venn diagram based on the labels (Figure 6-1).

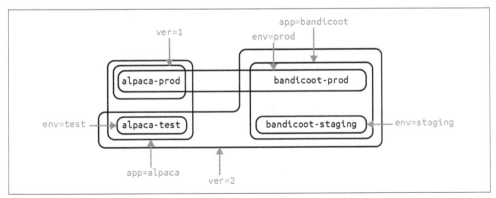

Figure 6-1. Visualization of labels applied to our deployments

Modifying Labels

You can also apply or update labels on objects after you create them:

```
$ kubectl label deployments alpaca-test "canary=true"
```

 There is a caveat here. In this example, the kubectl label command will only change the label on the deployment itself; it won't affect any objects that the deployment creates, such as ReplicaSets and Pods. To change those, you'll need to change the template embedded in the deployment (see Chapter 10).

You can also use the -L option to kubectl get to show a label value as a column:

```
$ kubectl get deployments -L canary
```

NAME	DESIRED	CURRENT	...	CANARY
alpaca-prod	2	2	...	<none>
alpaca-test	1	1	...	true
bandicoot-prod	2	2	...	<none>
bandicoot-staging	1	1	...	<none>

You can remove a label by applying a dash-suffix:

```
$ kubectl label deployments alpaca-test "canary-"
```

Label Selectors

Label selectors are used to filter Kubernetes objects based on a set of labels. Selectors use a simple syntax for Boolean expressions. They are used both by end users (via tools like kubectl) and by different types of objects (such as how a ReplicaSet relates to its Pods).

Each deployment (via a ReplicaSet) creates a set of Pods using the labels specified in the template embedded in the deployment. This is configured by the kubectl run command.

Running the kubectl get pods command should return all the Pods currently running in the cluster. We should have a total of six kuard Pods across our three environments:

```
$ kubectl get pods --show-labels
```

NAME	...	LABELS
alpaca-prod-3408831585-4nzfb	...	app=alpaca,env=prod,ver=1,...
alpaca-prod-3408831585-kga0a	...	app=alpaca,env=prod,ver=1,...
alpaca-test-1004512375-3r1m5	...	app=alpaca,env=test,ver=2,...
bandicoot-prod-373860099-0t1gp	...	app=bandicoot,env=prod,ver=2,...
bandicoot-prod-373860099-k2wcf	...	app=bandicoot,env=prod,ver=2,...
bandicoot-staging-1839769971-3ndv	...	app=bandicoot,env=staging,ver=2,...

You may see a new label that you haven't seen before: pod-template-hash. This label is applied by the deployment so it can keep track of which Pods were generated from which template versions. This allows the deployment to manage updates cleanly, as will be covered in depth in Chapter 10.

If we want to list only Pods that have the ver label set to 2, we could use the --selector flag:

```
$ kubectl get pods --selector="ver=2"
```

NAME	READY	STATUS	RESTARTS	AGE
alpaca-test-1004512375-3r1m5	1/1	Running	0	3m
bandicoot-prod-373860099-0t1gp	1/1	Running	0	3m
bandicoot-prod-373860099-k2wcf	1/1	Running	0	3m
bandicoot-staging-1839769971-3ndv5	1/1	Running	0	3m

If we specify two selectors separated by a comma, only the objects that satisfy both will be returned. This is a logical AND operation:

```
$ kubectl get pods --selector="app=bandicoot,ver=2"
```

NAME	READY	STATUS	RESTARTS	AGE
bandicoot-prod-373860099-0t1gp	1/1	Running	0	4m
bandicoot-prod-373860099-k2wcf	1/1	Running	0	4m
bandicoot-staging-1839769971-3ndv5	1/1	Running	0	4m

We can also ask if a label is one of a set of values. Here we ask for all Pods where the app label is set to alpaca or bandicoot (which will be all six Pods):

```
$ kubectl get pods --selector="app in (alpaca,bandicoot)"
```

NAME	READY	STATUS	RESTARTS	AGE
alpaca-prod-3408831585-4nzfb	1/1	Running	0	6m
alpaca-prod-3408831585-kga0a	1/1	Running	0	6m
alpaca-test-1004512375-3r1m5	1/1	Running	0	6m
bandicoot-prod-373860099-0t1gp	1/1	Running	0	6m
bandicoot-prod-373860099-k2wcf	1/1	Running	0	6m
bandicoot-staging-1839769971-3ndv5	1/1	Running	0	6m

Finally, we can ask if a label is set at all. Here we are asking for all of the deployments with the canary label set to anything:

```
$ kubectl get deployments --selector="canary"
```

NAME	DESIRED	CURRENT	UP-TO-DATE	AVAILABLE	AGE
alpaca-test	1	1	1	1	7m

There are also "negative" versions of each of these, as shown in Table 6-2.

Table 6-2. Selector operators

Operator	Description
key=value	key is set to value
key!=value	key is not set to value
key in (value1, value2)	key is one of value1 or value2
key notin (value1, value2)	key is not one of value1 or value2
key	key is set
!key	key is not set

For example, asking if a key, in this case `canary`, is not set can look like:

```
$ kubectl get deployments --selector='!canary'
```

You can combine positive and negative selectors:

```
$ kubectl get pods -l 'ver=2,!canary'
```

Label Selectors in API Objects

A Kubernetes object uses a label selector to refer to a set of other Kubernetes objects. Instead of a simple string as described in the previous section, we use a parsed structure.

For historical reasons (Kubernetes doesn't break API compatibility!), there are two forms. Most objects support a newer, more powerful set of selector operators. A selector of `app=alpaca,ver in (1, 2)` would be converted to this:

```
selector:
  matchLabels:
    app: alpaca
  matchExpressions:
    - {key: ver, operator: In, values: [1, 2]}
```

This example uses compact YAML syntax. This is an item in a list (`matchExpressions`) that is a map with three entries. The last entry (`values`) has a value that is a list with two items. All of the terms are evaluated as a logical AND. The only way to represent the `!=` operator is to convert it to a `NotIn` expression with a single value.

The older form of specifying selectors (used in `ReplicationControllers` and services) only supports the `=` operator. The `=` operator selects target objects where its set of key/value pairs all match the object. The selector `app=alpaca,ver=1` would be represented like this:

```
selector:
  app: alpaca
  ver: 1
```

Labels in the Kubernetes Architecture

In addition to enabling users to organize their infrastructure, labels play a critical role in linking various related Kubernetes objects. Kubernetes is a purposefully decoupled system. There is no hierarchy and all components operate independently. However, in many cases, objects need to relate to one another, and these relationships are defined by labels and label selectors.

For example, ReplicaSets, which create and maintain multiple replicas of a Pod, find the Pods that they are managing via a selector. Likewise, a service load balancer finds the Pods to which it should bring traffic via a selector query. When a Pod is created, it can use a node selector to identify a particular set of nodes onto which it can be scheduled. When people want to restrict network traffic in their cluster, they use Network Policy in conjunction with specific labels to identify Pods that should or should not be allowed to communicate with each other.

Labels are a powerful and ubiquitous glue that holds a Kubernetes application together. Though your application will likely start out with a simple set of labels and queries, you should expect it to grow in size and sophistication with time.

Annotations

Annotations provide a place to store additional metadata for Kubernetes objects where the sole purpose of the metadata is assisting tools and libraries. They are a way for other programs driving Kubernetes via an API to store some opaque data with an object. Annotations can be used for the tool itself or to pass configuration information between external systems.

While labels are used to identify and group objects, annotations are used to provide extra information about where an object came from, how to use it, or policy around that object. There is overlap, and it is a matter of taste as to when to use an annotation or a label. When in doubt, add information to an object as an annotation and promote it to a label if you find yourself wanting to use it in a selector.

Annotations are used to:

- Keep track of a "reason" for the latest update to an object.
- Communicate a specialized scheduling policy to a specialized scheduler.
- Extend data about the last tool to update the resource and how it was updated (used for detecting changes by other tools and doing a smart merge).
- Attach build, release, or image information that isn't appropriate for labels (may include a Git hash, timestamp, pull request number, etc.).
- Enable the Deployment object (see Chapter 10) to keep track of ReplicaSets that it is managing for rollouts.

- Provide extra data to enhance the visual quality or usability of a UI. For example, objects could include a link to an icon (or a base64-encoded version of an icon).

- Prototype alpha functionality in Kubernetes (instead of creating a first-class API field, the parameters for that functionality are encoded in an annotation).

Annotations are used in various places in Kubernetes, with the primary use case being rolling deployments. During rolling deployments, annotations are used to track rollout status and provide the necessary information required to roll back a deployment to a previous state.

Avoid using the Kubernetes API server as a general-purpose database. Annotations are good for small bits of data that are highly associated with a specific resource. If you want to store data in Kubernetes but you don't have an obvious object to associate it with, consider storing that data in some other, more appropriate database.

Annotation keys use the same format as label keys. However, because they are often used to communicate information between tools, the "namespace" part of the key is more important. Example keys include `deployment.kubernetes.io/revision` or `kubernetes.io/change-cause`.

The value component of an annotation is a free-form string field. While this allows maximum flexibility as users can store arbitrary data, because this is arbitrary text, there is no validation of any format. For example, it is not uncommon for a JSON document to be encoded as a string and stored in an annotation. It is important to note that the Kubernetes server has no knowledge of the required format of annotation values. If annotations are used to pass or store data, there is no guarantee the data is valid. This can make tracking down errors more difficult.

Annotations are defined in the common `metadata` section in every Kubernetes object:

```
...
metadata:
  annotations:
    example.com/icon-url: "https://example.com/icon.png"
...
```

 Annotations are very convenient and provide powerful loose coupling, but use them judiciously to avoid an untyped mess of data.

Cleanup

It is easy to clean up all of the deployments that we started in this chapter:

```
$ kubectl delete deployments --all
```

If you want to be more selective, you can use the `--selector` flag to choose which deployments to delete.

Summary

Labels are used to identify and optionally group objects in a Kubernetes cluster. They are also used in selector queries to provide flexible runtime grouping of objects, such as Pods.

Annotations provide object-scoped key/value metadata storage used by automation tooling and client libraries. They can also be used to hold configuration data for external tools such as third-party schedulers and monitoring tools.

Labels and annotations are vital to understanding how key components in a Kubernetes cluster work together to ensure the desired cluster state. Using them properly unlocks the true power of Kubernetes's flexibility and provides a starting point for building automation tools and deployment workflows.

## CHAPTER 7

Service Discovery

Kubernetes is a very dynamic system. The system is involved in placing Pods on nodes, making sure they are up and running, and rescheduling them as needed. There are ways to automatically change the number of Pods based on load (such as Horizontal Pod Autoscaling [see "Autoscaling a ReplicaSet" on page 110]). The API-driven nature of the system encourages others to create higher and higher levels of automation.

While the dynamic nature of Kubernetes makes it easy to run a lot of things, it creates problems when it comes to *finding* those things. Most of the traditional network infrastructure wasn't built for the level of dynamism that Kubernetes presents.

What Is Service Discovery?

The general name for this class of problems and solutions is *service discovery*. Service-discovery tools help solve the problem of finding which processes are listening at which addresses for which services. A good service-discovery system will enable users to resolve this information quickly and reliably. A good system is also low-latency; clients are updated soon after the information associated with a service changes. Finally, a good service-discovery system can store a richer definition of what that service is. For example, perhaps there are multiple ports associated with the service.

The Domain Name System (DNS) is the traditional system of service discovery on the internet. DNS is designed for relatively stable name resolution with wide and efficient caching. It is a great system for the internet but falls short in the dynamic world of Kubernetes.

Unfortunately, many systems (for example, Java, by default) look up a name in DNS directly and never re-resolve it. This can lead to clients caching stale mappings and talking to the wrong IP. Even with a short TTL (time-to-live) and a well-behaved client, there is a natural delay between when a name resolution changes and when the client notices. There are natural limits to the amount and type of information that can be returned in a typical DNS query too. Things start to break past 20 to 30 address (A) records for a single name. Service (SRV) records solve some problems, but are often very hard to use. Finally, the way that clients handle multiple IPs in a DNS record is usually to take the first IP address and rely on the DNS server to randomize or round-robin the order of records. This is no substitute for more purpose-built load balancing.

The Service Object

Real service discovery in Kubernetes starts with a Service object. A Service object is a way to create a named label selector. As we will see, the Service object does some other nice things for us too.

Just as the kubectl run command is an easy way to create a Kubernetes deployment, we can use kubectl expose to create a service. We'll talk about Deployments in detail in Chapter 10, but for now you can think of a Deployment as an instance of a microservice. Let's create some deployments and services so we can see how they work:

```
$ kubectl create deployment alpaca-prod \
  --image=gcr.io/kuar-demo/kuard-amd64:blue \
  --port=8080
$ kubectl scale deployment alpaca-prod --replicas 3
$ kubectl expose deployment alpaca-prod
$ kubectl create deployment bandicoot-prod \
  --image=gcr.io/kuar-demo/kuard-amd64:green \
  --port=8080
$ kubectl scale deployment bandicoot-prod --replicas 2
  kubectl expose deployment bandicoot-prod
$ kubectl get services -o wide

NAME             CLUSTER-IP      ... PORT(S)  ... SELECTOR
alpaca-prod      10.115.245.13 ... 8080/TCP ... app=alpaca
bandicoot-prod   10.115.242.3  ... 8080/TCP ... app=bandicoot
kubernetes       10.115.240.1  ... 443/TCP  ... <none>
```

After running these commands, we have three services. The ones we just created are alpaca-prod and bandicoot-prod. The kubernetes service is automatically created for you so that you can find and talk to the Kubernetes API from within the app.

If we look at the SELECTOR column, we see that the alpaca-prod service simply gives a name to a selector and specifies which ports to talk to for that service. The kubectl expose command will conveniently pull both the label selector and the relevant ports (8080, in this case) from the deployment definition.

Furthermore, that service is assigned a new type of virtual IP called a *cluster IP*. This is a special IP address the system will load balance across all of the Pods that are identified by the selector.

To interact with services, we are going to port-forward to one of the `alpaca` Pods. Start this command and leave it running in a terminal window. You can see the port-forward working by accessing the `alpaca` Pod at *http://localhost:48858*:

```
$ ALPACA_POD=$(kubectl get pods -l app=alpaca \
    -o jsonpath='{.items[0].metadata.name}')
$ kubectl port-forward $ALPACA_POD 48858:8080
```

Service DNS

Because the cluster IP is virtual, it is stable, and it is appropriate to give it a DNS address. All of the issues around clients caching DNS results no longer apply. Within a namespace, it is as easy as just using the service name to connect to one of the Pods identified by a service.

Kubernetes provides a DNS service exposed to Pods running in the cluster. This Kubernetes DNS service was installed as a system component when the cluster was first created. The DNS service is, itself, managed by Kubernetes and is a great example of Kubernetes building on Kubernetes. The Kubernetes DNS service provides DNS names for cluster IPs.

You can try this out by expanding the "DNS Query" section on the `kuard` server status page. Query the A record for `alpaca-prod`. The output should look something like this:

```
;; opcode: QUERY, status: NOERROR, id: 12071
;; flags: qr aa rd ra; QUERY: 1, ANSWER: 1, AUTHORITY: 0, ADDITIONAL: 0

;; QUESTION SECTION:
;alpaca-prod.default.svc.cluster.local. IN      A

;; ANSWER SECTION:
alpaca-prod.default.svc.cluster.local.  30      IN      A       10.115.245.13
```

The full DNS name here is `alpaca-prod.default.svc.cluster.local.`. Let's break this down:

`alpaca-prod`
> The name of the service in question.

`default`
> The namespace that this service is in.

`svc`

> Recognizing that this is a service. This allows Kubernetes to expose other types of things as DNS in the future.

`cluster.local.`

> The base domain name for the cluster. This is the default and what you will see for most clusters. Administrators may change this to allow unique DNS names across multiple clusters.

When referring to a service in your own namespace, you can just use the service name (`alpaca-prod`). You can also refer to a service in another namespace with `alpaca-prod.default`. And, of course, you can use the fully qualified service name (`alpaca-prod.default.svc.cluster.local.`). Try each of these out in the "DNS Query" section of kuard.

Readiness Checks

Often, when an application first starts up, it isn't ready to handle requests. There is usually some amount of initialization that can take anywhere from under a second to several minutes. One nice thing the Service object does is track which of your Pods are ready via a readiness check. Let's modify our deployment to add a readiness check that is attached to a Pod, as we discussed in Chapter 5:

```
$ kubectl edit deployment/alpaca-prod
```

This command will fetch the current version of the `alpaca-prod` deployment and bring it up in an editor. After you save and quit your editor, it'll write the object back to Kubernetes. This is a quick way to edit an object without saving it to a YAML file.

Add the following section:

```
spec:
  ...
  template:
    ...
    spec:
      containers:
        ...
        name: alpaca-prod
        readinessProbe:
          httpGet:
            path: /ready
            port: 8080
          periodSeconds: 2
          initialDelaySeconds: 0
          failureThreshold: 3
          successThreshold: 1
```

This sets up the Pods this deployment will create so that they will be checked for readiness via an HTTP GET to /ready on port 8080. This check is done every two seconds starting as soon as the Pod comes up. If three successive checks fail, then the Pod will be considered not ready. However, if only one check succeeds, the Pod will again be considered ready.

Only ready Pods are sent traffic.

Updating the deployment definition like this will delete and re-create the alpaca Pods. As such, we need to restart our port-forward command from earlier:

```
$ ALPACA_POD=$(kubectl get pods -l app=alpaca-prod \
    -o jsonpath='{.items[0].metadata.name}')
$ kubectl port-forward $ALPACA_POD 48858:8080
```

Point your browser to *http://localhost:48858*, and you should see the debug page for that instance of kuard. Expand the "Readiness Probe" section. You should see this page update every time there is a new readiness check from the system, which should happen every two seconds.

In another terminal window, start a watch command on the endpoints for the alpaca-prod service. Endpoints are a lower-level way of finding what a service is sending traffic to and are covered later in this chapter. The --watch option here causes the kubectl command to hang around and output any updates. This is an easy way to see how a Kubernetes object changes over time:

```
$ kubectl get endpoints alpaca-prod --watch
```

Now return to your browser and hit the "Fail" link for the readiness check. You should see that the server is now returning errors with codes in the 500s. After three of these, this server is removed from the list of endpoints for the service. Hit the "Succeed" link and notice that after a single readiness check, the endpoint is added back.

This readiness check is a way for an overloaded or sick server to signal to the system that it doesn't want to receive traffic anymore. This is a great way to implement graceful shutdown. The server can signal that it no longer wants traffic, wait until existing connections are closed, and then cleanly exit.

Press Ctrl-C to exit out of both the port-forward and watch commands in your terminals.

Looking Beyond the Cluster

So far, everything we've covered in this chapter has been about exposing services inside of a cluster. Oftentimes, the IPs for Pods are only reachable from within the cluster. At some point, we have to allow new traffic in!

The most portable way to do this is to use a feature called NodePorts, which enhance a service even further. In addition to a cluster IP, the system picks a port (or the user can specify one), and every node in the cluster then forwards traffic to that port to the service.

With this feature, if you can reach any node in the cluster, you can contact a service. You can use the NodePort without knowing where any of the Pods for that service are running. This can be integrated with hardware or software load balancers to expose the service further.

Try this out by modifying the `alpaca-prod` service:

```
$ kubectl edit service alpaca-prod
```

Change the `spec.type` field to `NodePort`. You can also do this when creating the service via kubectl expose by specifying `--type=NodePort`. The system will assign a new NodePort:

```
$ kubectl describe service alpaca-prod
Name:                alpaca-prod
Namespace:           default
Labels:              app=alpaca
Annotations:         <none>
Selector:            app=alpaca
Type:                NodePort
IP:                  10.115.245.13
Port:                <unset> 8080/TCP
NodePort:            <unset> 32711/TCP
Endpoints:           10.112.1.66:8080,10.112.2.104:8080,10.112.2.105:8080
Session Affinity:    None
No events.
```

Here we see that the system assigned port 32711 to this service. Now we can hit any of our cluster nodes on that port to access the service. If you are sitting on the same network, you can access it directly. If your cluster is in the cloud someplace, you can use SSH tunneling with something like this:

```
$ ssh <node> -L 8080:localhost:32711
```

Now if you point your browser to *http://localhost:8080*, you will be connected to that service. Each request that you send to the service will be randomly directed to one of the Pods that implements the service. Reload the page a few times, and you will see that you are randomly assigned to different Pods.

When you are done, exit the SSH session.

Load Balancer Integration

If you have a cluster that is configured to integrate with external load balancers, you can use the LoadBalancer type. This builds on the NodePort type by additionally configuring the cloud to create a new load balancer and direct it at nodes in your cluster. Most cloud-based Kubernetes clusters offer load balancer integration, and there are a number of projects that implement load balancer integration for common physical load balancers as well, although these may require more manual integration with your cluster.

Edit the alpaca-prod service again (kubectl edit service alpaca-prod) and change spec.type to LoadBalancer.

 Creating a service of type LoadBalancer exposes that service to the public internet. Before you do this, you should make certain that it is something that is secure to be exposed to everyone in the world. We will discuss security risks further in this section. Additionally, Chapters 9 and 20 provide guidance on how to secure your application.

If you do a kubectl get services right away, you'll see that the EXTERNAL-IP column for alpaca-prod now says <pending>. Wait a bit and you should see a public address assigned by your cloud. You can look in the console for your cloud account and see the configuration work that Kubernetes did for you:

```
$ kubectl describe service alpaca-prod

Name:                   alpaca-prod
Namespace:              default
Labels:                 app=alpaca
Selector:               app=alpaca
Type:                   LoadBalancer
IP:                     10.115.245.13
LoadBalancer Ingress:   104.196.248.204
Port:                   <unset> 8080/TCP
NodePort:               <unset> 32711/TCP
Endpoints:              10.112.1.66:8080,10.112.2.104:8080,10.112.2.105:8080
Session Affinity:       None
Events:
  FirstSeen ... Reason                  Message
  --------- ... ------                  -------
  3m        ... Type                    NodePort -> LoadBalancer
  3m        ... CreatingLoadBalancer    Creating load balancer
  2m        ... CreatedLoadBalancer     Created load balancer
```

Here we see that we have an address of 104.196.248.204 now assigned to the alpaca-prod service. Open up your browser and try!

This example is from a cluster launched and managed on the Google Cloud Platform via GKE. The way a load balancer is configured is specific to a cloud. Some clouds have DNS-based load balancers (e.g., AWS Elastic Load Balancing [ELB]). In this case, you'll see a hostname here instead of an IP. Depending on the cloud provider, it may still take a little while for the load balancer to be fully operational.

Creating a cloud-based load balancer can take some time. Don't be surprised if it takes a few minutes on most cloud providers.

The examples that we have seen so far use *external* load balancers; that is, load balancers that are connected to the public internet. While this is great for exposing services to the world, you'll often want to expose your application within only your private network. To achieve this, use an *internal* load balancer. Unfortunately, because support for internal load balancers was added to Kubernetes more recently, it is done in a somewhat ad hoc manner via object annotations. For example, to create an internal load balancer in an Azure Kubernetes Service cluster, you add the annotation `service.beta.kubernetes.io/azure-load-balancer-internal: "true"` to your Service resource. Here are the settings for some popular clouds:

Microsoft Azure
```
service.beta.kubernetes.io/azure-load-balancer-internal: "true"
```

Amazon Web Services
```
service.beta.kubernetes.io/aws-load-balancer-internal: "true"
```

Alibaba Cloud
```
service.beta.kubernetes.io/alibaba-cloud-loadbalancer-address-type:
"intranet"
```

Google Cloud Platform
```
cloud.google.com/load-balancer-type: "Internal"
```

When you add this annotation to your Service, it should look like this:

```
...
metadata:
    ...
    name: some-service
    annotations:
        service.beta.kubernetes.io/azure-load-balancer-internal: "true"
...
```

When you create a service with one of these annotations, an internally exposed service will be created instead of one on the public internet.

There are several other annotations that extend LoadBalancer behavior, including ones for using a preexisiting IP address. The specific extensions for your provider should be documented on its website.

Advanced Details

Kubernetes is built to be an extensible system. As such, there are layers that allow for more advanced integrations. Understanding the details of how a sophisticated concept like services is implemented may help you troubleshoot or create more advanced integrations. This section goes a bit below the surface.

Endpoints

Some applications (and the system itself) want to be able to use services without using a cluster IP. This is done with another type of object called an Endpoints object. For every Service object, Kubernetes creates a buddy Endpoints object that contains the IP addresses for that service:

```
$ kubectl describe endpoints alpaca-prod

Name:             alpaca-prod
Namespace:        default
Labels:           app=alpaca
Subsets:
  Addresses:              10.112.1.54,10.112.2.84,10.112.2.85
  NotReadyAddresses:      <none>
  Ports:
    Name       Port    Protocol
    ----       ----    --------
    <unset>    8080    TCP

No events.
```

To use a service, an advanced application can talk to the Kubernetes API directly to look up endpoints and call them. The Kubernetes API even has the capability to "watch" objects and be notified as soon as they change. In this way, a client can react immediately as soon as the IPs associated with a service change.

Let's demonstrate this. In a terminal window, start the following command and leave it running:

```
$ kubectl get endpoints alpaca-prod --watch
```

It will output the current state of the endpoint and then "hang":

```
NAME           ENDPOINTS                                                 AGE
alpaca-prod    10.112.1.54:8080,10.112.2.84:8080,10.112.2.85:8080        1m
```

Now open up *another* terminal window and delete and re-create the deployment backing alpaca-prod:

```
$ kubectl delete deployment alpaca-prod
$ kubectl create deployment alpaca-prod \
  --image=gcr.io/kuar-demo/kuard-amd64:blue \
  --port=8080
$ kubectl scale deployment alpaca-prod --replicas=3
```

If you look back at the output from the watched endpoint, you will see that as you deleted and re-created these Pods, the output of the command reflected the most up-to-date set of IP addresses associated with the service. Your output will look something like this:

```
NAME          ENDPOINTS                                              AGE
alpaca-prod   10.112.1.54:8080,10.112.2.84:8080,10.112.2.85:8080    1m
alpaca-prod   10.112.1.54:8080,10.112.2.84:8080                      1m
alpaca-prod   <none>                                                 1m
alpaca-prod   10.112.2.90:8080                                       1m
alpaca-prod   10.112.1.57:8080,10.112.2.90:8080                      1m
alpaca-prod   10.112.0.28:8080,10.112.1.57:8080,10.112.2.90:8080    1m
```

The Endpoints object is great if you are writing new code that is built to run on Kubernetes from the start. But most projects aren't in this position! Most existing systems are built to work with regular old IP addresses that don't change that often.

Manual Service Discovery

Kubernetes services are built on top of label selectors over Pods. That means that you can use the Kubernetes API to do rudimentary service discovery without using a Service object at all! Let's demonstrate.

With kubectl (and via the API) we can easily see what IPs are assigned to each Pod in our example deployments:

```
$ kubectl get pods -o wide --show-labels
```

```
NAME                          ... IP          ... LABELS
alpaca-prod-12334-87f8h       ... 10.112.1.54 ... app=alpaca
alpaca-prod-12334-jssmh       ... 10.112.2.84 ... app=alpaca
alpaca-prod-12334-tjp56       ... 10.112.2.85 ... app=alpaca
bandicoot-prod-5678-sbxzl     ... 10.112.1.55 ... app=bandicoot
bandicoot-prod-5678-x0dh8     ... 10.112.2.86 ... app=bandicoot
```

This is great, but what if you have a ton of Pods? You'll probably want to filter this based on the labels applied as part of the deployment. Let's do that for just the alpaca app:

```
$ kubectl get pods -o wide --selector=app=alpaca
```

```
NAME                          ... IP          ...
```

```
alpaca-prod-3408831585-bpzdz ... 10.112.1.54 ...
alpaca-prod-3408831585-kncwt ... 10.112.2.84 ...
alpaca-prod-3408831585-l9fsq ... 10.112.2.85 ...
```

At this point, you have the basics of service discovery! You can always use labels to identify the set of Pods you are interested in, get all of the Pods for those labels, and dig out the IP address. But keeping the correct set of labels to use in sync can be tricky. This is why the Service object was created.

kube-proxy and Cluster IPs

Cluster IPs are stable virtual IPs that load balance traffic across all of the endpoints in a service. This magic is performed by a component running on every node in the cluster called the kube-proxy (Figure 7-1).

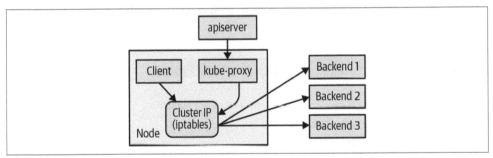

Figure 7-1. Configuring and using a cluster IP

In Figure 7-1, the kube-proxy watches for new services in the cluster via the API server. It then programs a set of iptables rules in the kernel of that host to rewrite the destinations of packets so they are directed at one of the endpoints for that service. If the set of endpoints for a service changes (due to Pods coming and going or due to a failed readiness check), the set of iptables rules is rewritten.

The cluster IP itself is usually assigned by the API server as the service is created. However, when creating the service, the user can specify a specific cluster IP. Once set, the cluster IP cannot be modified without deleting and re-creating the Service object.

> The Kubernetes service address range is configured using the `--service-cluster-ip-range` flag on the kube-apiserver binary. The service address range should not overlap with the IP subnets and ranges assigned to each Docker bridge or Kubernetes node. In addition, any explicit cluster IP requested must come from that range and not already be in use.

Cluster IP Environment Variables

While most users should be using the DNS services to find cluster IPs, there are some older mechanisms that may still be in use. One of these is injecting a set of environment variables into Pods as they start up.

To see this in action, let's look at the console for the `bandicoot` instance of `kuard`. Enter the following commands in your terminal:

```
$ BANDICOOT_POD=$(kubectl get pods -l app=bandicoot \
    -o jsonpath='{.items[0].metadata.name}')
$ kubectl port-forward $BANDICOOT_POD 48858:8080
```

Now point your browser to *http://localhost:48858* to see the status page for this server. Expand the "Server Env" section and note the set of environment variables for the `alpaca` service. The status page should show a table similar to Table 7-1.

Table 7-1. Service environment variables

Key	Value
ALPACA_PROD_PORT	tcp://10.115.245.13:8080
ALPACA_PROD_PORT_8080_TCP	tcp://10.115.245.13:8080
ALPACA_PROD_PORT_8080_TCP_ADDR	10.115.245.13
ALPACA_PROD_PORT_8080_TCP_PORT	8080
ALPACA_PROD_PORT_8080_TCP_PROTO	tcp
ALPACA_PROD_SERVICE_HOST	10.115.245.13
ALPACA_PROD_SERVICE_PORT	8080

The two main environment variables to use are `ALPACA_PROD_SERVICE_HOST` and `ALPACA_PROD_SERVICE_PORT`. The other environment variables are created to be compatible with (now deprecated) Docker link variables.

A problem with the environment variable approach is that it requires resources to be created in a specific order. The services must be created before the Pods that reference them. This can introduce quite a bit of complexity when deploying a set of services that make up a larger application. In addition, using *just* environment variables seems strange to many users. For this reason, DNS is probably a better option.

Connecting with Other Environments

While it is great to have service discovery within your own cluster, many real-world applications actually require that you integrate more cloud native applications deployed in Kubernetes with applications deployed to more legacy environments. Additionally, you may need to integrate a Kubernetes cluster in the cloud with infrastructure that has been deployed on-premise. This is an area of Kubernetes that is still undergoing a fair amount of exploration and development of solutions.

Connecting to Resources Outside of a Cluster

When you are connecting Kubernetes to legacy resources outside of the cluster, you can use selector-less services to declare a Kubernetes service with a manually assigned IP address that is outside of the cluster. That way, Kubernetes service discovery via DNS works as expected, but the network traffic itself flows to an external resource. To create a selector-less service, you remove the `spec.selector` field from your resource, while leaving the `metadata` and the `ports` sections unchanged. Because your service has no selector, no endpoints are automatically added to the service. This means that you must add them manually. Typically the endpoint that you will add will be a fixed IP address (e.g., the IP address of your database server) so you only need to add it once. But if the IP address that backs the service ever changes, you will need to update the corresponding endpoint resource. To create or update the endpoint resource, you use an endpoint that looks something like the following:

```
apiVersion: v1
kind: Endpoints
metadata:
  # This name must match the name of your service
  name: my-database-server
subsets:
  - addresses:
      # Replace this IP with the real IP of your server
      - ip: 1.2.3.4
    ports:
      # Replace this port with the port(s) you want to expose
      - port: 1433
```

Connecting External Resources to Services Inside a Cluster

Connecting external resources to Kubernetes services is somewhat trickier. If your cloud provider supports it, the easiest thing to do is to create an "internal" load balancer, as described above, that lives in your virtual private network and can deliver traffic from a fixed IP address into the cluster. You can then use traditional DNS to make this IP address available to the external resource. If an internal load balancer isn't available, you can use a `NodePort` service to expose the service on the IP addresses of the nodes in the cluster. You can then either program a physical load balancer to serve traffic to those nodes, or use DNS-based load-balancing to spread traffic between the nodes.

If neither of those solutions works for your use case, more complex options include running the full `kube-proxy` on an external resource and programming that machine to use the DNS server in the Kubernetes cluster. Such a setup is significantly more difficult to get right and should really only be used in on-premise environments. There are also a variety of open source projects (for example, HashiCorp's Consul) that can be used to manage connectivity between in-cluster and out-of-cluster resources. Such options require significant knowledge of both networking and Kubernetes to get right and should really be considered a last resort.

Cleanup

Run the following command to clean up all of the objects created in this chapter:

```
$ kubectl delete services,deployments -l app
```

Summary

Kubernetes is a dynamic system that challenges traditional methods of naming and connecting services over the network. The Service object provides a flexible and powerful way to expose services both within the cluster and beyond. With the techniques covered here, you can connect services to each other and expose them outside the cluster.

While using the dynamic service discovery mechanisms in Kubernetes introduces some new concepts and may, at first, seem complex, understanding and adapting these techniques is key to unlocking the power of Kubernetes. Once your application can dynamically find services and react to the dynamic placement of those applications, you are free to stop worrying about where things are running and when they move. Thinking about services in a logical way and letting Kubernetes take care of the details of container placement is a critical piece of the puzzle.

Of course, service discovery is just the beginning of how application networking works with Kubernetes. Chapter 8 covers Ingress networking, which is dedicated to Layer 7 (HTTP) load balancing and routing, and Chapter 15 is about service meshes, which are a more recently developed approach to cloud native networking that provide many additional capabilities in addition to service discovery and load balancing.

HTTP Load Balancing with Ingress

A critical part of any application is getting network traffic to and from that application. As described in Chapter 7, Kubernetes has a set of capabilities to enable services to be exposed outside of the cluster. For many users and simple use cases, these capabilities are sufficient.

But the Service object operates at Layer 4 (according to the OSI model).[1] This means that it only forwards TCP and UDP connections and doesn't look inside of those connections. Because of this, hosting many applications on a cluster uses many different exposed services. In the case where these services are `type: NodePort`, you'll have to have clients connect to a unique port per service. In the case where these services are `type: LoadBalancer`, you'll be allocating (often expensive or scarce) cloud resources for each service. But for HTTP (Layer 7)-based services, we can do better.

When solving a similar problem in non-Kubernetes situations, users often turn to the idea of "virtual hosting." This is a mechanism to host many HTTP sites on a single IP address. Typically, the user uses a load balancer or reverse proxy to accept incoming connections on HTTP (80) and HTTPS (443) ports. That program then parses the HTTP connection and, based on the `Host` header and the URL path that is requested, proxies the HTTP call to some other program. In this way, that load balancer or reverse proxy directs traffic for decoding and directing incoming connections to the right "upstream" server.

Kubernetes calls its HTTP-based load-balancing system *Ingress*. Ingress is a Kubernetes-native way to implement the "virtual hosting" pattern we just discussed.

---

1 The Open Systems Interconnection (OSI) model (*https://oreil.ly/czfCd*) is a standard way to describe how different networking layers build on each other. TCP and UDP are considered to be Layer 4, while HTTP is Layer 7.

One of the more complex aspects of the pattern is that the user has to manage the load balancer configuration file. In a dynamic environment and as the set of virtual hosts expands, this can be very complex. The Kubernetes Ingress system works to simplify this by (a) standardizing that configuration, (b) moving it to a standard Kubernetes object, and (c) merging multiple Ingress objects into a single config for the load balancer.

The typical software base implementation looks something like what is depicted in Figure 8-1. The Ingress controller is a software system made up of two parts. The first is the Ingress proxy, which is exposed outside the cluster using a service of type: LoadBalancer. This proxy sends requests to "upstream" servers. The other component is the Ingress reconciler, or operator. The Ingress operator is responsible for reading and monitoring Ingress objects in the Kubernetes API and reconfiguring the Ingress proxy to route traffic as specified in the Ingress resource. There are many different Ingress implementations. In some, these two components are combined in a single container; in others, they are distinct components that are deployed separately in the Kubernetes cluster. In Figure 8-1, we introduce one example of an Ingress controller.

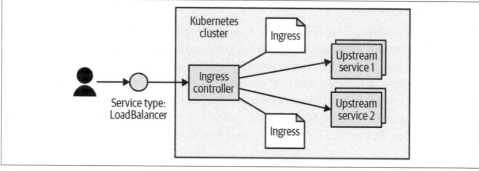

Figure 8-1. The typical software Ingress controller configuration

Ingress Spec Versus Ingress Controllers

While conceptually simple, at an implementation level, Ingress is very different from pretty much every other regular resource object in Kubernetes. Specifically, it is split into a common resource specification and a controller implementation. There is no "standard" Ingress controller that is built into Kubernetes, so the user must install one of many optional implementations.

Users can create and modify Ingress objects just like every other object. But, by default, there is no code running to actually act on those objects. It is up to the users (or the distribution they are using) to install and manage an outside controller. In this way, the controller is pluggable.

There are a couple of reasons that Ingress ended up like this. First of all, there is no one single HTTP load balancer that can be used universally. In addition to many software load balancers (both open source and proprietary), there are also load-balancing capabilities provided by cloud providers (e.g., ELB on AWS), and hardware-based load balancers. The second reason is that the Ingress object was added to Kubernetes before any of the common extensibility capabilities were added (see Chapter 17). As Ingress progresses, it is likely that it will evolve to use these mechanisms.

Installing Contour

While there are many available Ingress controllers, for the examples here, we use an Ingress controller called Contour. This is a controller built to configure the open source (and CNCF project) load balancer called Envoy. Envoy is built to be dynamically configured via an API. The Contour Ingress controller takes care of translating the Ingress objects into something that Envoy can understand.

 The Contour project (*https://oreil.ly/5IHmq*) was created by Heptio in collaboration with real-world customers and is used in production settings but is now an independent open source project.

You can install Contour with a simple one-line invocation:

```
$ kubectl apply -f https://projectcontour.io/quickstart/contour.yaml
```

Note that this requires execution by a user who has `cluster-admin` permissions.

This one line works for most configurations. It creates a namespace called `project contour`. Inside of that namespace it creates a deployment (with two replicas) and an external-facing service of `type: LoadBalancer`. In addition, it sets up the correct permissions via a service account and installs a CustomResourceDefinition (see Chapter 17) for some extended capabilities discussed in "The Future of Ingress" on page 101.

Because it is a global install, you need to ensure that you have wide admin permissions on the cluster you are installing into. After you install it, you can fetch the external address of Contour via:

```
$ kubectl get -n projectcontour service envoy -o wide
NAME      CLUSTER-IP    EXTERNAL-IP       PORT(S)      ...
contour   10.106.53.14  a477...amazonaws.com 80:30274/TCP ...
```

Look at the `EXTERNAL-IP` column. This can be either an IP address (for GCP and Azure) or a hostname (for AWS). Other clouds and environments may differ. If your Kubernetes cluster doesn't support services of `type: LoadBalancer`, you'll have to change the YAML for installing Contour to use `type: NodePort` and route traffic to machines on the cluster via a mechanism that works in your configuration.

If you are using `minikube`, you probably won't have anything listed for `EXTERNAL-IP`. To fix this, you need to open a separate terminal window and run `minikube tunnel`. This configures networking routes such that you have unique IP addresses assigned to every service of `type: LoadBalancer`.

Configuring DNS

To make Ingress work well, you need to configure DNS entries to the external address for your load balancer. You can map multiple hostnames to a single external endpoint and the Ingress controller will direct incoming requests to the appropriate upstream service based on that hostname.

For this chapter, we assume that you have a domain called `example.com`. You need to configure two DNS entries: `alpaca.example.com` and `bandicoot.example.com`. If you have an IP address for your external load balancer, you'll want to create A records. If you have a hostname, you'll want to configure CNAME records.

The ExternalDNS project (*https://oreil.ly/ILdEj*) is a cluster add-on that you can use to manage DNS records for you. ExternalDNS monitors your Kubernetes cluster and synchronizes IP addresses for Kubernetes Service resources with an external DNS provider. ExternalDNS supports a wide variety of DNS providers including traditional domain registrars as well as public cloud providers.

Configuring a Local hosts File

If you don't have a domain or if you are using a local solution such as `minikube`, you can set up a local configuration by editing your */etc/hosts* file to add an IP address. You need admin/root privileges on your workstation. The location of the file may differ on your platform, and making it take effect may require extra steps. For example, on Windows the file is usually at *C:\Windows\System32\drivers\etc\hosts*, and for recent versions of macOS, you need to run `sudo killall -HUP mDNSResponder` after changing the file.

Edit the file to add a line like the following:

```
<ip-address> alpaca.example.com bandicoot.example.com
```

For `<ip-address>`, fill in the external IP address for Contour. If all you have is a hostname (like from AWS), you can get an IP address (that may change in the future) by executing `host -t a <address>`.

Don't forget to undo these changes when you are done!

Using Ingress

Now that we have an Ingress controller configured, let's put it through its paces. First, we'll create a few upstream (also sometimes referred to as "backend") services to play with by executing the following commands:

```
$ kubectl create deployment be-default \
  --image=gcr.io/kuar-demo/kuard-amd64:blue \
  --replicas=3 \
  --port=8080
$ kubectl expose deployment be-default
$ kubectl create deployment alpaca \
  --image=gcr.io/kuar-demo/kuard-amd64:green \
  --replicas=3 \
  --port=8080
$ kubectl expose deployment alpaca
$ kubectl create deployment bandicoot \
  --image=gcr.io/kuar-demo/kuard-amd64:purple \
  --replicas=3 \
  --port=8080
$ kubectl expose deployment bandicoot
$ kubectl get services -o wide

NAME          CLUSTER-IP     ... PORT(S)   ... SELECTOR
alpaca        10.115.245.13 ... 8080/TCP ... run=alpaca
bandicoot     10.115.242.3  ... 8080/TCP ... run=bandicoot
be-default    10.115.246.6  ... 8080/TCP ... run=be-default
kubernetes    10.115.240.1  ... 443/TCP  ... <none>
```

Simplest Usage

The simplest way to use Ingress is to have it just blindly pass everything that it sees through to an upstream service. There is limited support for imperative commands to work with Ingress in kubectl, so we'll start with a YAML file (see Example 8-1).

Example 8-1. simple-ingress.yaml

```
apiVersion: networking.k8s.io/v1
kind: Ingress
metadata:
  name: simple-ingress
spec:
  defaultBackend:
    service:
      name: alpaca
      port:
        number: 8080
```

Create this Ingress with kubectl apply:

```
$ kubectl apply -f simple-ingress.yaml
ingress.extensions/simple-ingress created
```

You can verify that it was set up correctly using kubectl get and kubectl describe:

```
$ kubectl get ingress
NAME              HOSTS   ADDRESS   PORTS   AGE
simple-ingress    *                 80      13m

$ kubectl describe ingress simple-ingress
Name:            simple-ingress
Namespace:       default
Address:
Default backend: alpaca:8080
(172.17.0.6:8080,172.17.0.7:8080,172.17.0.8:8080)
Rules:
  Host  Path  Backends
  ----  ----  --------
  *     *     alpaca:8080 (172.17.0.6:8080,172.17.0.7:8080,172.17.0.8:8080)
Annotations:
  ...

Events:   <none>
```

This sets things up so that *any* HTTP request that hits the Ingress controller is forwarded on to the alpaca service. You can now access the alpaca instance of kuard on any of the raw IPs/CNAMEs of the service; in this case, either alpaca.example.com or bandicoot.example.com. This doesn't, at this point, add much value over a simple service of type: LoadBalancer. The following sections experiment with more complex configurations.

Using Hostnames

Things start to get interesting when we direct traffic based on properties of the request. The most common example of this is to have the Ingress system look at the HTTP host header (which is set to the DNS domain in the original URL) and direct traffic based on that header. Let's add *another* Ingress object for directing traffic to the alpaca service for any traffic directed to alpaca.example.com (see Example 8-2).

Example 8-2. host-ingress.yaml

```
apiVersion: networking.k8s.io/v1
kind: Ingress
metadata:
  name: host-ingress
spec:
  defaultBackend:
    service:
```

```
      name: be-default
      port:
        number: 8080
  rules:
  - host: alpaca.example.com
    http:
      paths:
      - pathType: Prefix
        path: /
        backend:
          service:
            name: alpaca
            port:
              number: 8080
```

Create this Ingress with kubectl apply:

```
$ kubectl apply -f host-ingress.yaml
ingress.extensions/host-ingress created
```

We can verify that things are set up correctly as follows:

```
$ kubectl get ingress
NAME             HOSTS                ADDRESS   PORTS   AGE
host-ingress     alpaca.example.com             80      54s
simple-ingress   *                              80      13m

$ kubectl describe ingress host-ingress
Name:            host-ingress
Namespace:       default
Address:
Default backend: be-default:8080 (<none>)
Rules:
  Host                 Path  Backends
  ----                 ----  --------
  alpaca.example.com
                       /     alpaca:8080 (<none>)
Annotations:
  ...

Events:  <none>
```

There are a couple of confusing things here. First, there is a reference to the default-http-backend. This is a convention that only some Ingress controllers use to handle requests that aren't handled in any other way. These controllers send those requests to a service called default-http-backend in the kube-system namespace. This convention is surfaced client-side in kubectl. Next, there are no endpoints listed for the alpaca backend service. This is a bug in kubectl that is fixed in Kubernetes v1.14.

Regardless, you should now be able to address the `alpaca` service via *http://alpaca.example.com*. If instead you reach the service endpoint via other methods, you should get the default service.

Using Paths

The next interesting scenario is to direct traffic based on not just the hostname, but also the path in the HTTP request. We can do this easily by specifying a path in the `paths` entry (see Example 8-3). In this example, we direct everything coming into *http://bandicoot.example.com* to the `bandicoot` service, but we also send *http://bandicoot.example.com/a* to the `alpaca` service. This type of scenario can be used to host multiple services on different paths of a single domain.

Example 8-3. path-ingress.yaml

```
apiVersion: networking.k8s.io/v1
kind: Ingress
metadata:
  name: path-ingress
spec:
  rules:
  - host: bandicoot.example.com
    http:
      paths:
      - pathType: Prefix
        path: "/"
        backend:
          service:
            name: bandicoot
            port:
              number: 8080
      - pathType: Prefix
        path: "/a/"
        backend:
          service:
            name: alpaca
            port:
              number: 8080
```

When there are multiple paths on the same host listed in the Ingress system, the longest prefix matches. So, in this example, traffic starting with /a/ is forwarded to the `alpaca` service, while all other traffic (starting with /) is directed to the `bandicoot` service.

As requests get proxied to the upstream service, the path remains unmodified. That means a request to `bandicoot.example.com/a/` shows up to the upstream server that is configured for that request hostname and path. The upstream service needs to be ready to serve traffic on that subpath. In this case, kuard has special code for testing, where it responds on the root path (/) along with a predefined set of subpaths (/a/, /b/, and /c/).

Cleanup

To clean up, execute the following:

```
$ kubectl delete ingress host-ingress path-ingress simple-ingress
$ kubectl delete service alpaca bandicoot be-default
$ kubectl delete deployment alpaca bandicoot be-default
```

Advanced Ingress Topics and Gotchas

Ingress supports some other fancy features. The level of support for these features differs based on the Ingress controller implementation, and two controllers may implement a feature in slightly different ways.

Many of the extended features are exposed via annotations on the Ingress object. Be careful; these annotations can be hard to validate and are easy to get wrong. Many of these annotations apply to the entire Ingress object and so can be more general than you might like. To scope the annotations down, you can always split a single Ingress object into multiple Ingress objects. The Ingress controller should read them and merge them together.

Running Multiple Ingress Controllers

There are multiple Ingress controller implementations, and you may want to run multiple Ingress controllers on a single cluster. To solve this case, the IngressClass resource exists so that an Ingress resource can request a particular implementation. When you create an Ingress resource, you use the spec.ingressClassName field to specify the specific Ingress resource.

In Kubernetes prior to version 1.18, the IngressClassName field did not exist and the kubernetes.io/ingress.class annotation was used instead. While this is still supported by many controllers, it is recommended that people move away from the annotation as it will likely be deprecated by controllers in the future.

If the spec.ingressClassName annotation is missing, a default Ingress controller is used. It is specified by adding the ingressclass.kubernetes.io/is-default-class annotation to the correct IngressClass resource.

Multiple Ingress Objects

If you specify multiple Ingress objects, the Ingress controllers should read them all and try to merge them into a coherent configuration. However, if you specify duplicate and conflicting configurations, the behavior is undefined. It is likely that different Ingress controllers will behave differently. Even a single implementation may do different things depending on nonobvious factors.

Ingress and Namespaces

Ingress interacts with namespaces in some nonobvious ways. First, due to an abundance of security caution, an Ingress object can refer to only an upstream service in the same namespace. This means that you can't use an Ingress object to point a subpath to a service in another namespace.

However, multiple Ingress objects in different namespaces can specify subpaths for the same host. These Ingress objects are then merged to come up with the final config for the Ingress controller.

This cross-namespace behavior means that coordinating Ingress globally across the cluster is necessary. If not coordinated carefully, an Ingress object in one namespace could cause problems (and undefined behavior) in other namespaces.

Typically there are no restrictions built into the Ingress controller around which namespaces are allowed to specify which hostnames and paths. Advanced users may try to enforce a policy for this using a custom admission controller. There are also evolutions of Ingress described in "The Future of Ingress" on page 101 that address this problem.

Path Rewriting

Some Ingress controller implementations support, optionally, doing path rewriting. This can be used to modify the path in the HTTP request as it gets proxied. This is usually specified by an annotation on the Ingress object and applies to all requests that are specified by that object. For example, if we were using the NGINX Ingress controller, we could specify an annotation of `nginx.ingress.kubernetes.io/rewrite-target: /`. This can sometimes make upstream services work on a subpath even if they weren't built to do so.

There are multiple implementations that not only implement path rewriting, but also support regular expressions when specifying the path. For example, the NGINX controller allows regular expressions to capture parts of the path and then use that captured content when doing rewriting. How this is done (and what variant of regular expressions is used) is implementation-specific.

Path rewriting isn't a silver bullet, though, and can often lead to bugs. Many web applications assume that they can link within themselves using absolute paths. In that case, the app in question may be hosted on /subpath but have requests show up to it on /. It may then send a user to /app-path. There is then the question of whether that is an "internal" link for the app (in which case it should instead be /subpath/app-path) or a link to some other app. For this reason, it is probably best to avoid subpaths for any complicated applications if you can help it.

Serving TLS

When serving websites, it is becoming increasingly necessary to do so securely using TLS and HTTPS. Ingress supports this (as do most Ingress controllers).

First, users need to specify a Secret with their TLS certificate and keys—something like what is outlined in Example 8-4. You can also create a Secret imperatively with kubectl create secret tls <secret-name> --cert <certificate-pem-file> --key <private-key-pem-file>.

Example 8-4. tls-secret.yaml

```
apiVersion: v1
kind: Secret
metadata:
  creationTimestamp: null
  name: tls-secret-name
type: kubernetes.io/tls
data:
  tls.crt: <base64 encoded certificate>
  tls.key: <base64 encoded private key>
```

Once you have the certificate uploaded, you can reference it in an Ingress object. This specifies a list of certificates along with the hostnames that those certificates should be used for (see Example 8-5). Again, if multiple Ingress objects specify certificates for the same hostname, the behavior is undefined.

Example 8-5. tls-ingress.yaml

```
apiVersion: networking.k8s.io/v1
kind: Ingress
metadata:
  name: tls-ingress
spec:
  tls:
  - hosts:
    - alpaca.example.com
    secretName: tls-secret-name
  rules:
```

```
 - host: alpaca.example.com
   http:
     paths:
     - backend:
         serviceName: alpaca
         servicePort: 8080
```

Uploading and managing TLS secrets can be difficult. In addition, certificates can often come at a significant cost. To help solve this problem, there is a nonprofit called "Let's Encrypt" (*https://letsencrypt.org*) running a free Certificate Authority that is API-driven. Since it is API-driven, it is possible to set up a Kubernetes cluster that automatically fetches and installs TLS certificates for you. It can be tricky to set up, but when working, it's very simple to use. The missing piece is an open source project called cert-manager (*https://cert-manager.io*) created by Jetstack, a UK startup, onboarded to the CNCF. The *cert-manager.io* website or GitHub repository (*https:// oreil.ly/S0PU4*) has details on how to install cert-manager and get started.

Alternate Ingress Implementations

There are many different implementations of Ingress controllers, each building on the base Ingress object with unique features. It is a vibrant ecosystem.

First, each cloud provider has an Ingress implementation that exposes the specific cloud-based L7 load balancer for that cloud. Instead of configuring a software load balancer running in a Pod, these controllers take Ingress objects and use them to configure, via an API, the cloud-based load balancers. This reduces the load on the cluster and the management burden for the operators, but can often come at a cost.

The most popular generic Ingress controller is probably the open source NGINX Ingress controller (*https://oreil.ly/EstHX*). Be aware that there is also a commercial controller based on the proprietary NGINX Plus. The open source controller essentially reads Ingress objects and merges them into an NGINX configuration file. It then signals to the NGINX process to restart with the new configuration (while responsibly serving existing in-flight connections). The open source NGINX controller has an enormous number of features and options exposed via annotations (*https:// oreil.ly/V8nM7*).

Emissary (*https://oreil.ly/5HDun*) and Gloo (*https://oreil.ly/rZDlX*) are two other Envoy-based Ingress controllers that are focused on being API gateways.

Traefik (*https://traefik.io*) is a reverse proxy implemented in Go that also can function as an Ingress controller. It has a set of features and dashboards that are very developer-friendly.

This just scratches the surface. The Ingress ecosystem is very active, and there are many new projects and commercial offerings that build on the humble Ingress object in unique ways.

The Future of Ingress

As you have seen, the Ingress object provides a very useful abstraction for configuring L7 load balancers—but it hasn't scaled to all the features that users want and various implementations are looking to offer. Many of the features in Ingress are underdefined. Implementations can surface these features in different ways, reducing the portability of configurations between implementations.

Another problem is that it is easy to misconfigure Ingress. The way that multiple objects compbine opens the door for conflicts that are resolved differently by different implementations. In addition, the way that these are merged across namespaces breaks the idea of namespace isolation.

Ingress was also created before the idea of a service mesh (exemplified by projects such as Istio and Linkerd) was well known. The intersection of Ingress and service meshes is still being defined. Service meshes are covered in greater detail in Chapter 15.

The future of HTTP load balancing for Kubernetes looks to be the *Gateway* API, which is in the midst of development by the Kubernetes special interest group (SIG) dedicated to networking. The Gateway API project is intended to develop a more modern API for routing in Kubernetes. Though it is more focused on HTTP balancing, Gateway also includes resources for controlling Layer 4 (TCP) balancing. The Gateway APIs are still very much under development, so it is strongly recommended that people stick to the existing Ingress and Service resources that are currently present in Kubernetes. The current state of the Gateway API can be found online (*https://oreil.ly/zhlil*).

Summary

Ingress is a unique system in Kubernetes. It is simply a schema, and the implementations of a controller for that schema must be installed and managed separately. But it is also a critical system for exposing services to users in a practical and cost-efficient way. As Kubernetes continues to mature, expect to see Ingress become more and more relevant.

## CHAPTER 9

ReplicaSets

We have covered how to run individual containers as Pods, but these Pods are essentially one-off singletons. More often than not, you want multiple replicas of a container running at a particular time for a variety of reasons:

Redundancy
  Failure toleration by running multiple instances.

Scale
  Higher request-processing capacity by running multiple instances.

Sharding
  Different replicas can handle different parts of a computation in parallel.

Of course, you could manually create multiple copies of a Pod using multiple different (though largely similar) Pod manifests, but doing so is both tedious and error-prone. Logically, a user managing a replicated set of Pods considers them as a single entity to be defined and managed—and that's precisely what a ReplicaSet is. A ReplicaSet acts as a cluster-wide Pod manager, ensuring that the right types and numbers of Pods are running at all times.

Because ReplicaSets make it easy to create and manage replicated sets of Pods, they are the building blocks for common application deployment patterns and for self-healing applications at the infrastructure level. Pods managed by ReplicaSets are automatically rescheduled under certain failure conditions, such as node failures and network partitions.

The easiest way to think of a ReplicaSet is that it combines a cookie cutter and a desired number of cookies into a single API object. When we define a ReplicaSet, we define a specification for the Pods we want to create (the "cookie cutter") and a desired number of replicas. Additionally, we need to define a way of finding Pods that the ReplicaSet should control. The actual act of managing the replicated Pods is an example of a *reconciliation loop*. Such loops are fundamental to most of the design and implementation of Kubernetes.

Reconciliation Loops

The central concept behind a reconciliation loop is the notion of *desired* state versus *observed* or *current* state. Desired state is the state you want. With a ReplicaSet, it is the desired number of replicas and the definition of the Pod to replicate. For example, "the desired state is that there are three replicas of a Pod running the kuard server." In contrast, the current state is the currently observed state of the system. For example, "there are only two kuard Pods currently running."

The reconciliation loop is constantly running, observing the current state of the world and taking action to try to make the observed state match the desired state. For instance, with the previous examples, the reconciliation loop would create a new kuard Pod in an effort to make the observed state match the desired state of three replicas.

There are many benefits to the reconciliation-loop approach to managing state. It is an inherently goal-driven, self-healing system, yet it can often be easily expressed in a few lines of code. For example, the reconciliation loop for ReplicaSets is a single loop, yet it handles user actions to scale up or scale down the ReplicaSet as well as node failures or nodes rejoining the cluster after being absent.

We'll see numerous examples of reconciliation loops in action throughout the rest of the book.

Relating Pods and ReplicaSets

Decoupling is a key theme in Kubernetes. In particular, it's important that all of the core concepts of Kubernetes are modular with respect to each other and that they are swappable and replaceable with other components. In this spirit, the relationship between ReplicaSets and Pods is loosely coupled. Though ReplicaSets create and manage Pods, they do not own the Pods they create. ReplicaSets use label queries to identify the set of Pods they should be managing. They then use the exact same Pod API that you used directly in Chapter 5 to create the Pods that they are managing. This notion of "coming in the front door" is another central design concept in Kubernetes. In a similar decoupling, ReplicaSets that create multiple Pods and the services that load balance to those Pods are also totally separate, decoupled API objects. In addition to supporting modularity, decoupling Pods and ReplicaSets enables several important behaviors, discussed in the following sections.

Adopting Existing Containers

Although declarative configuration is valuable, there are times when it is easier to build something up imperatively. In particular, early on you may be simply deploying a single Pod with a container image without a ReplicaSet managing it. You might even define a load balancer to serve traffic to that single Pod.

But at some point, you may want to expand your singleton container into a replicated service and create and manage an array of similar containers. If ReplicaSets owned the Pods they created, then the only way to start replicating your Pod would be to delete it and relaunch it via a ReplicaSet. This might be disruptive, as there would be a moment when there would be no copies of your container running. However, because ReplicaSets are decoupled from the Pods they manage, you can simply create a ReplicaSet that will "adopt" the existing Pod and scale out additional copies of those containers. In this way, you can seamlessly move from a single imperative Pod to a replicated set of Pods managed by a ReplicaSet.

Quarantining Containers

Oftentimes, when a server misbehaves, Pod-level health checks will automatically restart that Pod. But if your health checks are incomplete, a Pod can be misbehaving but still be part of the replicated set. In these situations, while it would work to simply kill the Pod, that would leave your developers with only logs to debug the problem. Instead, you can modify the set of labels on the sick Pod. Doing so will disassociate it from the ReplicaSet (and service) so that you can debug the Pod. The ReplicaSet controller will notice that a Pod is missing and create a new copy, but because the Pod is still running, it is available to developers for interactive debugging, which is significantly more valuable than debugging from logs.

Designing with ReplicaSets

ReplicaSets are designed to represent a single, scalable microservice inside your architecture. Their key characteristic is that every Pod the ReplicaSet controller creates is entirely homogeneous. Typically, these Pods are then fronted by a Kubernetes service load balancer, which spreads traffic across the Pods that make up the service. Generally speaking, ReplicaSets are designed for stateless (or nearly stateless) services. The elements they create are interchangeable; when a ReplicaSet is scaled down, an arbitrary Pod is selected for deletion. Your application's behavior shouldn't change because of such a scale-down operation.

Typically you will see applications use the Deployment object because it allows you to manage the release of new versions. ReplicaSets power Deployments under the hood, and it's important to understand how they operate so that you can debug them should you need to troubleshoot.

ReplicaSet Spec

Like all objects in Kubernetes, ReplicaSets are defined using a specification. All ReplicaSets must have a unique name (defined using the `metadata.name` field), a `spec` section that describes the number of Pods (replicas) that should be running cluster-wide at any given time, and a Pod template that describes the Pod to be created when the defined number of replicas is not met. Example 9-1 shows a minimal ReplicaSet definition. Pay attention to the replicas, selector, and template sections of the definition because they provide more insight into how ReplicaSets operate.

Example 9-1. kuard-rs.yaml

```
apiVersion: apps/v1
kind: ReplicaSet
metadata:
  labels:
    app: kuard
    version: "2"
  name: kuard
spec:
  replicas: 1
  selector:
    matchLabels:
      app: kuard
      version: "2"
  template:
    metadata:
      labels:
        app: kuard
        version: "2"
    spec:
      containers:
        - name: kuard
          image: "gcr.io/kuar-demo/kuard-amd64:green"
```

Pod Templates

As mentioned previously, when the number of Pods in the current state is less than the number of Pods in the desired state, the ReplicaSet controller will create new Pods using a template contained in the ReplicaSet specification. The Pods are created in exactly the same manner as when you created a Pod from a YAML file in previous chapters, but instead of using a file, the Kubernetes ReplicaSet controller creates and submits a Pod manifest based on the Pod template directly to the API server. Here is an example of a Pod template in a ReplicaSet:

```
template:
  metadata:
    labels:
      app: helloworld
      version: v1
  spec:
    containers:
      - name: helloworld
        image: kelseyhightower/helloworld:v1
        ports:
          - containerPort: 80
```

Labels

In any reasonably sized cluster, many different Pods are running simultaneously—so how does the ReplicaSet reconciliation loop discover the set of Pods for a particular ReplicaSet? ReplicaSets monitor cluster state using a set of Pod labels to filter Pod listings and track Pods running within a cluster. When initially created, a ReplicaSet fetches a Pod listing from the Kubernetes API and filters the results by labels. Based on the number of Pods the query returns, the ReplicaSet deletes or creates Pods to meet the desired number of replicas. These filtering labels are defined in the ReplicaSet spec section and are the key to understanding how ReplicaSets work.

The selector in the ReplicaSet spec should be a proper subset of the labels in the Pod template.

Creating a ReplicaSet

ReplicaSets are created by submitting a ReplicaSet object to the Kubernetes API. In this section, we will create a ReplicaSet using a configuration file and the kubectl apply command.

The ReplicaSet configuration file in Example 9-1 will ensure one copy of the gcr.io/kuar-demo/kuard-amd64:green container is running at any given time. Use the kubectl apply command to submit the kuard ReplicaSet to the Kubernetes API:

```
$ kubectl apply -f kuard-rs.yaml
replicaset "kuard" created
```

Once the kuard ReplicaSet has been accepted, the ReplicaSet controller will detect that there are no kuard Pods running that match the desired state and create a new kuard Pod based on the contents of the Pod template:

```
$ kubectl get pods
NAME          READY     STATUS     RESTARTS    AGE
kuard-yvzgd   1/1       Running    0           11s
```

Inspecting a ReplicaSet

As with Pods and other Kubernetes API objects, if you are interested in further details about a ReplicaSet, you can use the describe command to provide much more information about its state. Here is an example of using describe to obtain the details of the ReplicaSet we previously created:

```
$ kubectl describe rs kuard
Name:           kuard
Namespace:      default
Selector:       app=kuard,version=2
Labels:         app=kuard
                version=2
Annotations:    <none>
Replicas:       1 current / 1 desired
Pods Status:    1 Running / 0 Waiting / 0 Succeeded / 0 Failed
Pod Template:
```

You can see the label selector for the ReplicaSet, as well as the state of all of the replicas it manages.

Finding a ReplicaSet from a Pod

Sometimes you may wonder if a Pod is being managed by a ReplicaSet, and if it is, which one. To enable this kind of discovery, the ReplicaSet controller adds an ownerReferences section to every Pod that it creates. If you run the following, look for the ownerReferences section:

```
$ kubectl get pods <pod-name> -o=jsonpath='{.metadata.ownerReferences[0].name}'
```

If applicable, this will list the name of the ReplicaSet that is managing this Pod.

Finding a Set of Pods for a ReplicaSet

You can also determine the set of Pods managed by a ReplicaSet. First, get the set of labels using the kubectl describe command. In the previous example, the label selector was app=kuard,version=2. To find the Pods that match this selector, use the --selector flag or the shorthand -l:

```
$ kubectl get pods -l app=kuard,version=2
```

This is exactly the same query that the ReplicaSet executes to determine the current number of Pods.

Scaling ReplicaSets

You can scale ReplicaSets up or down by updating the `spec.replicas` key on the ReplicaSet object stored in Kubernetes. When you scale up a ReplicaSet, it submits new Pods to the Kubernetes API using the Pod template defined on the ReplicaSet.

Imperative Scaling with kubectl scale

The easiest way to achieve this is using the `scale` command in `kubectl`. For example, to scale up to four replicas, you could run:

```
$ kubectl scale replicasets kuard --replicas=4
```

While such imperative commands are useful for demonstrations and quick reactions to emergency situations (such as a sudden increase in load), it is important to also update any text file configurations to match the number of replicas that you set via the imperative `scale` command. The reason for this becomes obvious when you consider the following scenario.

Alice is on call, when suddenly there is a large increase in load on the service she is managing. Alice uses the `scale` command to increase the number of servers responding to requests to 10, and the situation is resolved. However, Alice forgets to update the ReplicaSet configurations checked into source control.

Several days later, Bob is preparing the weekly rollouts. Bob edits the ReplicaSet configurations stored in version control to use the new container image, but he doesn't notice that the number of replicas in the file is currently 5, not the 10 that Alice set in response to the increased load. Bob proceeds with the rollout, which both updates the container image and reduces the number of replicas by half. This causes an immediate overload, which leads to an outage.

This fictional case study illustrates the need to ensure that any imperative changes are immediately followed by a declarative change in source control. Indeed, if the need is not acute, we generally recommend only making declarative changes as described in the following section.

Declaratively Scaling with kubectl apply

In a declarative world, you make changes by editing the configuration file in version control and then applying those changes to your cluster. To scale the kuard Replica-Set, edit the *kuard-rs.yaml* configuration file and set the `replicas` count to 3:

```
...
spec:
  replicas: 3
...
```

In a multiuser setting, you would likely have a documented code review of this change and eventually check the changes into version control. Either way, you can then use the kubectl apply command to submit the updated kuard ReplicaSet to the API server:

```
$ kubectl apply -f kuard-rs.yaml
replicaset "kuard" configured
```

Now that the updated kuard ReplicaSet is in place, the ReplicaSet controller will detect that the number of desired Pods has changed and that it needs to take action to realize that desired state. If you used the imperative scale command in the previous section, the ReplicaSet controller will destroy one Pod to get the number to three. Otherwise, it will submit two new Pods to the Kubernetes API using the Pod template defined on the kuard ReplicaSet. Regardless, use the kubectl get pods command to list the running kuard Pods. You should see output similar to the following with three Pods in running state; two will have a smaller age because they were recently started:

```
$ kubectl get pods
NAME            READY      STATUS      RESTARTS    AGE
kuard-3a2sb     1/1        Running     0           26s
kuard-wuq9v     1/1        Running     0           26s
kuard-yvzgd     1/1        Running     0           2m
```

Autoscaling a ReplicaSet

While there will be times when you want to have explicit control over the number of replicas in a ReplicaSet, often you simply want to have "enough" replicas. The definition varies depending on the needs of the containers in the ReplicaSet. For example, with a web server like NGINX, you might want to scale due to CPU usage. For an in-memory cache, you might want to scale with memory consumption. In some cases, you might want to scale in response to custom application metrics. Kubernetes can handle all of these scenarios via *Horizontal Pod Autoscaling* (HPA).

"Horizontal Pod Autoscaling" is kind of a mouthful, and you might wonder why it is not simply called "autoscaling." Kubernetes makes a distinction between *horizontal* scaling, which involves creating additional replicas of a Pod, and *vertical* scaling, which involves increasing the resources required for a particular Pod (such as increasing the CPU required for the Pod). Many solutions also enable *cluster* autoscaling, where the number of machines in the cluster is scaled in response to resource needs, but that solution is outside the scope of this chapter.

Autoscaling requires the presence of the metrics-server in your cluster. The metrics-server keeps track of metrics and provides an API for consuming metrics that HPA uses when making scaling decisions. Most installations of Kubernetes include metrics-server by default. You can validate its presence by listing the Pods in the kube-system namespace:

```
$ kubectl get pods --namespace=kube-system
```

You should see a Pod with a name that starts with metrics-server somewhere in that list. If you do not see it, autoscaling will not work correctly.

Scaling based on CPU usage is the most common use case for Pod autoscaling. You can also scale based on memory usage. CPU-based autoscaling is most useful for request-based systems that consume CPU proportionally to the number of requests they are receiving, while using a relatively static amount of memory.

To scale a ReplicaSet, you can run a command like the following:

```
$ kubectl autoscale rs kuard --min=2 --max=5 --cpu-percent=80
```

This command creates an autoscaler that scales between two and five replicas with a CPU threshold of 80%. To view, modify, or delete this resource, you can use the standard kubectl commands and the horizontalpodautoscalers resource. It is quite a bit to type horizontalpodautoscalers, but it can be shortened to hpa:

```
$ kubectl get hpa
```

Because of the decoupled nature of Kubernetes, there is no direct link between the HPA and the ReplicaSet. While this is great for modularity and composition, it also enables some antipatterns. In particular, it's a bad idea to combine autoscaling with imperative or declarative management of the number of replicas. If both you and an autoscaler are attempting to modify the number of replicas, it's highly likely that you will clash, resulting in unexpected behavior.

Deleting ReplicaSets

When a ReplicaSet is no longer required, it can be deleted using the kubectl delete command. By default, this also deletes the Pods that are managed by the ReplicaSet:

```
$ kubectl delete rs kuard
replicaset "kuard" deleted
```

Running the kubectl get pods command shows that all the kuard Pods created by the kuard ReplicaSet have also been deleted:

```
$ kubectl get pods
```

If you don't want to delete the Pods that the ReplicaSet is managing, you can set the `--cascade` flag to `false` to ensure only the ReplicaSet object is deleted and not the Pods:

```
$ kubectl delete rs kuard --cascade=false
```

Summary

Composing Pods with ReplicaSets provides the foundation for building robust applications with automatic failover, and makes deploying those applications a breeze by enabling scalable and sane deployment patterns. Use ReplicaSets for any Pod you care about, even if it is a single Pod! Some people even default to using ReplicaSets instead of Pods. A typical cluster will have many ReplicaSets, so apply them liberally to the affected area.

## CHAPTER 10

Deployments

So far, you have seen how to package your applications as containers, create replicated sets of containers, and use Ingress controllers to load balance traffic to your services. You can use all of these objects (Pods, ReplicaSets, and Services) to build a single instance of your application. However, they do little to help you manage the daily or weekly cadence of releasing new versions of your application. Indeed, both Pods and ReplicaSets are expected to be tied to specific container images that don't change.

The Deployment object exists to manage the release of new versions. Deployments represent deployed applications in a way that transcends any particular version. Additionally, Deployments enable you to easily move from one version of your code to the next. This "rollout" process is specifiable and careful. It waits for a user-configurable amount of time between upgrading individual Pods. It also uses health checks to ensure that the new version of the application is operating correctly and stops the deployment if too many failures occur.

Using Deployments, you can simply and reliably roll out new software versions without downtime or errors. The actual mechanics of the software rollout performed by a Deployment are controlled by a Deployment controller that runs in the Kubernetes cluster itself. This means you can let a Deployment proceed unattended and it will still operate correctly and safely. This makes it easy to integrate Deployments with numerous continuous delivery tools and services. Further, running server-side makes it safe to perform a rollout from places with poor or intermittent internet connectivity. Imagine rolling out a new version of your software from your phone while riding on the subway. Deployments make this possible and safe!

When Kubernetes was first released, one of the most popular demonstrations of its power was the "rolling update," which showed how you could use a single command to seamlessly update a running application without any downtime and without losing requests. This original demo was based on the kubectl rolling-update command, which is still available in the command-line tool, although its functionality has largely been subsumed by the Deployment object.

Your First Deployment

Like all objects in Kubernetes, a Deployment can be represented as a declarative YAML object that provides the details about what you want to run. In the following case, the Deployment is requesting a single instance of the kuard application:

```yaml
apiVersion: apps/v1
kind: Deployment
metadata:
  name: kuard
  labels:
    run: kuard
spec:
  selector:
    matchLabels:
      run: kuard
  replicas: 1
  template:
    metadata:
      labels:
        run: kuard
    spec:
      containers:
      - name: kuard
        image: gcr.io/kuar-demo/kuard-amd64:blue
```

Save this YAML file as *kuard-deployment.yaml*, then you can create it using:

```
$ kubectl create -f kuard-deployment.yaml
```

Let's explore how Deployments actually work. Just as we learned that ReplicaSets manage Pods, Deployments manage ReplicaSets. As with all relationships in Kubernetes, this relationship is defined by labels and a label selector. You can see the label selector by looking at the Deployment object:

```
$ kubectl get deployments kuard \
  -o jsonpath --template {.spec.selector.matchLabels}

{"run":"kuard"}
```

From this you can see that the Deployment is managing a ReplicaSet with the label run=kuard. You can use this in a label selector query across ReplicaSets to find that specific ReplicaSet:

```
$ kubectl get replicasets --selector=run=kuard

NAME              DESIRED   CURRENT   READY   AGE
kuard-1128242161  1         1         1       13m
```

Now let's look at the relationship between a Deployment and a ReplicaSet in action. We can resize the Deployment using the imperative `scale` command:

```
$ kubectl scale deployments kuard --replicas=2

deployment.apps/kuard scaled
```

Now if we list that ReplicaSet again, we should see:

```
$ kubectl get replicasets --selector=run=kuard

NAME              DESIRED   CURRENT   READY   AGE
kuard-1128242161  2         2         2       13m
```

Scaling the Deployment has also scaled the ReplicaSet it controls.

Now let's try the opposite, scaling the ReplicaSet:

```
$ kubectl scale replicasets kuard-1128242161 --replicas=1

replicaset.apps/kuard-1128242161 scaled
```

Now get that ReplicaSet again:

```
$ kubectl get replicasets --selector=run=kuard

NAME              DESIRED   CURRENT   READY   AGE
kuard-1128242161  2         2         2       13m
```

That's odd. Despite scaling the ReplicaSet to one replica, it still has two replicas as its desired state. What's going on?

Remember, Kubernetes is an online, self-healing system. The top-level Deployment object is managing this ReplicaSet. When you adjust the number of replicas to one, it no longer matches the desired state of the Deployment, which has `replicas` set to 2. The Deployment controller notices this and takes action to ensure the observed state matches the desired state, in this case readjusting the number of replicas back to two.

If you ever want to manage that ReplicaSet directly, you need to delete the Deployment. (Remember to set `--cascade` to `false`, or else it will delete the ReplicaSet and Pods as well!)

Creating Deployments

Of course, as stated in the introduction, you should have a preference for declarative management of your Kubernetes configurations. This means maintaining the state of your Deployments in YAML or JSON files on disk.

As a starting point, download this Deployment into a YAML file:

```
$ kubectl get deployments kuard -o yaml > kuard-deployment.yaml
$ kubectl replace -f kuard-deployment.yaml --save-config
```

If you look in the file, you will see something like this (note that we've removed a lot of read-only and default fields for readability). Pay attention to the annotations, selector, and strategy fields as they provide insight into Deployment-specific functionality:

```
apiVersion: apps/v1
kind: Deployment
metadata:
  annotations:
    deployment.kubernetes.io/revision: "1"
  creationTimestamp: null
  generation: 1
  labels:
    run: kuard
  name: kuard
spec:
  progressDeadlineSeconds: 600
  replicas: 1
  revisionHistoryLimit: 10
  selector:
    matchLabels:
      run: kuard
  strategy:
    rollingUpdate:
      maxSurge: 25%
      maxUnavailable: 25%
    type: RollingUpdate
  template:
    metadata:
      creationTimestamp: null
      labels:
        run: kuard
    spec:
      containers:
      - image: gcr.io/kuar-demo/kuard-amd64:blue
        imagePullPolicy: IfNotPresent
        name: kuard
        resources: {}
        terminationMessagePath: /dev/termination-log
        terminationMessagePolicy: File
      dnsPolicy: ClusterFirst
      restartPolicy: Always
```

```
      schedulerName: default-scheduler
      securityContext: {}
      terminationGracePeriodSeconds: 30
  status: {}
```

 You also need to run kubectl replace --save-config. This
adds an annotation so that, when applying changes in the future,
kubectl will know what the last applied configuration was for
smarter merging of configs. If you always use kubectl apply, this
step is only required after the first time you create a Deployment
using kubectl create -f.

The Deployment spec has a very similar structure to the ReplicaSet spec. There is a
Pod template, which contains a number of containers that are created for each replica
managed by the Deployment. In addition to the Pod specification, there is also a
strategy object:

```
...
  strategy:
    rollingUpdate:
      maxSurge: 25%
      maxUnavailable: 25%
    type: RollingUpdate
...
```

The strategy object dictates the different ways in which a rollout of new software
can proceed. There are two strategies supported by Deployments: Recreate and
RollingUpdate. These are discussed in detail later in this chapter.

Managing Deployments

As with all Kubernetes objects, you can get detailed information about your Deployment via the kubectl describe command. This command provides an overview
of the Deployment configuration, which includes interesting fields like the Selector,
Replicas, and Events:

```
$ kubectl describe deployments kuard

Name:                   kuard
Namespace:              default
CreationTimestamp:      Tue, 01 Jun 2021 21:19:46 -0700
Labels:                 run=kuard
Annotations:            deployment.kubernetes.io/revision: 1
Selector:               run=kuard
Replicas:               1 desired | 1 updated | 1 total | 1 available | 0 ...
StrategyType:           RollingUpdate
MinReadySeconds:        0
RollingUpdateStrategy:  25% max unavailable, 25% max surge
```

```
Pod Template:
  Labels:  run=kuard
  Containers:
   kuard:
    Image:        gcr.io/kuar-demo/kuard-amd64:blue
    Port:         <none>
    Host Port:    <none>
    Environment:  <none>
    Mounts:       <none>
   Volumes:       <none>
  Conditions:
   Type           Status  Reason
   ----           ------  ------
   Available      True    MinimumReplicasAvailable
  OldReplicaSets:  <none>
  NewReplicaSet:   kuard-6d69d9fc5c (2/2 replicas created)
  Events:
   Type    Reason            Age                 From             Message
   ----    ------            ----                ----             -------
   Normal  ScalingReplicaSet  4m6s                deployment-con...  ...
   Normal  ScalingReplicaSet  113s (x2 over 3m20s) deployment-con...  ...
```

In the output of describe, there is a great deal of important information. Two of the most important pieces of information in the output are OldReplicaSets and New ReplicaSet. These fields point to the ReplicaSet objects this Deployment is currently managing. If a Deployment is in the middle of a rollout, both fields will be set to a value. If a rollout is complete, OldReplicaSets will be set to <none>.

In addition to the describe command, there is also the kubectl rollout command for Deployments. We will go into this command in more detail later on, but for now, know that you can use kubectl rollout history to obtain the history of rollouts associated with a particular Deployment. If you have a current Deployment in progress, you can use kubectl rollout status to obtain the current status of that rollout.

Updating Deployments

Deployments are declarative objects that describe a deployed application. The two most common operations on a Deployment are scaling and application updates.

Scaling a Deployment

Although we previously showed how to imperatively scale a Deployment using the kubectl scale command, the best practice is to manage your Deployments declaratively via the YAML files, then use those files to update your Deployment. To scale up a Deployment, you would edit your YAML file to increase the number of replicas:

```
...
spec:
  replicas: 3
...
```

Once you have saved and committed this change, you can update the Deployment using the kubectl apply command:

```
$ kubectl apply -f kuard-deployment.yaml
```

This will update the desired state of the Deployment, causing it to increase the size of the ReplicaSet it manages and eventually create a new Pod managed by the Deployment:

```
$ kubectl get deployments kuard
```

```
NAME    READY   UP-TO-DATE   AVAILABLE   AGE
kuard   3/3     3            3           10m
```

Updating a Container Image

The other common use case for updating a Deployment is to roll out a new version of the software running in one or more containers. To do this, you should likewise edit the Deployment YAML file, though in this case you are updating the container image, rather than the number of replicas:

```
...
      containers:
      - image: gcr.io/kuar-demo/kuard-amd64:green
        imagePullPolicy: Always
...
```

Annotate the template for the Deployment to record some information about the update:

```
...
spec:
  ...
  template:
    metadata:
      annotations:
        kubernetes.io/change-cause: "Update to green kuard"
...
```

> Make sure you add this annotation to the template and not the Deployment itself, since the kubectl apply command uses this field in the Deployment object. Also, do not update the change-cause annotation when doing simple scaling operations. A modification of change-cause is a significant change to the template and will trigger a new rollout.

Again, you can use kubectl apply to update the Deployment:

```
$ kubectl apply -f kuard-deployment.yaml
```

After you update the Deployment, it will trigger a rollout, which you can then monitor via the kubectl rollout command:

```
$ kubectl rollout status deployments kuard
deployment "kuard" successfully rolled out
```

You can see the old and new ReplicaSets managed by the Deployment along with the images being used. Both the old and new ReplicaSets are kept around in case you want to roll back:

```
$ kubectl get replicasets -o wide

NAME                DESIRED   CURRENT   READY   ...   IMAGE(S)            ...
kuard-1128242161    0         0         0       ...   gcr.io/kuar-demo/   ...
kuard-1128635377    3         3         3       ...   gcr.io/kuar-demo/   ...
```

If you are in the middle of a rollout and you want to temporarily pause it (e.g., if you start seeing weird behavior in your system that you want to investigate), you can use the pause command:

```
$ kubectl rollout pause deployments kuard
deployment.apps/kuard paused
```

If, after investigation, you believe the rollout can safely proceed, you can use the resume command to start up where you left off:

```
$ kubectl rollout resume deployments kuard
deployment.apps/kuard resumed
```

Rollout History

Kubernetes Deployments maintain a history of rollouts, which can be useful both for understanding the previous state of the Deployment and for rolling back to a specific version.

You can see the Deployment history by running:

```
$ kubectl rollout history deployment kuard

deployment.apps/kuard
REVISION   CHANGE-CAUSE
1          <none>
2          Update to green kuard
```

The revision history is given in oldest to newest order. A unique revision number is incremented for each new rollout. So far we have two: the initial Deployment and the update of the image to kuard:green.

If you are interested in more details about a particular revision, you can add the `--revision` flag to view details about that specific revision:

```
$ kubectl rollout history deployment kuard --revision=2

deployment.apps/kuard with revision #2
Pod Template:
  Labels:        pod-template-hash=54b74ddcd4
          run=kuard
  Annotations:  kubernetes.io/change-cause: Update to green kuard
  Containers:
   kuard:
    Image:      gcr.io/kuar-demo/kuard-amd64:green
    Port:       <none>
    Host Port:  <none>
    Environment:        <none>
    Mounts:     <none>
   Volumes:     <none>
```

Let's do one more update for this example. Update the kuard version back to `blue` by modifying the container version number and updating the `change-cause` annotation. Apply it with `kubectl apply`. The history should now have three entries:

```
$ kubectl rollout history deployment kuard

deployment.apps/kuard
REVISION   CHANGE-CAUSE
1          <none>
2          Update to green kuard
3          Update to blue kuard
```

Let's say there is an issue with the latest release and you want to roll back while you investigate. You can simply undo the last rollout:

```
$ kubectl rollout undo deployments kuard
deployment.apps/kuard rolled back
```

The undo command works regardless of the stage of the rollout. You can undo both partially completed and fully completed rollouts. An undo of a rollout is actually simply a rollout in reverse (for example from v2 to v1, instead of from v1 to v2), and all of the same policies that control the rollout strategy apply to the undo strategy as well. You can see that the Deployment object simply adjusts the desired replica counts in the managed ReplicaSets:

```
$ kubectl get replicasets -o wide

NAME               DESIRED  CURRENT  READY  ...  IMAGE(S)            ...
kuard-1128242161   0        0        0      ...  gcr.io/kuar-demo/   ...
kuard-1570155864   0        0        0      ...  gcr.io/kuar-demo/   ...
kuard-2738859366   3        3        3      ...  gcr.io/kuar-demo/   ...
```

When using declarative files to control your production systems, you should, as much as possible, ensure that the checked-in manifests match what is actually running in your cluster. When you do a `kubectl rollout undo`, you are updating the production state in a way that isn't reflected in your source control.

An alternative (and perhaps preferable) way to undo a rollout is to revert your YAML file and `kubectl apply` the previous version. In this way, your "change tracked configuration" more closely tracks what is really running in your cluster.

Let's look at the Deployment history again:

```
$ kubectl rollout history deployment kuard

deployment.apps/kuard
REVISION   CHANGE-CAUSE
1          <none>
3          Update to blue kuard
4          Update to green kuard
```

Revision 2 is missing! It turns out that when you roll back to a previous revision, the Deployment simply reuses the template and renumbers it so that it is the latest revision. What was revision 2 before is now revision 4.

We previously saw that you can use the `kubectl rollout undo` command to roll back to a previous version of a Deployment. Additionally, you can roll back to a specific revision in the history using the `--to-revision` flag:

```
$ kubectl rollout undo deployments kuard --to-revision=3
deployment.apps/kuard rolled back
$ kubectl rollout history deployment kuard
deployment.apps/kuard
REVISION   CHANGE-CAUSE
1          <none>
4          Update to green kuard
5          Update to blue kuard
```

Again, the undo took revision 3, applied it, and renumbered it as revision 5.

Specifying a revision of 0 is a shorthand way of specifying the previous revision. In this way, `kubectl rollout undo` is equivalent to `kubectl rollout undo --to-revision=0`.

By default, the last 10 revisions of a Deployment are kept attached to the Deployment object itself. It is recommended that if you have Deployments that you expect to keep around for a long time, you set a maximum history size for the Deployment revision history. For example, if you do a daily update, you may limit your revision history to 14, to keep a maximum of two weeks' worth of revisions (if you don't expect to need to roll back beyond two weeks).

To accomplish this, use the `revisionHistoryLimit` property in the Deployment specification:

```
...
spec:
  # We do daily rollouts, limit the revision history to two weeks of
  # releases as we don't expect to roll back beyond that.
  revisionHistoryLimit: 14
...
```

Deployment Strategies

When it comes time to change the version of the software implementing your service, a Kubernetes deployment supports two different rollout strategies, `Recreate` and `RollingUpdate`. Let's look at each in turn.

Recreate Strategy

The `Recreate` strategy is the simpler of the two. It simply updates the ReplicaSet it manages to use the new image and terminates all of the Pods associated with the Deployment. The ReplicaSet notices that it no longer has any replicas and re-creates all Pods using the new image. Once the Pods are re-created, they are running the new version.

While this strategy is fast and simple, it will result in workload downtime. Because of this, the `Recreate` strategy should be used only for test Deployments where a service downtime is acceptable.

RollingUpdate Strategy

The `RollingUpdate` strategy is the generally preferable strategy for any user-facing service. While it is slower than `Recreate`, it is also significantly more sophisticated and robust. Using `RollingUpdate`, you can roll out a new version of your service while it is still receiving user traffic, without any downtime.

As you might infer from the name, the `RollingUpdate` strategy works by updating a few Pods at a time, moving incrementally until all of the Pods are running the new version of your software.

Managing multiple versions of your service

Importantly, this means that for a while, both the new and the old version of your service will be receiving requests and serving traffic. This has important implications for how you build your software. Namely, it is critically important that each version of your software, and each of its clients, is capable of talking interchangeably with both a slightly older and a slightly newer version of your software.

Consider the following scenario: you are in the middle of rolling out your frontend software; half of your servers are running version 1, and half are running version 2. A user makes an initial request to your service and downloads a client-side JavaScript library that implements your UI. This request is serviced by a version 1 server, and thus the user receives the version 1 client library. This client library runs in the user's browser and makes subsequent API requests to your service. These API requests happen to be routed to a version 2 server; thus, version 1 of your JavaScript client library is talking to version 2 of your API server. If you haven't ensured compatibility between these versions, your application won't function correctly.

At first, this might seem like an extra burden. But in truth, you always had this problem; you may just not have noticed. Concretely, a user can make a request at time t just before you initiate an update. This request is serviced by a version 1 server. At t_1, you update your service to version 2. At t_2, the version 1 client code running on the user's browser runs and hits an API endpoint being operated by a version 2 server. No matter how you update your software, you have to maintain backward and forward compatibility for reliable updates. The nature of the `RollingUpdate` strategy simply makes that more clear and explicit.

This doesn't just apply to JavaScript clients—it's true of client libraries that are compiled into other services that make calls to your service. Just because you updated doesn't mean they have updated their client libraries. This sort of backward compatibility is critical to decoupling your service from systems that depend on your service. If you don't formalize your APIs and decouple yourself, you are forced to carefully manage your rollouts with all of the other systems that call into your service. This kind of tight coupling makes it extremely hard to produce the necessary agility to be able to push out new software every week, let alone every hour or every day. In the decoupled architecture shown in Figure 10-1, the frontend is isolated from the backend via an API contract and a load balancer, whereas in the coupled architecture, a thick client compiled into the frontend is used to connect directly to the backends.

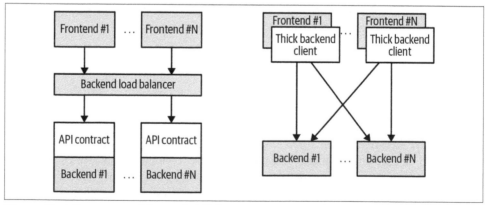

Figure 10-1. Diagrams of decoupled (left) and coupled (right) application architectures

Configuring a rolling update

RollingUpdate is a fairly generic strategy; it can be used to update a variety of applications in a variety of settings. Consequently, the rolling update itself is quite configurable; you can tune its behavior to suit your particular needs. There are two parameters you can use to tune the rolling update behavior: maxUnavailable and maxSurge.

The maxUnavailable parameter sets the maximum number of Pods that can be unavailable during a rolling update. It can either be set to an absolute number (e.g., 3, meaning a maximum of three Pods can be unavailable) or to a percentage (e.g., 20%, meaning a maximum of 20% of the desired number of replicas can be unavailable). Generally speaking, using a percentage is a good approach for most services, since the value is correctly applied regardless of the desired number of replicas in the Deployment. However, there are times when you may want to use an absolute number (e.g., limiting the maximum unavailable Pods to one).

At its core, the maxUnavailable parameter helps tune how quickly a rolling update proceeds. For example, if you set maxUnavailable to 50%, then the rolling update will immediately scale the old ReplicaSet down to 50% of its original size. If you have four replicas, it will scale it down to two replicas. The rolling update will then replace the removed Pods by scaling the new ReplicaSet up to two replicas, for a total of four replicas (two old, two new). It will then scale the old ReplicaSet down to zero replicas, for a total size of two new replicas. Finally, it will scale the new ReplicaSet up to four replicas, completing the rollout. Thus, with maxUnavailable set to 50%, the rollout completes in four steps, but with only 50% of the service capacity at times.

Consider what happens if we instead set maxUnavailable to 25%. In this situation, each step is only performed with a single replica at a time and thus it takes twice as many steps for the rollout to complete, but availability only drops to a minimum of 75% during the rollout. This illustrates how maxUnavailable allows us to trade rollout speed for availability.

> The observant among you will notice that the Recreate strategy is identical to the RollingUpdate strategy with maxUnavailable set to 100%.

Using reduced capacity to achieve a successful rollout is useful either when your service has cyclical traffic patterns (for example, if there's much less traffic at night) or when you have limited resources, so scaling to larger than the current maximum number of replicas isn't possible.

However, there are situations where you don't want to fall below 100% capacity, but you are willing to temporarily use additional resources to perform a rollout. In these situations, you can set the maxUnavailable parameter to 0, and instead control the rollout using the maxSurge parameter. Like maxUnavailable, maxSurge can be specified either as a specific number or a percentage.

The maxSurge parameter controls how many extra resources can be created to achieve a rollout. To illustrate how this works, imagine a service with 10 replicas. We set maxUnavailable to 0 and maxSurge to 20%. The first thing the rollout will do is scale the new ReplicaSet up by 2 replicas, for a total of 12 (120%) in the service. It will then scale the old ReplicaSet down to 8 replicas, for a total of 10 (8 old, 2 new) in the service. This process proceeds until the rollout is complete. At any time, the capacity of the service is guaranteed to be at least 100% and the maximum extra resources used for the rollout are limited to an additional 20% of all resources.

Setting maxSurge to 100% is equivalent to a blue/green Deployment. The Deployment controller first scales the new version up to 100% of the old version. Once the new version is healthy, it immediately scales the old version down to 0%.

Slowing Rollouts to Ensure Service Health

Staged rollouts are meant to ensure that the rollout results in a healthy, stable service running the new software version. To do this, the Deployment controller always waits until a Pod reports that it is ready before moving on to update the next Pod.

The Deployment controller examines the Pod's status as determined by its readiness checks. Readiness checks are part of the Pod's health checks, described in detail in Chapter 5. If you want to use Deployments to reliably roll out your software, you *have* to specify readiness health checks for the containers in your Pod. Without these checks, the Deployment controller is running without knowing the Pod's status.

Sometimes, however, simply noticing that a Pod has become ready doesn't give you sufficient confidence that the Pod is actually behaving correctly. Some error conditions don't occur immediately. For example, you could have a serious memory leak that takes a few minutes to show up, or you could have a bug that is only triggered by 1% of all requests. In most real-world scenarios, you want to wait a period of time to have high confidence that the new version is operating correctly before you move on to updating the next Pod.

For Deployments, this time to wait is defined by the `minReadySeconds` parameter:

```
...
spec:
  minReadySeconds: 60
...
```

Setting `minReadySeconds` to `60` indicates that the Deployment must wait for 60 seconds *after* seeing a Pod become healthy before moving on to updating the next Pod.

In addition to waiting for a Pod to become healthy, you also want to set a timeout that limits how long the system will wait. Suppose, for example, the new version of your service has a bug and immediately deadlocks. It will never become ready, and in the absence of a timeout, the Deployment controller will stall your rollout forever.

The correct behavior in such a situation is to time out the rollout. This in turn marks the rollout as failed. This failure status can be used to trigger alerting that can indicate to an operator that there is a problem with the rollout.

At first blush, timing out a rollout might seem like an unnecessary complication. However, increasingly, things like rollouts are being triggered by fully automated systems with little to no human involvement. In such a situation, timing out becomes a critical exception, which can either trigger an automated rollback of the release or create a ticket/event that triggers human intervention.

In order to set the timeout period, you will use the Deployment parameter `progress DeadlineSeconds`:

```
...
spec:
  progressDeadlineSeconds: 600
...
```

This example sets the progress deadline to 10 minutes. If any particular stage in the rollout fails to progress in 10 minutes, then the Deployment is marked as failed, and all attempts to move the Deployment forward are halted.

It is important to note that this timeout is given in terms of Deployment *progress*, not the overall length of a Deployment. In this context, progress is defined as any time the Deployment creates or deletes a Pod. When that happens, the timeout clock is reset to zero. Figure 10-2 shows the Deployment life cycle.

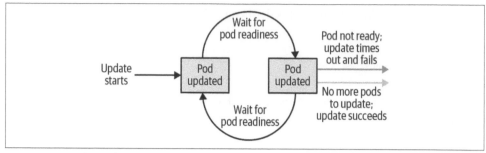

Figure 10-2. The Kubernetes Deployment life cycle

Deleting a Deployment

If you ever want to delete a Deployment, you can do it with the imperative command:

```
$ kubectl delete deployments kuard
```

You can also do it using the declarative YAML file you created earlier:

```
$ kubectl delete -f kuard-deployment.yaml
```

In either case, by default, deleting a Deployment deletes the entire service. The means it will delete not just the Deployment, but also any ReplicaSets it manages, as well as any Pods the ReplicaSets manage. As with ReplicaSets, if this is not the desired behavior, you can use the `--cascade=false` flag to delete only the Deployment object.

Monitoring a Deployment

If a Deployment fails to make progress after a specified amount of time, it will time out. When this happens, the status of the Deployment will transition to a failed state. This status can be obtained from the `status.conditions` array, where there will be a `Condition` whose `Type` is `Progressing` and whose `Status` is `False`. A Deployment in such a state has failed and will not progress further. To set how long the Deployment controller should wait before transitioning into this state, use the `spec.progressDeadlineSeconds` field.

Summary

Ultimately, the primary goal of Kubernetes is to make it easy for you to build and deploy reliable distributed systems. This means not just instantiating the application once, but managing the regularly scheduled rollout of new versions of that software service. Deployments are a critical piece of reliable rollouts and rollout management for your services. In the next chapter we will cover DaemonSets, which ensure only a single copy of a Pod is running across a set of nodes in a Kubernetes cluster.

## CHAPTER 11

DaemonSets

Deployments and ReplicaSets are generally about creating a service (such as a web server) with multiple replicas for redundancy. But that is not the only reason to replicate a set of Pods within a cluster. Another reason is to schedule a single Pod on every node within the cluster. Generally, the motivation for replicating a Pod to every node is to land some sort of agent or daemon on each node, and the Kubernetes object for achieving this is the DaemonSet.

A DaemonSet ensures that a copy of a Pod is running across a set of nodes in a Kubernetes cluster. DaemonSets are used to deploy system daemons such as log collectors and monitoring agents, which typically must run on every node. DaemonSets share similar functionality with ReplicaSets; both create Pods that are expected to be long-running services and ensure that the desired state and the observed state of the cluster match.

Given the similarities between DaemonSets and ReplicaSets, it's important to understand when to use one over the other. ReplicaSets should be used when your application is completely decoupled from the node and you can run multiple copies on a given node without special consideration. DaemonSets should be used when a single copy of your application must run on all or a subset of the nodes in the cluster.

You should generally not use scheduling restrictions or other parameters to ensure that Pods do not colocate on the same node. If you find yourself wanting a single Pod per node, then a DaemonSet is the correct Kubernetes resource to use. Likewise, if you find yourself building a homogeneous replicated service to serve user traffic, then a ReplicaSet is probably the right Kubernetes resource to use.

You can use labels to run DaemonSet Pods on specific nodes; for example, you may want to run specialized intrusion-detection software on nodes that are exposed to the edge network.

You can also use DaemonSets to install software on nodes in a cloud-based cluster. For many cloud services, an upgrade or scaling of a cluster can delete and/or re-create new virtual machines. This dynamic *immutable infrastructure* approach can cause problems if you want (or are required by central IT) to have specific software on every node. To ensure that specific software is installed on every machine despite upgrades and scale events, a DaemonSet is the right approach. You can even mount the host filesystem and run scripts that install RPM/DEB packages onto the host operating system. In this way, you can have a cloud native cluster that still meets the enterprise requirements of your IT department.

DaemonSet Scheduler

By default, a DaemonSet will create a copy of a Pod on every node unless a node selector is used, which will limit eligible nodes to those with a matching set of labels. DaemonSets determine which node a Pod will run on at Pod creation time by specifying the nodeName field in the Pod spec. As a result, Pods created by DaemonSets are ignored by the Kubernetes scheduler.

Like ReplicaSets, DaemonSets are managed by a reconciliation control loop that measures the desired state (a Pod is present on all nodes) with the observed state (is the Pod present on a particular node?). Given this information, the DaemonSet controller creates a Pod on each node that doesn't currently have a matching Pod.

If a new node is added to the cluster, then the DaemonSet controller notices that it is missing a Pod and adds the Pod to the new node.

DaemonSets and ReplicaSets are a great demonstration of the value of decoupled architecture. It might seem that the right design would be for a ReplicaSet to own the Pods it manages, and for Pods to be subresources of a ReplicaSet. Likewise, the Pods managed by a DaemonSet would be subresources of that DaemonSet. However, this kind of encapsulation would require that tools for dealing with Pods be written twice: once for DaemonSets and once for ReplicaSets. Instead, Kubernetes uses a decoupled approach where Pods are top-level objects. This means that every tool you have learned for introspecting Pods in the context of ReplicaSets (e.g., kubectl logs <pod-name>) is equally applicable to Pods created by DaemonSets.

Creating DaemonSets

DaemonSets are created by submitting a DaemonSet configuration to the Kubernetes API server. The DaemonSet in Example 11-1 will create a `fluentd` logging agent on every node in the target cluster.

Example 11-1. fluentd.yaml

```
apiVersion: apps/v1
kind: DaemonSet
metadata:
  name: fluentd
  labels:
    app: fluentd
spec:
  selector:
    matchLabels:
      app: fluentd
  template:
    metadata:
      labels:
        app: fluentd
    spec:
      containers:
      - name: fluentd
        image: fluent/fluentd:v0.14.10
        resources:
          limits:
            memory: 200Mi
          requests:
            cpu: 100m
            memory: 200Mi
        volumeMounts:
        - name: varlog
          mountPath: /var/log
        - name: varlibdockercontainers
          mountPath: /var/lib/docker/containers
          readOnly: true
      terminationGracePeriodSeconds: 30
      volumes:
      - name: varlog
        hostPath:
          path: /var/log
      - name: varlibdockercontainers
        hostPath:
          path: /var/lib/docker/containers
```

DaemonSets require a unique name across all DaemonSets in a given Kubernetes namespace. Each DaemonSet must include a Pod template spec, which will be used to create Pods as needed. This is where the similarities between ReplicaSets and

DaemonSets end. Unlike ReplicaSets, DaemonSets will create Pods on every node in the cluster by default unless a node selector is used.

Once you have a valid DaemonSet configuration in place, you can use the kubectl apply command to submit the DaemonSet to the Kubernetes API. In this section, we will create a DaemonSet to ensure the fluentd HTTP server is running on every node in our cluster:

```
$ kubectl apply -f fluentd.yaml
daemonset.apps/fluentd created
```

Once the fluentd DaemonSet has been successfully submitted to the Kubernetes API, you can query its current state using the kubectl describe command:

```
$ kubectl describe daemonset fluentd
Name:          fluentd
Selector:      app=fluentd
Node-Selector: <none>
Labels:        app=fluentd
Annotations:   deprecated.daemonset.template.generation: 1
Desired Number of Nodes Scheduled: 3
Current Number of Nodes Scheduled: 3
Number of Nodes Scheduled with Up-to-date Pods: 3
Number of Nodes Scheduled with Available Pods: 3
Number of Nodes Misscheduled: 0
Pods Status:  3 Running / 0 Waiting / 0 Succeeded / 0 Failed
...
```

This output indicates a fluentd Pod was successfully deployed to all three nodes in our cluster. We can verify this using the kubectl get pods command with the -o flag to print the nodes where each fluentd Pod was assigned:

```
$ kubectl get pods -l app=fluentd -o wide
NAME           READY  STATUS   RESTARTS  AGE   IP             NODE
fluentd-1q6c6  1/1    Running  0         13m   10.240.0.101   k0-default...
fluentd-mwi7h  1/1    Running  0         13m   10.240.0.80    k0-default...
fluentd-zr6l7  1/1    Running  0         13m   10.240.0.44    k0-default...
```

With the fluentd DaemonSet in place, adding a new node to the cluster will result in a fluentd Pod being deployed to that node automatically:

```
$ kubectl get pods -l app=fluentd -o wide
NAME           READY  STATUS   RESTARTS  AGE   IP             NODE
fluentd-1q6c6  1/1    Running  0         13m   10.240.0.101   k0-default...
fluentd-mwi7h  1/1    Running  0         13m   10.240.0.80    k0-default...
fluentd-oipmq  1/1    Running  0         43s   10.240.0.96    k0-default...
fluentd-zr6l7  1/1    Running  0         13m   10.240.0.44    k0-default...
```

This is exactly the behavior you want when managing logging daemons and other cluster-wide services. No action was required from our end; this is how the Kubernetes DaemonSet controller reconciles its observed state with our desired state.

Limiting DaemonSets to Specific Nodes

The most common use case for DaemonSets is to run a Pod across every node in a Kubernetes cluster. However, there are some cases where you want to deploy a Pod to only a subset of nodes. For example, maybe you have a workload that requires a GPU or access to fast storage only available on a subset of nodes in your cluster. In cases like these, node labels can be used to tag specific nodes that meet workload requirements.

Adding Labels to Nodes

The first step in limiting DaemonSets to specific nodes is to add the desired set of labels to a subset of nodes. This can be achieved using the `kubectl label` command.

The following command adds the `ssd=true` label to a single node:

```
$ kubectl label nodes k0-default-pool-35609c18-z7tb ssd=true
node/k0-default-pool-35609c18-z7tb labeled
```

Just like with other Kubernetes resources, listing nodes without a label selector returns all nodes in the cluster:

```
$ kubectl get nodes
NAME                              STATUS   ROLES   AGE   VERSION
k0-default-pool-35609c18-0xnl     Ready    agent   23m   v1.21.1
k0-default-pool-35609c18-pol3     Ready    agent   1d    v1.21.1
k0-default-pool-35609c18-ydae     Ready    agent   1d    v1.21.1
k0-default-pool-35609c18-z7tb     Ready    agent   1d    v1.21.1
```

Using a label selector, we can filter nodes based on labels. To list only the nodes that have the `ssd` label set to `true`, use the `kubectl get nodes` command with the `--selector` flag:

```
$ kubectl get nodes --selector ssd=true
NAME                              STATUS   ROLES   AGE   VERSION
k0-default-pool-35609c18-z7tb     Ready    agent   1d    v1.21.1
```

Node Selectors

Node selectors can be used to limit what nodes a Pod can run on in a given Kubernetes cluster. Node selectors are defined as part of the Pod spec when creating a DaemonSet. The DaemonSet configuration in Example 11-2 limits NGINX to running only on nodes with the `ssd=true` label set.

Example 11-2. nginx-fast-storage.yaml

```yaml
apiVersion: apps/v1
kind: "DaemonSet"
metadata:
  labels:
    app: nginx
    ssd: "true"
  name: nginx-fast-storage
spec:
  selector:
    matchLabels:
      app: nginx
      ssd: "true"
  template:
    metadata:
      labels:
        app: nginx
        ssd: "true"
    spec:
      nodeSelector:
        ssd: "true"
      containers:
        - name: nginx
          image: nginx:1.10.0
```

Let's see what happens when we submit the `nginx-fast-storage` DaemonSet to the Kubernetes API:

```
$ kubectl apply -f nginx-fast-storage.yaml
daemonset.apps/nginx-fast-storage created
```

Since there is only one node with the `ssd=true` label, the `nginx-fast-storage` Pod will only run on that node:

```
$ kubectl get pods -l app=nginx -o wide
NAME                       READY   STATUS    RESTARTS   AGE   IP            NODE
nginx-fast-storage-7b90t   1/1     Running   0          44s   10.240.0.48   ...
```

Adding the `ssd=true` label to additional nodes will cause the `nginx-fast-storage` Pod to be deployed on those nodes. The inverse is also true: if a required label is removed from a node, the Pod will be removed by the DaemonSet controller.

> Removing labels from a node that are required by a DaemonSet's node selector will cause the Pod being managed by that DaemonSet to be removed from the node.

Updating a DaemonSet

DaemonSets are great for deploying services across an entire cluster, but what about upgrades? Prior to Kubernetes 1.6, the only way to update Pods managed by a DaemonSet was to update the DaemonSet and then manually delete each Pod that was managed by the DaemonSet so that it would be re-created with the new configuration. With the release of Kubernetes 1.6, DaemonSets gained an equivalent to the Deployment object that manages a ReplicaSet rollout inside the cluster.

DaemonSets can be rolled out using the same `RollingUpdate` strategy that Deployments use. You can configure the update strategy using the `spec.update Strategy.type` field, which should have the value `RollingUpdate`. When a Daemon-Set has an update strategy of `RollingUpdate`, any change to the `spec.template` field (or subfields) in the DaemonSet will initiate a rolling update.

As with rolling updates of Deployments (see Chapter 10), the `RollingUpdate` strategy gradually updates members of a DaemonSet until all of the Pods are running the new configuration. There are two parameters that control the rolling update of a DaemonSet:

`spec.minReadySeconds`
   Determines how long a Pod must be "ready" before the rolling update proceeds to upgrade subsequent Pods

`spec.updateStrategy.rollingUpdate.maxUnavailable`
   Indicates how many Pods may be simultaneously updated by the rolling update

You will likely want to set `spec.minReadySeconds` to a reasonably long value, for example 30–60 seconds, to ensure that your Pod is truly healthy before the rollout proceeds.

The setting for `spec.updateStrategy.rollingUpdate.maxUnavailable` is more likely to be application-dependent. Setting it to 1 is a safe, general-purpose strategy, but it also takes a while to complete the rollout (number of nodes × `minReady Seconds`). Increasing the maximum unavailability will make your rollout move faster, but increases the "blast radius" of a failed rollout. The characteristics of your application and cluster environment dictate the relative values of speed versus safety. A good approach might be to set `maxUnavailable` to 1 and only increase it if users or administrators complain about DaemonSet rollout speed.

Once a rolling update has started, you can use the `kubectl rollout` commands to see the current status of a DaemonSet rollout. For example, `kubectl rollout status daemonSets my-daemon-set` will show the current rollout status of a DaemonSet named `my-daemon-set`.

Deleting a DaemonSet

Deleting a DaemonSet using the `kubectl delete` command is pretty straightfoward. Just be sure to supply the correct name of the DaemonSet you would like to delete:

```
$ kubectl delete -f fluentd.yaml
```

 Deleting a DaemonSet will also delete all the Pods being managed by that DaemonSet. Set the `--cascade` flag to `false` to ensure only the DaemonSet is deleted and not the Pods.

Summary

DaemonSets provide an easy-to-use abstraction for running a set of Pods on every node in a Kubernetes cluster, or, if the case requires it, on a subset of nodes based on labels. The DaemonSet provides its own controller and scheduler to ensure key services like monitoring agents are always up and running on the right nodes in your cluster.

For some applications, you simply want to schedule a certain number of replicas; you don't really care where they run as long as they have sufficient resources and distribution to operate reliably. However, there is a different class of applications, like agents and monitoring applications, that needs to be present on every machine in a cluster to function properly. These DaemonSets aren't really traditional serving applications, but rather add additional capabilities and features to the Kubernetes cluster itself. Because the DaemonSet is an active declarative object managed by a controller, it makes it easy to declare your intent that an agent run on every machine without explicitly placing it on every machine. This is especially useful in the context of an autoscaled Kubernetes cluster where nodes may constantly be coming and going without user intervention. In such cases, the DaemonSet automatically adds the proper agents to each node as the autoscaler adds the node to the cluster.

## CHAPTER 12

Jobs

So far we have focused on long-running processes, such as databases and web applications. These types of workloads run until they are either upgraded or the service is no longer needed. While long-running processes make up the large majority of workloads that run on a Kubernetes cluster, there is often a need to run short-lived, one-off tasks. The Job object is made for handling these types of tasks.

A Job creates Pods that run until successful termination (for instance, exit with 0). In contrast, a regular Pod will continually restart regardless of its exit code. Jobs are useful for things you only want to do once, such as database migrations or batch jobs. If run as a regular Pod, your database migration task would run in a loop, continually repopulating the database after every exit.

In this chapter, we'll explore the most common job patterns Kubernetes affords. We will also show you how to leverage these patterns in real-life scenarios.

The Job Object

The Job object is responsible for creating and managing Pods defined in a template in the job specification. These Pods generally run until successful completion. The Job object coordinates running a number of Pods in parallel.

If the Pod fails before a successful termination, the job controller will create a new Pod based on the Pod template in the job specification. Given that Pods have to be scheduled, there is a chance that your job will not execute if the scheduler does not find the required resources. Also, due to the nature of distributed systems, there is a small chance that duplicate Pods will be created for a specific task during certain failure scenarios.

Job Patterns

Jobs are designed to manage batch-like workloads where work items are processed by one or more Pods. By default, each job runs a single Pod once until successful termination. This job pattern is defined by two primary attributes of a job: the number of job completions and the number of Pods to run in parallel. In the case of the "run once until completion" pattern, the `completions` and `parallelism` parameters are set to 1. Table 12-1 highlights job patterns based on the combination of `completions` and `parallelism` for a job configuration.

Table 12-1. Job patterns

Type	Use case	Behavior	comple tions	paral lelism
One shot	Database migrations	A single Pod running once until successful termination	1	1
Parallel fixed completions	Multiple Pods processing a set of work in parallel	One or more Pods running one or more times until reaching a fixed completion count	1+	1+
Work queue: parallel jobs	Multiple Pods processing from a centralized work queue	One or more Pods running once until successful termination	1	2+

One Shot

One-shot jobs provide a way to run a single Pod once until successful termination. While this may sound like an easy task, there is some work involved in pulling this off. First, a Pod must be created and submitted to the Kubernetes API. This is done using a Pod template defined in the job configuration. Once a job is up and running, the Pod backing the job must be monitored for successful termination. A job can fail for any number of reasons, including an application error, an uncaught exception during runtime, or a node failure before the job has a chance to complete. In all cases, the job controller is responsible for re-creating the Pod until a successful termination occurs.

There are multiple ways to create a one-shot job in Kubernetes. The easiest is to use the kubectl command-line tool:

```
$ kubectl run -i oneshot \
  --image=gcr.io/kuar-demo/kuard-amd64:blue \
  --restart=OnFailure \
  --command /kuard \
  -- --keygen-enable \
     --keygen-exit-on-complete \
     --keygen-num-to-gen 10

...
(ID 0) Workload starting
```

```
(ID 0 1/10) Item done: SHA256:nAsUsG54XoKRkJwyN+OShkUPKew3mwq7OCc
(ID 0 2/10) Item done: SHA256:HVKX1ANns6SgF/er1lyo+ZCdnB8geFGt0/8
(ID 0 3/10) Item done: SHA256:irjCLRov3mTT0P0JfsvUyhKRQ1TdGR8H1jg
(ID 0 4/10) Item done: SHA256:nbQAIVY/yrhmEGk3Ui2sAHuxb/o6mYO0qRk
(ID 0 5/10) Item done: SHA256:CCpBoXNlXOMQvR2v38yqimXGAa/w2Tym+aI
(ID 0 6/10) Item done: SHA256:wEY2TTIDz4ATjcr1iimxavCzZzNjRmbOQp8
(ID 0 7/10) Item done: SHA256:t3JSrCt7sQweBgqG5CrbMoBulwk4lfDWiTI
(ID 0 8/10) Item done: SHA256:E84/Vze7KKyjCh9OZh02MkXJGoty9PhaCec
(ID 0 9/10) Item done: SHA256:UOmYex79qqbI1MhcIfG4hDnGKonlsij2k3s
(ID 0 10/10) Item done: SHA256:WCR8wIGOFag84Bsa8f/9QHuKqF+0mEnCADY
(ID 0) Workload exiting
```

There are some things to note here:

- The -i option to kubectl indicates that this is an interactive command. kubectl will wait until the job is running and then show the log output from the first (and in this case only) Pod in the job.

- --restart=OnFailure is the option that tells kubectl to create a Job object.

- All of the options after -- are command-line arguments to the container image. These instruct our test server (kuard) to generate ten 4,096-bit SSH keys and then exit.

- Your output may not match this exactly. kubectl often misses the first couple of lines of output with the -i option.

After the job has completed, the Job object and related Pod are retained so that you can inspect the log output. Note that this job won't show up in kubectl get jobs unless you pass the -a flag. Without this flag, kubectl hides completed jobs. Delete the job before continuing:

```
$ kubectl delete pods oneshot
```

The other option for creating a one-shot job is using a configuration file, as shown in Example 12-1.

Example 12-1. job-oneshot.yaml

```
apiVersion: batch/v1
kind: Job
metadata:
  name: oneshot
spec:
  template:
    spec:
      containers:
      - name: kuard
        image: gcr.io/kuar-demo/kuard-amd64:blue
        imagePullPolicy: Always
        command:
```

```
- "/kuard"
args:
- "--keygen-enable"
- "--keygen-exit-on-complete"
- "--keygen-num-to-gen=10"
restartPolicy: OnFailure
```

Submit the job using the kubectl apply command:

```
$ kubectl apply -f job-oneshot.yaml
job.batch/oneshot created
```

Then describe the oneshot job:

```
$ kubectl describe jobs oneshot

Name:          oneshot
Namespace:     default
Selector:      controller-uid=a2ed65c4-cfda-43c8-bb4a-707c4ed29143
Labels:        controller-uid=a2ed65c4-cfda-43c8-bb4a-707c4ed29143
               job-name=oneshot
Annotations:   <none>
Parallelism:   1
Completions:   1
Start Time:    Wed, 02 Jun 2021 21:23:23 -0700
Completed At:  Wed, 02 Jun 2021 21:23:51 -0700
Duration:      28s
Pods Statuses: 0 Running / 1 Succeeded / 0 Failed
Pod Template:
  Labels:  controller-uid=a2ed65c4-cfda-43c8-bb4a-707c4ed29143
           job-name=oneshot
Events:
  ... Reason            Message
  ... ------            -------
  ... SuccessfulCreate  Created pod: oneshot-4kfdt
```

You can view the results of the job by looking at the logs of the Pod that was created:

```
$ kubectl logs oneshot-4kfdt

...
Serving on :8080
(ID 0) Workload starting
(ID 0 1/10) Item done: SHA256:+r6b4W81DbEjxMcD3LHjU+EIGnLEzbpxITKn8IqhkPI
(ID 0 2/10) Item done: SHA256:mzHewajaY1KA8VluSLOnNMk9fDE5zdn7vvBS5Ne8AxM
(ID 0 3/10) Item done: SHA256:TRtEQHfflJmwkqnNyGgQm/IvXNykSBIg8c03h0g3onE
(ID 0 4/10) Item done: SHA256:tSwPYH/J347il/mgqTxRRdeZcOazEtgZlA8A3/HWbro
(ID 0 5/10) Item done: SHA256:IP8XtguJ6GbWwLHqjKecVfdS96B17nnO21I/TNc1j9k
(ID 0 6/10) Item done: SHA256:ZfNxdQvuST/6ZzEVkyxdRG98p73c/5TM99SEbPeRWfc
(ID 0 7/10) Item done: SHA256:tH+CNl/IUl/HUuKdMsq2XEmDQ8oAvmhMO6Iwj8ZEOj0
(ID 0 8/10) Item done: SHA256:3GfsUaALVEHQcGNLBOu4Qd1zqqqJ8j738i5r+I5XwVI
(ID 0 9/10) Item done: SHA256:5wV4L/xEiHSJXwLUT2fHf0SCKM2g3XH3sVtNbgskCXw
(ID 0 10/10) Item done: SHA256:bPqqOonwSbjzLqe9ZuVRmZkz+DBjaNTZ9HwmQhbdWLI
(ID 0) Workload exiting
```

Congratulations, your job has run successfully!

 Notice that we didn't specify any labels when creating the Job object. Like with other controllers (such as DaemonSets, Replica-Sets, and Deployments) that use labels to identify a set of Pods, unexpected behaviors can occur if a Pod is reused across objects.

Because jobs have a finite beginning and ending, users often create many of them. This makes picking unique labels more difficult and more critical. For this reason, the Job object will automatically pick a unique label and use it to identify the Pods it creates. In advanced scenarios (such as swapping out a running job without killing the Pods it is managing), users can choose to turn off this automatic behavior and manually specify labels and selectors.

We just saw how a job can complete successfully. But what happens if something fails? Let's try that out and see what happens. Modify the arguments to kuard in our configuration file to cause it to fail with a nonzero exit code after generating three keys, as shown in Example 12-2.

Example 12-2. job-oneshot-failure1.yaml

```
...
spec:
  template:
    spec:
      containers:
        ...
        args:
        - "--keygen-enable"
        - "--keygen-exit-on-complete"
        - "--keygen-exit-code=1"
        - "--keygen-num-to-gen=3"
...
```

Now launch this with `kubectl apply -f job-oneshot-failure1.yaml`. Let it run for a bit and then look at the Pod status:

```
$ kubectl get pod -l job-name=oneshot

NAME            READY    STATUS             RESTARTS    AGE
oneshot-3ddk0   0/1      CrashLoopBackOff   4           3m
```

Here we see that the same Pod has restarted four times. Kubernetes is in `CrashLoop BackOff` for this Pod. It is not uncommon to have a bug someplace that causes a program to crash as soon as it starts. In that case, Kubernetes will wait a bit before restarting the Pod to avoid a crash loop that would eat resources on the node. This is all handled local to the node by the `kubelet` without the job being involved at all.

Kill the job (`kubectl delete jobs oneshot`), and let's try something else. Modify the config file again and change the `restartPolicy` from `OnFailure` to `Never`. Launch this with `kubectl apply -f jobs-oneshot-failure2.yaml`.

If we let this run for a bit and then look at related Pods, we'll find something interesting:

```
$ kubectl get pod -l job-name=oneshot -a

NAME             READY   STATUS    RESTARTS   AGE
oneshot-0wm49    0/1     Error     0          1m
oneshot-6h9s2    0/1     Error     0          39s
oneshot-hkzw0    1/1     Running   0          6s
oneshot-k5swz    0/1     Error     0          28s
oneshot-m1rdw    0/1     Error     0          19s
oneshot-x157b    0/1     Error     0          57s
```

What we see is that we have multiple Pods here that have errored out. By setting `restartPolicy: Never`, we are telling the `kubelet` not to restart the Pod on failure, but rather just declare the Pod as failed. The Job object then notices and creates a replacement Pod. If you aren't careful, this'll create a lot of "junk" in your cluster. For this reason, we suggest you use `restartPolicy: OnFailure` so failed Pods are rerun in place. Clean this up with `kubectl delete jobs oneshot`.

So far we've seen a program fail by exiting with a nonzero exit code. But workers can fail in other ways. Specifically, they can get stuck and not make any forward progress. To help cover this case, you can use liveness probes with jobs. If the liveness probe policy determines that a Pod is dead, it'll be restarted or replaced for you.

Parallelism

Generating keys can be slow. Let's start a bunch of workers together to make key generation faster. We're going to use a combination of the `completions` and `parallelism` parameters. Our goal is to generate 100 keys by having 10 runs of kuard, with each run generating 10 keys. But we don't want to swamp our cluster, so we'll limit ourselves to only five Pods at a time.

This translates to setting `completions` to `10` and `parallelism` to `5`. The config is shown in Example 12-3.

Example 12-3. job-parallel.yaml

```
apiVersion: batch/v1
kind: Job
metadata:
  name: parallel
  labels:
    chapter: jobs
```

```
spec:
  parallelism: 5
  completions: 10
  template:
    metadata:
      labels:
        chapter: jobs
    spec:
      containers:
      - name: kuard
        image: gcr.io/kuar-demo/kuard-amd64:blue
        imagePullPolicy: Always
        command:
        - "/kuard"
        args:
        - "--keygen-enable"
        - "--keygen-exit-on-complete"
        - "--keygen-num-to-gen=10"
      restartPolicy: OnFailure
```

Start it up:

```
$ kubectl apply -f job-parallel.yaml
job.batch/parallel created
```

Now watch as the Pods come up, do their thing, and exit. New Pods are created until 10 have completed altogether. Here we use the --watch flag to have kubectl stay around and list changes as they happen:

```
$ kubectl get pods -w
NAME              READY    STATUS              RESTARTS   AGE
parallel-55tlv    1/1      Running             0          5s
parallel-5s7s9    1/1      Running             0          5s
parallel-jp7bj    1/1      Running             0          5s
parallel-lssmn    1/1      Running             0          5s
parallel-qxcxp    1/1      Running             0          5s
NAME              READY    STATUS              RESTARTS   AGE
parallel-jp7bj    0/1      Completed           0          26s
parallel-tzp9n    0/1      Pending             0          0s
parallel-tzp9n    0/1      Pending             0          0s
parallel-tzp9n    0/1      ContainerCreating   0          1s
parallel-tzp9n    1/1      Running             0          1s
parallel-tzp9n    0/1      Completed           0          48s
parallel-x1kmr    0/1      Pending             0          0s
...
```

Feel free to study the completed jobs and check out their logs to see the fingerprints of the keys they generated. Clean up by deleting the finished Job object with kubectl delete job parallel.

Work Queues

A common use case for jobs is to process work from a work queue. In this scenario, some task creates a number of work items and publishes them to a work queue. A worker job can be run to process each work item until the work queue is empty (Figure 12-1).

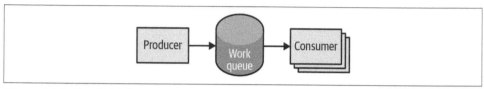

Figure 12-1. Parallel jobs

Starting a work queue

We start by launching a centralized work queue service. kuard has a simple memory-based work queue system built in. We will start an instance of kuard to act as a coordinator for all the work.

Next, we create a simple ReplicaSet to manage a singleton work queue daemon. We are using a ReplicaSet to ensure that a new Pod will get created in the face of machine failure, as shown in Example 12-4.

Example 12-4. rs-queue.yaml

```
apiVersion: apps/v1
kind: ReplicaSet
metadata:
  labels:
    app: work-queue
    component: queue
    chapter: jobs
  name: queue
spec:
  replicas: 1
  selector:
    matchLabels:
      app: work-queue
      component: queue
      chapter: jobs
  template:
    metadata:
      labels:
        app: work-queue
        component: queue
        chapter: jobs
    spec:
      containers:
```

```
- name: queue
  image: "gcr.io/kuar-demo/kuard-amd64:blue"
  imagePullPolicy: Always
```

Run the work queue with the following command:

```
$ kubectl apply -f rs-queue.yaml
replicaset.apps/queue created
```

At this point, the work queue daemon should be up and running. Let's use port-forwarding to connect to it. Leave this command running in a terminal window:

```
$ kubectl port-forward rs/queue 8080:8080
Forwarding from 127.0.0.1:8080 -> 8080
Forwarding from [::1]:8080 -> 8080
```

You can open your browser to *http://localhost:8080* and see the kuard interface. Switch to the "MemQ Server" tab to keep an eye on what is going on.

With the work queue server in place, the next step is to expose it using a service. This will make it easy for producers and consumers to locate the work queue via DNS, as Example 12-5 shows.

Example 12-5. service-queue.yaml

```
apiVersion: v1
kind: Service
metadata:
  labels:
    app: work-queue
    component: queue
    chapter: jobs
  name: queue
spec:
  ports:
  - port: 8080
    protocol: TCP
    targetPort: 8080
  selector:
    app: work-queue
    component: queue
```

Create the queue service with kubectl:

```
$ kubectl apply -f service-queue.yaml
service/queue created
```

Loading up the queue

We are now ready to put a bunch of work items in the queue. For the sake of simplicity, we'll just use curl to drive the API for the work queue server and insert a bunch of work items. curl will communicate to the work queue through the kubectl port-forward we set up earlier, as shown in Example 12-6.

Example 12-6. load-queue.sh

```
# Create a work queue called 'keygen'
curl -X PUT localhost:8080/memq/server/queues/keygen

# Create 100 work items and load up the queue.
for i in work-item-{0..99}; do
  curl -X POST localhost:8080/memq/server/queues/keygen/enqueue \
    -d "$i"
done
```

Run these commands, and you should see 100 JSON objects output to your terminal with a unique message identifier for each work item. You can confirm the status of the queue by looking at the "MemQ Server" tab in the UI, or you can ask the work queue API directly:

```
$ curl 127.0.0.1:8080/memq/server/stats
{
    "kind": "stats",
    "queues": [
        {
            "depth": 100,
            "dequeued": 0,
            "drained": 0,
            "enqueued": 100,
            "name": "keygen"
        }
    ]
}
```

Now we are ready to kick off a job to consume the work queue until it's empty.

Creating the consumer job

This is where things get interesting! kuard can also act in consumer mode. We can set it up to draw work items from the work queue, create a key, and then exit once the queue is empty, as shown in Example 12-7.

Example 12-7. job-consumers.yaml

```
apiVersion: batch/v1
kind: Job
metadata:
  labels:
    app: message-queue
    component: consumer
```

```
        chapter: jobs
    name: consumers
spec:
  parallelism: 5
  template:
    metadata:
      labels:
          app: message-queue
          component: consumer
          chapter: jobs
      spec:
        containers:
        - name: worker
          image: "gcr.io/kuar-demo/kuard-amd64:blue"
          imagePullPolicy: Always
          command:
          - "/kuard"
          args:
          - "--keygen-enable"
          - "--keygen-exit-on-complete"
          - "--keygen-memq-server=http://queue:8080/memq/server"
          - "--keygen-memq-queue=keygen"
        restartPolicy: OnFailure
```

Here, we are telling the job to start up five Pods in parallel. As the completions parameter is unset, we put the job into worker-pool mode. Once the first Pod exits with a zero exit code, the job will start winding down and will not start any new Pods. This means that none of the workers should exit until the work is done and they are all in the process of finishing up.

Now, create the consumers job:

```
$ kubectl apply -f job-consumers.yaml
job.batch/consumers created
```

Then you can view the Pods backing the job:

```
$ kubectl get pods
NAME             READY   STATUS    RESTARTS   AGE
queue-43s87      1/1     Running   0          5m
consumers-6wjxc  1/1     Running   0          2m
consumers-7l5mh  1/1     Running   0          2m
consumers-hvz42  1/1     Running   0          2m
consumers-pc8hr  1/1     Running   0          2m
consumers-w20cc  1/1     Running   0          2m
```

Note there are five Pods running in parallel. These Pods will continue to run until the work queue is empty. You can watch as it happens in the UI on the work queue server. As the queue empties, the consumer Pods will exit cleanly and the consumers job will be considered complete.

Cleanup

Using labels, we can clean up all of the stuff we created in this section:

```
$ kubectl delete rs,svc,job -l chapter=jobs
```

CronJobs

Sometimes you want to schedule a job to be run at a certain interval. To achieve this, you can declare a CronJob in Kubernetes, which is responsible for creating a new Job object at a particular interval. Example 12-8 is an example CronJob declaration:

Example 12-8. job-cronjob.yaml

```
apiVersion: batch/v1
kind: CronJob
metadata:
  name: example-cron
spec:
  # Run every fifth hour
  schedule: "0 */5 * * *"
  jobTemplate:
    spec:
      template:
        spec:
          containers:
          - name: batch-job
            image: my-batch-image
          restartPolicy: OnFailure
```

Note the `spec.schedule` field, which contains the interval for the CronJob in standard cron format.

You can save this file as *job-cronjob.yaml*, and create the CronJob with `kubectl create -f cron-job.yaml`. If you are interested in the current state of a CronJob, you can use `kubectl describe <cron-job>` to get the details.

Summary

On a single cluster, Kubernetes can handle both long-running workloads such as web applications and short-lived workloads such as batch jobs. The job abstraction allows you to model batch job patterns ranging from simple, one-time tasks to parallel jobs that process many items until the work has been exhausted.

Jobs are a low-level primitive and can be used directly for simple workloads. However, Kubernetes is built from the ground up to be extensible by higher-level objects. Jobs are no exception; higher-level orchestration systems can easily use them to take on more complex tasks.

## CHAPTER 13

ConfigMaps and Secrets

It's good practice to make container images as reusable as possible. The same image should be able to be used for development, staging, and production. It's even better if the same image is general-purpose enough to be used across applications and services. Testing and versioning are more risky and complicated if images need to be re-created for each new environment. How then do we specialize the use of that image at runtime?

This is where ConfigMaps and Secrets come into play. ConfigMaps are used to provide configuration information for workloads. This can be either fine-grained information like a string or a composite value in the form of a file. Secrets are similar to ConfigMaps but focus on making sensitive information available to the workload. They can be used for things like credentials or TLS certificates.

ConfigMaps

One way to think of a ConfigMap is as a Kubernetes object that defines a small filesystem. Another way is as a set of variables that can be used when defining the environment or command line for your containers. The key thing to note is that the ConfigMap is combined with the Pod right before it is run. This means that the container image and the Pod definition can be reused by many workloads just by changing the ConfigMap that is used.

Creating ConfigMaps

Let's jump right in and create a ConfigMap. Like many objects in Kubernetes, you can create these in an immediate, imperative way, or you can create them from a manifest on disk. We'll start with the imperative method.

First, suppose we have a file on disk (called *my-config.txt*) that we want to make available to the Pod in question, as shown in Example 13-1.

Example 13-1. my-config.txt

```
# This is a sample config file that I might use to configure an application
parameter1 = value1
parameter2 = value2
```

Next, let's create a ConfigMap with that file. We'll also add a couple of simple key/value pairs here. These are referred to as literal values on the command line:

```
$ kubectl create configmap my-config \
  --from-file=my-config.txt \
  --from-literal=extra-param=extra-value \
  --from-literal=another-param=another-value
```

The equivalent YAML for the ConfigMap object we just created is as follows:

```
$ kubectl get configmaps my-config -o yaml

apiVersion: v1
data:
  another-param: another-value
  extra-param: extra-value
  my-config.txt: |
    # This is a sample config file that I might use to configure an application
    parameter1 = value1
    parameter2 = value2
kind: ConfigMap
metadata:
  creationTimestamp: ...
  name: my-config
  namespace: default
  resourceVersion: "13556"
  selfLink: /api/v1/namespaces/default/configmaps/my-config
  uid: 3641c553-f7de-11e6-98c9-06135271a273
```

As you can see, the ConfigMap is just some key/value pairs stored in an object. The interesting part is when you try to *use* a ConfigMap.

Using a ConfigMap

There are three main ways to use a ConfigMap:

Filesystem
> You can mount a ConfigMap into a Pod. A file is created for each entry based on the key name. The contents of that file are set to the value.

Environment variable

A ConfigMap can be used to dynamically set the value of an environment variable.

Command-line argument

Kubernetes supports dynamically creating the command line for a container based on ConfigMap values.

Let's create a manifest for kuard that pulls all of these together, as shown in Example 13-2.

Example 13-2. kuard-config.yaml

```
apiVersion: v1
kind: Pod
metadata:
  name: kuard-config
spec:
  containers:
    - name: test-container
      image: gcr.io/kuar-demo/kuard-amd64:blue
      imagePullPolicy: Always
      command:
        - "/kuard"
        - "$(EXTRA_PARAM)"
      env:
        # An example of an environment variable used inside the container
        - name: ANOTHER_PARAM
          valueFrom:
            configMapKeyRef:
              name: my-config
              key: another-param
        # An example of an environment variable passed to the command to start
        # the container (above).
        - name: EXTRA_PARAM
          valueFrom:
            configMapKeyRef:
              name: my-config
              key: extra-param
      volumeMounts:
        # Mounting the ConfigMap as a set of files
        - name: config-volume
          mountPath: /config
  volumes:
    - name: config-volume
      configMap:
        name: my-config
  restartPolicy: Never
```

For the filesystem method, we create a new volume inside the Pod and give it the name config-volume. We then define this volume to be a ConfigMap volume and point at the ConfigMap to mount. We have to specify where this gets mounted into the kuard container with a volumeMount. In this case, we are mounting it at /config.

Environment variables are specified with a special valueFrom member. This references the ConfigMap and the data key to use within that ConfigMap. Command-line arguments build on environment variables. Kubernetes will perform the correct substitution with a special $(<env-var-name>) syntax.

Run this Pod, and let's port-forward to examine how the app sees the world:

```
$ kubectl apply -f kuard-config.yaml
$ kubectl port-forward kuard-config 8080
```

Now point your browser to *http://localhost:8080*. We can look at how we've injected configuration values into the program in all three ways. Click the "Server Env" tab on the left. This will show the command line that the app was launched with along with its environment, as shown in Figure 13-1.

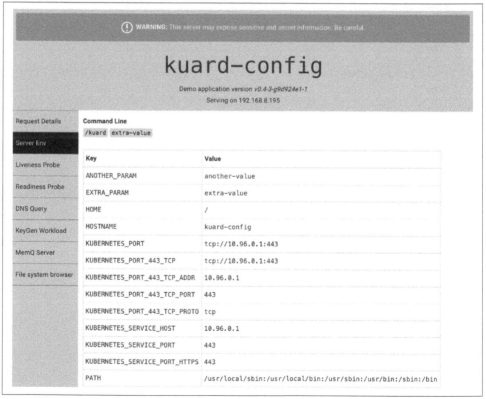

Figure 13-1. kuard, showing its environment

Here we can see that we've added two environment variables (ANOTHER_PARAM and EXTRA_PARAM) whose values are set via the ConfigMap. We've also added an argument to the command line of kuard based on the EXTRA_PARAM value.

Next, click the "File system browser" tab (Figure 13-2). This lets you explore the filesystem as the application sees it. You should see an entry called /config. This is a volume created based on our ConfigMap. If you navigate into that, you'll see that a file has been created for each entry of the ConfigMap. You'll also see some hidden files (prepended with ..) that are used to do a clean swap of new values when the ConfigMap is updated.

Figure 13-2. The /config directory as seen through kuard

Secrets

While ConfigMaps are great for most configuration data, there is certain data that is extra sensitive. This includes passwords, security tokens, or other types of private keys. Collectively, we call this type of data "Secrets." Kubernetes has native support for storing and handling this data with care.

Secrets enable container images to be created without bundling sensitive data. This allows containers to remain portable across environments. Secrets are exposed to Pods via explicit declaration in Pod manifests and the Kubernetes API. In this way, the Kubernetes Secrets API provides an application-centric mechanism for exposing sensitive configuration information to applications in a way that's easy to audit and leverages native OS isolation primitives.

The remainder of this section will explore how to create and manage Kubernetes Secrets, and also lay out best practices for exposing Secrets to Pods that require them.

By default, Kubernetes Secrets are stored in plain text in the etcd storage for the cluster. Depending on your requirements, this may not be sufficient security for you. In particular, anyone who has cluster administration rights in your cluster will be able to read all of the Secrets in the cluster.

In recent versions of Kubernetes, support has been added for encrypting the Secrets with a user-supplied key, generally integrated into a cloud key store. Additionally, most cloud key stores have integration with Kubernetes Secrets Store CSI Driver (*https://oreil.ly/DRHt6*) volumes, enabling you to skip Kubernetes Secrets entirely and rely exclusively on the cloud provider's key store. All of these options should provide you with sufficient tools to craft a security profile that suits your needs.

Creating Secrets

Secrets are created using the Kubernetes API or the kubectl command-line tool. Secrets hold one or more data elements as a collection of key/value pairs.

In this section, we will create a Secret to store a TLS key and certificate for the kuard application that meets the storage requirements listed previously.

The kuard container image does not bundle a TLS certificate or key. This allows the kuard container to remain portable across environments and distributable through public Docker repositories.

The first step in creating a Secret is to obtain the raw data we want to store. The TLS key and certificate for the kuard application can be downloaded by running the following commands:

```
$ curl -o kuard.crt  https://storage.googleapis.com/kuar-demo/kuard.crt
$ curl -o kuard.key https://storage.googleapis.com/kuar-demo/kuard.key
```

These certificates are shared with the world and they provide no actual security. Please do not use them except as a learning tool in these examples.

With the *kuard.crt* and *kuard.key* files stored locally, we are ready to create a Secret. Create a Secret named kuard-tls using the create secret command:

```
$ kubectl create secret generic kuard-tls \
  --from-file=kuard.crt \
  --from-file=kuard.key
```

The `kuard-tls` Secret has been created with two data elements. Run the following command to get details:

```
$ kubectl describe secrets kuard-tls

Name:         kuard-tls
Namespace:    default
Labels:       <none>
Annotations:  <none>

Type:         Opaque

Data
====
kuard.crt:    1050 bytes
kuard.key:    1679 bytes
```

With the `kuard-tls` Secret in place, we can consume it from a Pod by using a Secrets volume.

Consuming Secrets

Secrets can be consumed using the Kubernetes REST API by applications that know how to call that API directly. However, our goal is to keep applications portable. Not only should they run well in Kubernetes, but they should run, unmodified, on other platforms.

Instead of accessing Secrets through the API server, we can use a *Secrets volume*. Secret data can be exposed to Pods using the Secrets volume type. Secrets volumes are managed by the `kubelet` and are created at Pod creation time. Secrets are stored on `tmpfs` volumes (aka RAM disks), and as such are not written to disk on nodes.

Each data element of a Secret is stored in a separate file under the target mount point specified in the volume mount. The `kuard-tls` Secret contains two data elements: *kuard.crt* and *kuard.key*. Mounting the `kuard-tls` Secrets volume to `/tls` results in the following files:

```
/tls/kuard.crt
/tls/kuard.key
```

The Pod manifest in Example 13-3 demonstrates how to declare a Secrets volume, which exposes the `kuard-tls` Secret to the `kuard` container under `/tls`.

Example 13-3. kuard-secret.yaml

```
apiVersion: v1
kind: Pod
metadata:
  name: kuard-tls
```

```
spec:
  containers:
    - name: kuard-tls
      image: gcr.io/kuar-demo/kuard-amd64:blue
      imagePullPolicy: Always
      volumeMounts:
      - name: tls-certs
        mountPath: "/tls"
        readOnly: true
  volumes:
    - name: tls-certs
      secret:
        secretName: kuard-tls
```

Create the kuard-tls Pod using kubectl and observe the log output from the running Pod:

```
$ kubectl apply -f kuard-secret.yaml
```

Connect to the Pod by running:

```
$ kubectl port-forward kuard-tls 8443:8443
```

Now navigate your browser to *https://localhost:8443*. You should see some invalid certificate warnings because this is a self-signed certificate for *kuard.example.com*. If you navigate past this warning, you should see the kuard server hosted via HTTPS. Use the "File system browser" tab to find the certificates on disk in the /tls directory.

Private Container Registries

A special use case for Secrets is to store access credentials for private container registries. Kubernetes supports using images stored on private registries, but access to those images requires credentials. Private images can be stored across one or more private registries. This presents a challenge for managing credentials for each private registry on every possible node in the cluster.

Image pull Secrets leverage the Secrets API to automate the distribution of private registry credentials. Image pull Secrets are stored just like regular Secrets but are consumed through the spec.imagePullSecrets Pod specification field.

Use kubectl create secret docker-registry to create this special kind of Secret:

```
$ kubectl create secret docker-registry my-image-pull-secret \
  --docker-username=<username> \
  --docker-password=<password> \
  --docker-email=<email-address>
```

Enable access to the private repository by referencing the image pull secret in the Pod manifest file, as shown in Example 13-4.

Example 13-4. kuard-secret-ips.yaml

```
apiVersion: v1
kind: Pod
metadata:
  name: kuard-tls
spec:
  containers:
    - name: kuard-tls
      image: gcr.io/kuar-demo/kuard-amd64:blue
      imagePullPolicy: Always
      volumeMounts:
      - name: tls-certs
        mountPath: "/tls"
        readOnly: true
  imagePullSecrets:
  - name:  my-image-pull-secret
  volumes:
    - name: tls-certs
      secret:
        secretName: kuard-tls
```

If you are repeatedly pulling from the same registry, you can add the Secrets to the default service account associated with each Pod to avoid having to specify the Secrets in every Pod you create.

Naming Constraints

The key names for data items inside of a Secret or ConfigMap are defined to map to valid environment variable names. They may begin with a dot, then are followed by a letter or number, followed by characters including dots, dashes, and underscores. Dots cannot be repeated, and dots and underscores or dashes cannot be adjacent to each other. More formally, this means that they must conform to the regular expression `^[.]?[a-zAZ0-9]([.]?[a-zA-Z0-9]+[-_a-zA-Z0-9]?)*$`. Some examples of valid and invalid names for ConfigMaps and Secrets are given in Table 13-1.

Table 13-1. ConfigMap and Secret key examples

Valid key name	Invalid key name
.auth_token	Token..properties
Key.pem	auth file.json
config_file	_password.txt

When selecting a key name, remember that these keys can be exposed to Pods via a volume mount. Pick a name that is going to make sense when specified on a command line or in a config file. Storing a TLS key as key.pem is clearer than tls-key when configuring applications to access Secrets.

ConfigMap data values are simple UTF-8 text specified directly in the manifest. Secret data values hold arbitrary data encoded using base64. The use of base64 encoding makes it possible to store binary data. This does, however, make it more difficult to manage Secrets that are stored in YAML files as the base64-encoded value must be put in the YAML. Note that the maximum size for a ConfigMap or Secret is 1 MB.

Managing ConfigMaps and Secrets

ConfigMaps and Secrets are managed through the Kubernetes API. The usual `create`, `delete`, `get`, and `describe` commands work for manipulating these objects.

Listing

You can use the `kubectl get secrets` command to list all Secrets in the current namespace:

```
$ kubectl get secrets
```

```
NAME                  TYPE                                   DATA   AGE
default-token-f5jq2   kubernetes.io/service-account-token    3      1h
kuard-tls             Opaque                                 2      20m
```

Similarly, you can list all of the ConfigMaps in a namespace:

```
$ kubectl get configmaps
```

```
NAME        DATA   AGE
my-config   3      1m
```

`kubectl describe` can be used to get more details on a single object:

```
$ kubectl describe configmap my-config
```

```
Name:          my-config
Namespace:     default
Labels:        <none>
Annotations:   <none>

Data
====
another-param:  13 bytes
```

```
extra-param:    11 bytes
my-config.txt:  116 bytes
```

Finally, you can see the raw data (including values in Secrets!) by using a command similar to the following: kubectl get configmap my-config -o yaml or kubectl get secret kuard-tls -o yaml.

Creating

The easiest way to create a Secret or a ConfigMap is via kubectl create secret generic or kubectl create configmap. There are a variety of ways to specify the data items that go into the Secret or ConfigMap. These can be combined in a single command:

--from-file=<filename>
: Load from the file with the Secret data key that's the same as the filename.

--from-file=<key>=<filename>
: Load from the file with the Secret data key explicitly specified.

--from-file=<directory>
: Load all the files in the specified directory where the filename is an acceptable key name.

--from-literal=<key>=<value>
: Use the specified key/value pair directly.

Updating

You can update a ConfigMap or Secret and have it reflected in running applications. There is no need to restart if the application is configured to reread configuration values. Next, we will describe three ways to update ConfigMaps or Secrets.

Update from file

If you have a manifest for your ConfigMap or Secret, you can just edit it directly and replace it with a new version using kubectl replace -f <filename>. You can also use kubectl apply -f <filename> if you previously created the resource with kubectl apply.

Due to the way that datafiles are encoded into these objects, updating a configuration can be a bit cumbersome; there is no kubectl command that supports loading data from an external file. The data must be stored directly in the YAML manifest.

The most common use case is when the ConfigMap is defined as part of a directory or list of resources and everything is created and updated together. Oftentimes these manifests will be checked into source control.

It is generally a bad idea to check Secret YAML files into source control because it is too easy to inadvertently push these files someplace public and leak your Secrets.

Re-create and update

If you store the inputs into your ConfigMaps or Secrets as separate files on disk (as opposed to embedded into YAML directly), you can use kubectl to re-create the manifest and then use it to update the object, which will look something like this:

```
$ kubectl create secret generic kuard-tls \
  --from-file=kuard.crt --from-file=kuard.key \
  --dry-run -o yaml | kubectl replace -f -
```

This command line first creates a new Secret with the same name as our existing Secret. If we just stopped there, the Kubernetes API server would return an error complaining that we are trying to create a Secret that already exists. Instead, we tell kubectl not to actually send the data to the server but instead to dump the YAML that it *would have* sent to the API server to stdout. We then pipe that to kubectl replace and use -f - to tell it to read from stdin. In this way, we can update a Secret from files on disk without having to manually base64-encode data.

Edit current version

The final way to update a ConfigMap is to use kubectl edit to bring up a version of the ConfigMap in your editor so you can tweak it (you could also do this with a Secret, but you'd be stuck managing the base64 encoding of values on your own):

```
$ kubectl edit configmap my-config
```

You should see the ConfigMap definition in your editor. Make your desired changes and then save and close your editor. The new version of the object will be pushed to the Kubernetes API server.

Live updates

Once a ConfigMap or Secret is updated using the API, it'll be automatically pushed to all volumes that use that ConfigMap or Secret. It may take a few seconds, but the file listing and contents of the files, as seen by kuard, will be updated with these new values. Using this live update feature, you can update the configuration of applications without restarting them.

Currently there is no built-in way to signal an application when a new version of a ConfigMap is deployed. It is up to the application (or some helper script) to look for the config files to change and reload them.

Using the file browser in kuard (accessed through `kubectl port-forward`) is a great way to interactively play with dynamically updating Secrets and ConfigMaps.

Summary

ConfigMaps and Secrets are a great way to provide dynamic configuration in your application. They allow you to create a container image (and Pod definition) once and reuse it in different contexts. This can include using the exact same image as you move from development to staging to production. It can also include using a single image across multiple teams and services. Separating configuration from application code will make your applications more reliable and reusable.

## CHAPTER 14

Role-Based Access Control for Kubernetes

At this point, nearly every Kubernetes cluster you encounter has role-based access control (RBAC) enabled. So you have likely encountered RBAC before. Perhaps you initially couldn't access your cluster until you used some magical command to add a RoleBinding to map a user to a role. Even though you may have had some exposure to RBAC, you may not have had a great deal of experience understanding RBAC in Kubernetes, including what it is for and how to use it.

Role-based access control provides a mechanism for restricting both access to and actions on Kubernetes APIs to ensure that only authorized users have access. RBAC is a critical component to both harden access to the Kubernetes cluster where you are deploying your application and (possibly more importantly) prevent unexpected accidents where one person in the wrong namespace mistakenly takes down production when they think they are destroying their test cluster.

 While RBAC can be quite useful in limiting access to the Kubernetes API, it's important to remember that anyone who can run arbitrary code inside the Kubernetes cluster can effectively obtain root privileges on the entire cluster. There are approaches that you can take to make such attacks harder and more expensive, and a correct RBAC setup is part of this defense. But if you are focused on hostile multitenant security, RBAC by itself is sufficient to protect you. You must isolate the Pods running in your cluster to provide effective multitenant security. Generally this is done using hypervisor isolated containers or a container sandbox.

Before we dive into the details of RBAC in Kubernetes, it's valuable to have a high-level understanding of RBAC as a concept, as well as authentication and authorization more generally.

Every request to Kubernetes is first *authenticated*. Authentication provides the identity of the caller issuing the request. It could be as simple as saying that the request is unauthenticated, or it could integrate deeply with a pluggable authentication provider (e.g., Azure Active Directory) to establish an identity within that third-party system. Interestingly enough, Kubernetes does not have a built-in identity store, focusing instead on integrating other identity sources within itself.

Once users have been authenticated, the authorization phase determines whether they are authorized to perform the request. Authorization is a combination of the identity of the user, the resource (effectively the HTTP path), and the verb or action the user is attempting to perform. If the particular user is authorized to perform that action on that resource, then the request is allowed to proceed. Otherwise, an HTTP 403 error is returned. Let's dive into this process.

Role-Based Access Control

To properly manage access in Kubernetes, it's critical to understand how identity, roles, and role bindings interact to control who can do what with which resources. At first, RBAC can seem like a challenge to understand, with a series of interconnected, abstract concepts; but once it's understood, you can be confident in your ability to manage cluster access.

Identity in Kubernetes

Every request to Kubernetes is associated with some identity. Even a request with no identity is associated with the system:unauthenticated group. Kubernetes makes a distinction between user identities and service account identities. Service accounts are created and managed by Kubernetes itself and are generally associated with components running inside the cluster. User accounts are all other accounts associated with actual users of the cluster, and often include automation like continuous delivery services that run outside the cluster.

Kubernetes uses a generic interface for authentication providers. Each of the providers supplies a username and, optionally, the set of groups to which the user belongs. Kubernetes supports a number of authentication providers, including:

- HTTP Basic Authentication (largely deprecated)
- x509 client certificates
- Static token files on the host
- Cloud authentication providers, such as Azure Active Directory and AWS Identity and Access Management (IAM)
- Authentication webhooks

While most managed Kubernetes installations configure authentication for you, if you are deploying your own authentication, you will need to configure flags on the Kubernetes API server appropriately.

You should always use different identities for different applications in your cluster. For example, you should have one identity for your production frontends, a different identity for the production backends, and all production identities should be distinct from development identities. You should also have different identities for different clusters. All of these identities should be machine identities that are not shared with users. You can either use Kubernetes Service Accounts for achieving this, or you can use a Pod identity provider supplied by your identity system; for example, Azure Active Directory supplies an open source identity provider for Pods (*https://oreil.ly/ YLymu*) as do other popular identity providers.

Understanding Roles and Role Bindings

Identity is just the beginning of authorization in Kubernetes. Once Kubernetes knows the identity of the request, it needs to determine if the request is authorized for that user. To achieve this, it uses roles and role bindings.

A *role* is a set of abstract capabilities. For example, the appdev role might represent the ability to create Pods and Services. A *role binding* is an assignment of a role to one or more identities. Thus, binding the appdev role to the user identity alice indicates that Alice has the ability to create Pods and Services.

Roles and Role Bindings in Kubernetes

In Kubernetes, two pairs of related resources represent roles and role bindings. One pair is scoped to a namespace (Role and RoleBinding), while the other pair is scoped to the cluster (ClusterRole and ClusterRoleBinding).

Let's examine Role and RoleBinding first. Role resources are namespaced and represent capabilities within that single namespace. You cannot use namespaced roles for nonnamespaced resources (e.g., CustomResourceDefinitions), and binding a Role-Binding to a role only provides authorization within the Kubernetes namespace that contains both the Role and the RoleBinding.

As a concrete example, here is a simple role that gives an identity the ability to create and modify Pods and Services:

```
kind: Role
apiVersion: rbac.authorization.k8s.io/v1
metadata:
  namespace: default
  name: pod-and-services
rules:
- apiGroups: [""]
```

```
    resources: ["pods", "services"]
    verbs: ["create", "delete", "get", "list", "patch", "update", "watch"]
```

To bind this Role to the user alice, we need to create a RoleBinding that looks as follows. This role binding also binds the group mydevs to the same role:

```
apiVersion: rbac.authorization.k8s.io/v1
kind: RoleBinding
metadata:
  namespace: default
  name: pods-and-services
subjects:
- apiGroup: rbac.authorization.k8s.io
  kind: User
  name: alice
- apiGroup: rbac.authorization.k8s.io
  kind: Group
  name: mydevs
roleRef:
  apiGroup: rbac.authorization.k8s.io
  kind: Role
  name: pod-and-services
```

Sometimes you need to create a role that applies to the entire cluster, or you want to limit access to cluster-level resources. To achieve this, you use the ClusterRole and ClusterRoleBinding resources. They are largely identical to their namespaced peers, but are cluster-scoped.

Verbs for Kubernetes roles

Roles are defined in terms of both a resource (e.g., Pods) and a verb that describes an action that can be performed on that resource. The verbs correspond roughly to HTTP methods. The commonly used verbs in Kubernetes RBAC are listed in Table 14-1.

Table 14-1. Common Kubernetes RBAC verbs

Verb	HTTP method	Description
create	POST	Create a new resource.
delete	DELETE	Delete an existing resource.
get	GET	Get a resource.
list	GET	List a collection of resources.
patch	PATCH	Modify an existing resource via a partial change.
update	PUT	Modify an existing resource via a complete object.
watch	GET	Watch for streaming updates to a resource.
proxy	GET	Connect to resource via a streaming WebSocket proxy.

Using built-in roles

Designing your own roles can be complicated and time-consuming. Kubernetes has a large number of built-in cluster roles for well-known system identities (e.g., a scheduler) that require a known set of capabilities. You can view these by running:

```
$ kubectl get clusterroles
```

While most of these built-in roles are for system utilities, four are designed for generic end users:

- The `cluster-admin` role provides complete access to the entire cluster.
- The `admin` role provides complete access to a complete namespace.
- The `edit` role allows an end user to modify resources in a namespace.
- The `view` role allows for read-only access to a namespace.

Most clusters already have numerous ClusterRole bindings set up, and you can view these bindings with `kubectl get clusterrolebindings`.

Auto-reconciliation of built-in roles

When the Kubernetes API server starts up, it automatically installs a number of default ClusterRoles that are defined in the code of the API server itself. This means that if you modify any built-in cluster role, those modifications are transient. Whenever the API server is restarted (e.g., for an upgrade), your changes will be overwritten.

To prevent this from happening, before you make any other modifications, you need to add the `rbac.authorization.kubernetes.io/autoupdate` annotation with a value of `false` to the built-in ClusterRole resource. If this annotation is set to `false`, the API server will not overwrite the modified ClusterRole resource.

> By default, the Kubernetes API server installs a cluster role that allows `system:unauthenticated` users access to the API server's API discovery endpoint. For any cluster exposed to a hostile environment (e.g., the public internet) this is a bad idea, and there has been at least one serious security vulnerability via this exposure. If you are running a Kubernetes service on the public internet or an other hostile environment, you should ensure that the `--anonymous-auth=false` flag is set on your API server.

Techniques for Managing RBAC

Managing RBAC for a cluster can be complicated and frustrating. Possibly more concerning is that misconfigured RBAC can lead to security issues. Fortunately, there are several tools and techniques that make managing RBAC easier.

Testing Authorization with can-i

The first useful tool is the `auth can-i` command for `kubectl`. This tool is used for testing whether a specific user can perform a specific action. You can use `can-i` to validate configuration settings as you configure your cluster, or you can ask users to use the tool to validate their access when filing errors or bug reports.

In its simplest usage, the `can-i` command takes a verb and a resource. For example, this command will indicate if the current `kubectl` user is authorized to create Pods:

```
$ kubectl auth can-i create pods
```

You can also test subresources like logs or port-forwarding with the `--subresource` command-line flag:

```
$ kubectl auth can-i get pods --subresource=logs
```

Managing RBAC in Source Control

Like all resources in Kubernetes, RBAC resources are modeled using YAML. Given this text-based representation, it makes sense to store these resources in version control, which allows for accountability, auditability, and rollback.

The `kubectl` command-line tool provides a `reconcile` command that operates somewhat like `kubectl apply` and will reconcile a set of roles and role bindings with the current state of the cluster. You can run:

```
$ kubectl auth reconcile -f some-rbac-config.yaml
```

If you want to see changes before they are made, you can add the `--dry-run` flag to the command to output, but not apply, the changes.

Advanced Topics

Once you orient to the basics of role-based access control, it is relatively easy to manage access to a Kubernetes cluster. But when managing a large number of users or roles, there are additional advanced capabilities you can use to manage RBAC at scale.

Aggregating ClusterRoles

Sometimes you want to be able to define roles that are combinations of other roles. One option would be to simply clone all of the rules from one ClusterRole into another ClusterRole, but this is complicated and error-prone, since changes to one ClusterRole aren't automatically reflected in the other. Instead, Kubernetes RBAC supports the usage of an *aggregation rule* to combine multiple roles in a new role. This new role combines all of the capabilities of all of the aggregate roles, and any changes to any of the constituent subroles will automatically be propogated back into the aggregate role.

As with other aggregations or groupings in Kubernetes, the ClusterRoles to be aggregated are specified using label selectors. In this particular case, the `aggregationRule` field in the ClusterRole resource contains a `clusterRoleSelector` field, which in turn is a label selector. All ClusterRole resources that match this selector are dynamically aggregated into the `rules` array in the aggregate ClusterRole resource.

A best practice for managing ClusterRole resources is to create a number of fine-grained cluster roles and then aggregate them to form higher-level or broader cluster roles. This is how the built-in cluster roles are defined. For example, you can see that the built-in `edit` role looks like this:

```
apiVersion: rbac.authorization.k8s.io/v1
kind: ClusterRole
metadata:
  name: edit
  ...
aggregationRule:
  clusterRoleSelectors:
  - matchLabels:
      rbac.authorization.k8s.io/aggregate-to-edit: "true"
...
```

This means that the `edit` role is defined to be the aggregate of all ClusterRole objects that have a label of `rbac.authorization.k8s.io/aggregate-to-edit` set to `true`.

Using Groups for Bindings

When managing a large number of people in different organizations with similar access to the cluster, it's generally a best practice to use groups to manage the roles that define access, rather than individually adding bindings to specific identities. When you bind a group to a Role or ClusterRole, anyone who is a member of that group gains access to the resources and verbs defined by that role. Thus, to enable any individual to gain access to the group's role, that individual needs to be added to the group.

Using groups is a preferred strategy for managing access at scale for several reasons. The first is that in any large organization, access to the cluster is defined in terms of the team that someone is part of, rather than their specific identity. For example, someone who is part of the frontend operations team will need access to both view and edit the resources associated with the frontends, while they may only need view/read access to resources associated with the backend. Granting privileges to a group makes the association between the specific team and its capabilities clear. When granting roles to individuals, it's much harder to clearly understand the appropriate (i.e., minimal) privileges required for each team, especially when an individual may be part of multiple teams.

Additional benefits of binding roles to groups instead of individuals are simplicity and consistency. When someone joins or leaves a team, it is straightforward to simply add or remove them to or from a group in a single operation. If you instead have to remove a number of different role bindings for their identity, you may either remove too few or too many bindings, resulting in unnecessary access or preventing them from being able to do necessary actions. Additionally, because there is only a single set of group role bindings to maintain, you don't have to do lots of work to ensure that all team members have the same, consistent set of permissions.

 Many cloud providers support integrations onto their identity and access management platforms so that users and groups from those platforms can be used in conjunction with Kubernetes RBAC.

Many group systems enable "just in time" (JIT) access, such that people are only temporarily added to a group in response to an event (say, a page in the middle of the night) rather than having standing access. This means that you can both audit who had access at any particular time and ensure that, in general, even a compromised identity can't have access to your production infrastructure.

Finally, in many cases, these same groups are used to manage access to other resources, from facilities to documents and machine logins. Thus, using the same groups for access control to Kubernetes dramatically simplifies management.

To bind a group to a ClusterRole, use a Group kind for the `subject` in the binding:

```
...
subjects:
- apiGroup: rbac.authorization.k8s.io
  kind: Group
  name: my-great-groups-name
...
```

In Kubernetes, groups are supplied by authentication providers. There is no strong notion of a group within Kubernetes, only that an identity can be part of one or more groups, and those groups can be associated with a Role or ClusterRole via a binding.

Summary

When you begin with a small cluster and a small team, it is sufficient to have every member of the team have equivalent access to the cluster. But as teams grow and products become more mission critical, limiting access to parts of the cluster is crucial. In a well-designed cluster, access is limited to the minimal set of people and capabilities needed to efficiently manage the applications in the cluster.

Understanding how Kubernetes implements RBAC and how those capabilities can be used to control access to your cluster is important for both developers and cluster administrators. As with building out testing infrastructure, best practice is to set up RBAC earlier rather than later. It's far easier to start with the right foundation than to try to retrofit it later on. Hopefully, the information in this chapter has provided the necessary grounding for adding RBAC to your cluster.

Service Meshes

Perhaps second only to containers, the term *service mesh* has become synonymous with cloud native development. However, just like containers, service mesh is a broad term that encompasses a variety of open source projects as well as commercial products. Understanding the general role of a service mesh in a cloud native architecture is useful. This chapter will show you what a service mesh is, how different software projects implement them, and finally (and most importantly) when it makes sense to incorporate a service mesh, versus a less complex architecture, into your application.

 In many abstract cloud native architecture diagrams, it seems that a service mesh is necessary for a cloud native architecture. This is very much not true. When considering adopting a service mesh, you have to balance the complexity of adding a new component (generally provided by a third party) to your list of dependencies. In many cases, it is easier and more reliable to simply depend on the existing Kubernetes resources, if they meet the needs of your application.

We have previously discussed other networking primitives in Kubernetes like Services and Ingress. Given the presence of these networking capabilities in the core of Kubernetes, why is there a need to inject additional capabilities (and complexities) into the networking layer? Fundamentally it comes down to the needs of the software application that is using these networking primitives.

Networking in the core of Kubernetes is really only aware of the application as a destination. Both Service and Ingress resources have label selectors that route traffic to a particular set of Pods, but beyond that there is comparatively little in the way of additional capabilities that these resources bring. As an HTTP load balancer, Ingress goes a little beyond this, but the challenge of defining a common API that fits a wide variety of different existing implementations limits the capabilities in the Ingress API. How can a truly "cloud native" HTTP-routing API be compatible with load balancers and proxies ranging from bare-metal networking devices through to public cloud APIs that were built without thinking about cloud native development?

In a very real way, the development of service mesh APIs outside the core of Kubernetes is a result of this challenge. The Ingress APIs bring HTTP(S) traffic from the outside world into a cloud native application. Within a cloud native application in Kubernetes, freed of the need to be compatible with existing infrastructure, the service mesh APIs provide additional cloud native networking capabilities. So what are these capabilities? There are three general capabilities provided by most service mesh implementations: network encryption and authorization, traffic shaping, and observability. The following sections look at each of these in turn.

Encryption and Authentication with Mutal TLS

Encryption of network traffic between Pods is a key component to security in a microservice architecture. Encryptions provided by Mutual Transport Layer Security, or *mTLS*, is one of the most popular use cases for a service mesh. While it is possible for developers to implement this encryption themselves, certificate handling and traffic encryption is complicated and hard to get right. Leaving the implementation of encryption to individual development teams leads to developers forgetting to add encryption at all, or doing it poorly. When poorly implemented, encryption can negatively impact both reliability and, in the worst case, provide no real security. By contrast, installing a service mesh on your Kubernetes cluster automatically provides encryption to network traffic between every Pod in the cluster. The service mesh adds a sidecar container to every Pod, which transparently intercepts all network communication. In addition to securing the communication, mTLS adds identity to the encryption using client certificates so your application securely knows the identity of every network client.

Traffic Shaping

When you first think about your application design, it is typically a clean diagram with a single box for each microservice or layer in the system (e.g., the frontend service, user preferences service, etc). When implemented in practice, there are actually often multiple instances of any particular microservice running within the application. For example, when you are doing a rollout from version X of your service to version Y, there is a point in the middle of the rollout when you are simultaneously running two different versions of that service. While the middle of a rollout is a temporary state, there are many times when you need to create a longer-running experiment that persists for an extended period. A common model used in the software industry is "dog-fooding" your own software, meaning that a new version of the software is tried internally before anywhere else. In a dog-fooding model, you may run version Y of your service for a day to a week (or longer) for a subset of users before you roll it out broadly to your full set of users.

Such experiments require the ability to do *traffic shaping*, or routing of requests to different service implementations based on the characteristics of the request. In this example, you would create an experiment where all traffic from your company's internal users went to service Y, while all traffic from the rest of the world still went to service X.

Experiments are useful for a variety of scenarios, including development, where a programmer can send a limited set (typically 1% or less) of real-world traffic to an experimental backend, or you can run an A/B experiment where 50% of users get one experience and 50% of users get another, so that you can build statistical models of which approach is more effective. Experiments are an incredibly useful way to add reliability, agility, and insight to your application, but they are often difficult to implement in practice and thus not used as often as they might otherwise be.

Service meshes change this by building experimentation into the mesh itself. Instead of writing code to implement your experiment, or deploying an entirely new copy of your application on new infrastructure, you declaratively define the parameters of the experiment (10% of traffic to version Y, 90% of traffic to version X), and the service mesh implements it for you. Although, as a developer, you are involved in defining the experiment, the implementation is transparent and automatic, meaning that many more experiments will be run with a corresponding increase in reliability, agility, and insight.

Introspection

If you are like most programmers, once you write a program, you repeatedly debug it as new errors manifest themselves. Finding errors in your code is a large part of how most developers spend their days. Debugging is even more difficult when applications are spread across multiple microservices. It is hard to stitch together a single request when it spans multiple Pods. The information needed for debugging must be stitched back together from multiple sources, assuming that the relevant information was collected in the first place.

Automatic introspection is another important capability provided by a service mesh. Because it is involved in all communication between Pods, the service mesh knows where requests were routed, and it can keep track of the information required to put a complete request trace back together. Instead of seeing a flurry of requests to a bunch of different microservices, the developer can see a single aggregate request that defines the user experience of their complete application. Furthermore, the service mesh is implemented once for an entire cluster. This means that the same request tracing works no matter which team developed the service. The monitoring data is entirely consistent across all of the different services joined together by a cluster-wide service mesh.

Do You Really Need a Service Mesh?

The advantages described here may have you eager to start installing a service mesh on your cluster. However, before you do that, it's worth considering whether a service mesh is really necessary for your application. A service mesh is a distributed system that adds complexity to your application design. The service mesh is deeply integrated into the core communication of your microservices. When a service mesh fails, your entire application stops working. Before you adopt a service mesh, you must be confident that you can fix problems when they occur. You must also be ready to monitor the software releases for the service mesh to make sure that you pick up the latest security and bug fixes, and, of course, when fixes become available, you must also be ready to roll out the new version without impacting your application. This additional operational overhead means that for many small applications, a service mesh is an unnecessary complexity.

If you are using Kubernetes provided as a managed service that also provides a service mesh, it is much easier to use that mesh, knowing that the cloud provider will provide the support, debugging, and seamless new releases for the service mesh. But even with a service mesh supplied by a cloud provider, there is additional complexity for your developers to learn. Ultimately, weighing the costs versus benefits of a service mesh is something each application or platform team needs to do at a cluster level. To maximize the benefits of a service mesh, it's helpful for all microservices in the cluster to adopt it at the same time.

Introspecting a Service Mesh Implementation

There are many different service mesh projects and implementations in the cloud native ecosystem, but most share many of the same design patterns and technology. Because the service mesh is transparently intercepting network traffic from your application Pod, modifying it and rerouting it through the cluster, a part of the service mesh needs to be present within every one of your Pods. Forcing developers to add something to each container image would introduce significant friction as well as make it much more difficult to centrally manage the service mesh version. As a result, most service mesh implementations add a sidecar container to every Pod in the mesh. Because the sidecar sits in the same network stack as the application Pod, it can use tools like `iptables` or, more recently, eBPF to introspect and intercept network traffic coming from your application container and process it into the service mesh.

Of course, requiring every developer to add a container image to their Pod definition introduces nearly as much friction as requiring them to modify their container image. To address this, most service mesh implementations depend on a mutating admission controller to automatically add the service mesh sidecar to all Pods that are created in a particular cluster. Any REST API request to create a Pod is first routed to this admission controller. The service mesh admission controller modifies the Pod definition by adding the sidecar. Because this admission controller is installed by the cluster administrator, it transparently and consistently implements a service mesh for an entire cluster.

But the service mesh isn't just about modifying the Pod network. You also need to be able to control how the service mesh behaves; for example, by defining routing rules for experiments or access restrictions for services in the mesh. Like everything else in Kubernetes, these resource definitions are declaratively specified via JSON or YAML object definitions that you create using kubectl or other tools that communicate with the Kubernetes API server. Service mesh implementations take advantages of *custom resource definitions* (CRDs) to add specialized resources to your Kubernetes cluster that are not part of the default installation. In most cases, the specific custom resources are tightly tied to the service mesh itself. An ongoing effort in the CNCF is defining a standard vendor-neutral Service Mesh Interface (SMI) that many different service meshes can implement.

Service Mesh Landscape

The most daunting aspect of the service mesh landscape may be figuring out which mesh to choose. So far, no one mesh has emerged as the de facto standard. Though concrete statistics are hard to come by, the most popular service mesh is likely the Istio project. In addition to Istio, there are many other open source meshes, including Linkerd, Consul Connect, Open Service Mesh, and others. There are also proprietary meshes like AWS App Mesh. We expect efforts to standardize these interfaces to continue in the coming years in the cloud native community.

How is a developer or cluster administrator to choose? The truth is that the best service mesh for you is likely the one that your cloud provider supplies for you. Adding operating a service mesh to the already complicated duties of your cluster operators is generally unnecessary. It is much better to let a cloud provider manage it for you.

If that isn't an option for you, do your research. Don't be drawn in by flashy demos and promises of functionality. A service mesh lives deep within your infrastructure, and any failures can significantly impact the availability of your application. Additionally, because service mesh APIs tend to be implementation specific, it is difficult to change your choice of service mesh once you have spent time developing applications around it. In the end, you may find that the right mesh for you is no mesh at all.

Summary

Service meshes contain powerful functionality that adds security and flexibility to your application. At the same time, a service mesh adds complexity to the operations of your cluster and is another potential source of outages for your application. Carefully consider the pros and cons of adding service meshes to your infrastructure. If you have the choice, use a managed service mesh where someone else takes responsibility for the operational details while enabling your applications access to service mesh capabilities.

## CHAPTER 16

Integrating Storage Solutions and Kubernetes

In many cases, decoupling state from applications and building your microservices to be as stateless as possible results in maximally reliable, manageable systems.

However, nearly every system that has any complexity has state in the system somewhere, from the records in a database to the index shards that serve results for a web search engine. At some point, you have to have data stored somewhere.

Integrating this data with containers and container orchestration solutions is often the most complicated aspect of building a distributed system. This complexity largely stems from the fact that the move to containerized architectures is also a move toward decoupled, immutable, and declarative application development. These patterns are relatively easy to apply to stateless web applications, but even "cloud native" storage solutions like Cassandra or MongoDB involve some sort of manual or imperative steps to set up a reliable, replicated solution.

As an example of this, consider setting up a ReplicaSet in MongoDB, which involves deploying the Mongo daemon and then running an imperative command to identify the leader, as well as the participants, in the Mongo cluster. Of course, these steps can be scripted, but in a containerized world, it is difficult to see how to integrate such commands into a deployment. Likewise, even getting DNS-resolvable names for individual containers in a replicated set of containers is challenging.

Additional complexity comes from the fact that there is data gravity. Most containerized systems aren't built in a vacuum; they are usually adapted from existing systems deployed onto VMs, and these systems likely include data that has to be imported or migrated.

Finally, evolution to the cloud often means that storage is an externalized cloud service, and, in that context, it can never really exist inside of the Kubernetes cluster.

This chapter covers a variety of approaches for integrating storage into containerized microservices in Kubernetes. First, we cover how to import existing external storage solutions (either cloud services or running on VMs) into Kubernetes. Next, we explore how to run reliable singletons inside of Kubernetes that enable you to have an environment that largely matches the VMs where you previously deployed storage solutions. Finally, we cover StatefulSets, which are the Kubernetes resource most people use for stateful workloads in Kubernetes.

Importing External Services

In many cases, you have an existing machine running in your network that has some sort of database running on it. In this situation, you may not want to immediately move that database into containers and Kubernetes. Perhaps it is run by a different team, or you are doing a gradual move, or the task of migrating the data is simply more trouble than it's worth.

Regardless of the reasons for staying put, this legacy server and service are not going to move into Kubernetes—but it's still worthwhile to represent this server in Kubernetes. When you do this, you get to take advantage of all the built-in naming and service-discovery primitives provided by Kubernetes. Additionally, this enables you to configure all your applications so that it looks like the database that is running on a machine somewhere is actually a Kubernetes service. This means that it is trivial to replace it with a database that is a Kubernetes service. For example, in production, you may rely on your legacy database that is running on a machine, but for continuous testing, you may deploy a test database as a transient container. Since it is created and destroyed for each test run, data persistence isn't important in the continuous testing case. Representing both databases as Kubernetes services enables you to maintain identical configurations in both testing and production. High fidelity between test and production ensures that passing tests will lead to successful deployment in production.

To see concretely how you maintain high fidelity between development and production, remember that all Kubernetes objects are deployed into *namespaces*. Imagine that we have `test` and `production` namespaces defined. The test service is imported using an object like this:

```
kind: Service
metadata:
  name: my-database
  # note 'test' namespace here
  namespace: test
...
```

The production service looks the same, except it uses a different namespace:

```
kind: Service
metadata:
  name: my-database
  # note 'prod' namespace here
  namespace: prod
...
```

When you deploy a Pod into the `test` namespace and it looks up the service named `my-database`, it will receive a pointer to `my-database.test.svc.cluster.internal`, which in turn points to the test database. In contrast, when a Pod deployed in the `prod` namespace looks up the same name (`my-database`), it will receive a pointer to `my-database.prod.svc.cluster.internal`, which is the production database. Thus, the same service name, in two different namespaces, resolves to two different services. For more details on how this works, see Chapter 7.

 The following techniques all use database or other storage services, but these approaches can be used equally well with other services that aren't running inside your Kubernetes cluster.

Services Without Selectors

When we first introduced services, we talked at length about label queries and how they were used to identify the dynamic set of Pods that were the backends for a particular service. With external services, however, there is no such label query. Instead, you generally have a DNS name that points to the specific server running the database. For our example, let's assume that this server is named `database.company.com`. To import this external database service into Kubernetes, we start by creating a service without a Pod selector that references the DNS name of the database server (Example 16-1).

Example 16-1. dns-service.yaml

```
kind: Service
apiVersion: v1
metadata:
  name: external-database
spec:
  type: ExternalName
  externalName: database.company.com
```

When a typical Kubernetes service is created, an IP address is also created, and the Kubernetes DNS service is populated with an A record that points to that IP address. When you create a service of type `ExternalName`, the Kubernetes DNS service is instead populated with a CNAME record that points to the external name you specified (database.company.com in this case). When an application in the cluster does a DNS lookup for the hostname external-database.svc.default.cluster, the DNS protocol aliases that name to database.company.com. This then resolves to the IP address of your external database server. In this way, all containers in Kubernetes believe that they are talking to a service that is backed with other containers, when in fact they are being redirected to an external database.

Note that this is not restricted to databases you are running on your own infrastructure. Many cloud databases and other services provide you with a DNS name to use when accessing the database (e.g., my-database.databases.cloudprovider.com). You can use this DNS name as the externalName. This imports the cloud-provided database into the namespace of your Kubernetes cluster.

Sometimes, however, you don't have a DNS address for an external database service, just an IP address. In such cases, it is still possible to import this service as a Kubernetes service, but the operation is a little different. First, you create a Service without a label selector, but also without the ExternalName type we used before (Example 16-2).

Example 16-2. external-ip-service.yaml

```
kind: Service
apiVersion: v1
metadata:
  name: external-ip-database
```

Kubernetes will allocate a virtual IP address for this service and populate an A record for it. However, because there is no selector for the service, there will be no endpoints populated for the load balancer to redirect traffic to.

Given that this is an external service, the user is responsible for populating the endpoints manually with an Endpoints resource (Example 16-3).

Example 16-3. external-ip-endpoints.yaml

```
kind: Endpoints
apiVersion: v1
metadata:
  name: external-ip-database
subsets:
  - addresses:
    - ip: 192.168.0.1
    ports:
    - port: 3306
```

If you have more than one IP address for redundancy, you can repeat them in the `addresses` array. Once the endpoints are populated, the load balancer will start redirecting traffic from your Kubernetes service to the IP address endpoint(s).

 Because the user has assumed responsibility for keeping the IP address of the server up-to-date, you need to either ensure that it never changes or make sure that some automated process updates the `Endpoints` record.

Limitations of External Services: Health Checking

External services in Kubernetes have one significant restriction: they do not perform any health checking. The user is responsible for ensuring that the endpoint or DNS name supplied to Kubernetes is as reliable as necessary for the application.

Running Reliable Singletons

The challenge of running storage solutions in Kubernetes is often that primitives like ReplicaSet expect that every container is identical and replaceable, but for most storage solutions, this isn't the case. One option to address this is to use Kubernetes primitives, but not attempt to replicate the storage. Instead, simply run a single Pod that runs the database or other storage solution. In this way, the challenges of running replicated storage in Kubernetes don't occur because there is no replication.

At first blush, this might seem to run counter to the principles of building reliable distributed systems, but in general, it is no less reliable than running your database or storage infrastructure on a single virtual or physical machine, which is how many systems are currently built. Indeed, in reality, if you structure the system properly, the only thing you are sacrificing is potential downtime for upgrades or in case of machine failure. While for large-scale or mission-critical systems this may not be acceptable, for many smaller-scale applications, this kind of limited downtime is a reasonable trade-off for the reduced complexity. If this is not true for you, feel free to skip this section and either import existing services as described in the previous section, or move on to "Kubernetes-Native Storage with StatefulSets" on page 188. For everyone else, we'll review how to build reliable singletons for data storage.

Running a MySQL Singleton

In this section, we'll describe how to run a reliable singleton instance of the MySQL database as a Pod in Kubernetes and how to expose that singleton to other applications in the cluster. To do this, we are going to create three basic objects:

- A persistent volume to manage the lifespan of the on-disk storage independently from the lifespan of the running MySQL application

- A MySQL Pod that will run the MySQL application

- A service that will expose this Pod to other containers in the cluster

In Chapter 5, we described persistent volumes: storage locations that have a lifetime independent of any Pod or container. Persistent volume is useful in the case of persistent storage solutions where the on-disk representation of a database should survive even if the containers running the database application crash, or move to different machines. If the application moves to a different machine, the volume should move with it, and data should be preserved. Separating the data storage out as a persistent volume makes this possible.

To begin, we'll create a persistent volume for our MySQL database to use. This example uses NFS for maximum portability, but Kubernetes supports many different persistent volume driver types. For example, there are persistent volume drivers for all major public cloud providers as well as many private cloud providers. To use these solutions, simply replace nfs with the appropriate cloud provider volume type (e.g., azure, awsElasticBlockStore, or gcePersistentDisk). In all cases, this change is all you need. Kubernetes knows how to create the appropriate storage disk in the respective cloud provider. This is a great example of how Kubernetes simplifies the development of reliable distributed systems. Example 16-4 shows the PersistentVolume object.

Example 16-4. nfs-volume.yaml

```
apiVersion: v1
kind: PersistentVolume
metadata:
  name: database
  labels:
    volume: my-volume
spec:
  accessModes:
  - ReadWriteMany
  capacity:
    storage: 1Gi
  nfs:
    server: 192.168.0.1
    path: "/exports"
```

This defines an NFS PersistentVolume object with 1 GB of storage space. We can create this persistent volume as usual with:

```
$ kubectl apply -f nfs-volume.yaml
```

Now that we have created a persistent volume, we need to claim that persistent volume for our Pod. We do this with a PersistentVolumeClaim object (Example 16-5).

Example 16-5. nfs-volume-claim.yaml

```
kind: PersistentVolumeClaim
apiVersion: v1
metadata:
  name: database
spec:
  accessModes:
  - ReadWriteMany
  resources:
    requests:
      storage: 1Gi
  selector:
    matchLabels:
      volume: my-volume
```

The `selector` field uses labels to find the matching volume we defined previously.

This kind of indirection may seem overly complicated, but it has a purpose—it serves to isolate our Pod definition from our storage definition. You can declare volumes directly inside a Pod specification, but this locks that Pod specification to a particular volume provider (e.g., a specific public or private cloud). By using volume claims, you can keep your Pod specifications cloud-agnostic; simply create different volumes, specific to the cloud, and use a PersistentVolumeClaim to bind them together. Furthermore, in many cases, the persistent volume controller will actually automatically create a volume for you. There are more details of this process in the following section.

Now that we've claimed our volume, we can use a ReplicaSet to construct our singleton Pod. It might seem odd that we are using a ReplicaSet to manage a single Pod, but it is necessary for reliability. Remember that once scheduled to a machine, a bare Pod is bound to that machine forever. If the machine fails, then any Pods that are on that machine that are not being managed by a higher-level controller like a ReplicaSet vanish along with the machine and are not rescheduled elsewhere. Consequently, to ensure that our database Pod is rescheduled in the presence of machine failures, we use the higher-level ReplicaSet controller, with a replica size of 1, to manage our database (Example 16-6).

Example 16-6. mysql-replicaset.yaml

```
apiVersion: extensions/v1
kind: ReplicaSet
metadata:
  name: mysql
```

```
  # Labels so that we can bind a Service to this Pod
  labels:
    app: mysql
spec:
  replicas: 1
  selector:
    matchLabels:
      app: mysql
  template:
    metadata:
      labels:
        app: mysql
    spec:
      containers:
      - name: database
        image: mysql
        resources:
          requests:
            cpu: 1
            memory: 2Gi
        env:
        # Environment variables are not a best practice for security,
        # but we're using them here for brevity in the example.
        # See Chapter 11 for better options.
        - name: MYSQL_ROOT_PASSWORD
          value: some-password-here
        livenessProbe:
          tcpSocket:
            port: 3306
        ports:
        - containerPort: 3306
        volumeMounts:
          - name: database
            # /var/lib/mysql is where MySQL stores its databases
            mountPath: "/var/lib/mysql"
      volumes:
      - name: database
        persistentVolumeClaim:
          claimName: database
```

Once we create the ReplicaSet, it will, in turn, create a Pod running MySQL using the persistent disk we originally created. The final step is to expose this as a Kubernetes service (Example 16-7).

Example 16-7. mysql-service.yaml

```
apiVersion: v1
kind: Service
metadata:
  name: mysql
spec:
```

```
  ports:
  - port: 3306
    protocol: TCP
  selector:
    app: mysql
```

Now we have a reliable singleton MySQL instance running in our cluster and exposed as a service named `mysql`, which we can access at the full domain name `mysql.svc.default.cluster`.

Similar instructions can be used for a variety of data stores, and if your needs are simple and you can survive limited downtime in the face of a machine failure or when you need to upgrade the database software, a reliable singleton may be the right approach to storage for your application.

Dynamic Volume Provisioning

Many clusters also include *dynamic volume provisioning*. With dynamic volume provisioning, the cluster operator creates one or more `StorageClass` objects. In Kubernetes, a `StorageClass` encapsulates the characteristics of a particular type of storage. A cluster can have multiple different storage classes installed. For example, you might have a storage class for an NFS server on your network and a storage class for iSCSI block store. Storage classes can also encapsulate different levels of reliability or performance. Example 16-8 shows a default storage class that automatically provisions disk objects on the Microsoft Azure platform.

Example 16-8. storageclass.yaml

```
apiVersion: storage.k8s.io/v1
kind: StorageClass
metadata:
  name: default
  annotations:
    storageclass.beta.kubernetes.io/is-default-class: "true"
  labels:
    kubernetes.io/cluster-service: "true"
provisioner: kubernetes.io/azure-disk
```

Once a storage class has been created for a cluster, you can refer to this storage class in your persistent volume claim, rather than referring to any specific persistent volume. When the dynamic provisioner sees this storage claim, it uses the appropriate volume driver to create the volume and bind it to your persistent volume claim.

Example 16-9 shows an example of a PersistentVolumeClaim that uses the `default` storage class we just defined to claim a newly created persistent volume.

Example 16-9. dynamic-volume-claim.yaml

```
kind: PersistentVolumeClaim
apiVersion: v1
metadata:
  name: my-claim
  annotations:
    volume.beta.kubernetes.io/storage-class: default
spec:
  accessModes:
  - ReadWriteOnce
  resources:
    requests:
      storage: 10Gi
```

The `volume.beta.kubernetes.io/storage-class` annotation is what links this claim back up to the storage class we created.

Automatic provisioning of a persistent volume is a great feature that makes it significantly easier to build and manage stateful applications in Kubernetes. However, the lifespan of these persistent volumes is dictated by the reclamation policy of the PersistentVolumeClaim, and the default is to bind that lifespan to the lifespan of the Pod that creates the volume.

This means that if you happen to delete the Pod (e.g., via a scaledown or other event), then the volume is deleted as well. While this may be what you want in certain circumstances, you need to be careful to ensure that you don't accidentally delete your persistent volumes.

Persistent volumes are great for traditional applications that require storage, but if you need to develop high-availability, scalable storage in a Kubernetes-native fashion, the newly released StatefulSet object can be used instead. We'll describe how to deploy MongoDB using StatefulSets in the next section.

Kubernetes-Native Storage with StatefulSets

When Kubernetes was first developed, there was a heavy emphasis on homogeneity for all replicas in a replicated set. In this design, no replica had an individual identity or configuration. It was up to the application developer to determine a design that could establish this identity for their application.

While this approach provides a great deal of isolation for the orchestration system, it also makes it quite difficult to develop stateful applications. After significant input from the community and a great deal of experimentation with various existing stateful applications, StatefulSets were introduced in Kubernetes version 1.5.

Properties of StatefulSets

StatefulSets are replicated groups of Pods, similar to ReplicaSets. But unlike a Replica-Set, they have certain unique properties:

- Each replica gets a persistent hostname with a unique index (e.g., `database-0`, `database-1`, etc.).
- Each replica is created in order from lowest to highest index, and creation will pause until the Pod at the previous index is healthy and available. This also applies to scaling up.
- When a StatefulSet is deleted, each of the managed replica Pods is also deleted in order from highest to lowest. This also applies to scaling down the number of replicas.

It turns out that this simple set of requirements makes it drastically easier to deploy storage applications on Kubernetes. For example, the combination of stable host-names (e.g., `database-0`) and the ordering constraints mean that all replicas, other than the first one, can reliably reference `database-0` for the purposes of discovery and establishing a replication quorum.

Manually Replicated MongoDB with StatefulSets

In this section, we'll deploy a replicated MongoDB cluster. For now, the replication setup itself will be done manually to give you a feel for how StatefulSets work. Eventually, we will automate this setup as well.

To start, we'll create a replicated set of three MongoDB Pods using a StatefulSet object (Example 16-10).

Example 16-10. mongo-simple.yaml

```
apiVersion: apps/v1
kind: StatefulSet
metadata:
  name: mongo
spec:
  serviceName: "mongo"
  replicas: 3
  selector:
    matchLabels:
      app: mongo
  template:
    metadata:
      labels:
        app: mongo
    spec:
```

```
containers:
- name: mongodb
  image: mongo:3.4.24
  command:
  - mongod
  - --replSet
  - rs0
  ports:
  - containerPort: 27017
    name: peer
```

As you can see, the definition is similar to the ReplicaSet definitions we've seen previously. The only changes are in the `apiVersion` and `kind` fields.

Create the StatefulSet:

```
$ kubectl apply -f mongo-simple.yaml
```

Once created, the differences between a ReplicaSet and a StatefulSet become apparent. Run `kubectl get pods` and you will likely see this:

```
NAME      READY   STATUS             RESTARTS   AGE
mongo-0   1/1     Running            0          1m
mongo-1   0/1     ContainerCreating  0          10s
```

There are two important differences between this and what you would see with a ReplicaSet. The first is that each replicated Pod has a numeric index (0, 1, ...), instead of the random suffix that is added by the ReplicaSet controller. The second is that the Pods are being slowly created in order, not all at once as they would be with a ReplicaSet.

After the StatefulSet is created, we also need to create a "headless" service to manage the DNS entries for the StatefulSet. In Kubernetes, a service is called "headless" if it doesn't have a cluster virtual IP address. Since with StatefulSets, each Pod has a unique identity, it doesn't really make sense to have a load-balancing IP address for the replicated service. You can create a headless service using `clusterIP: None` in the service specification (Example 16-11).

Example 16-11. mongo-service.yaml

```
apiVersion: v1
kind: Service
metadata:
  name: mongo
spec:
  ports:
  - port: 27017
    name: peer
  clusterIP: None
```

```
selector:
  app: mongo
```

Once you create that service, four DNS entries are usually populated. As usual, `mongo.default.svc.cluster.local` is created, but unlike with a standard service, doing a DNS lookup on this hostname provides all the addresses in the StatefulSet. In addition, entries are created for `mongo-0.mongo.default.svc.cluster.local` as well as `mongo-1.mongo` and `mongo-2.mongo`. Each of these resolves to the specific IP address of the replica index in the StatefulSet. Thus, with StatefulSets you get well-defined, persistent names for each replica in the set. This is often very useful when you are configuring a replicated storage solution. You can see these DNS entries in action by running the following command in one of the Mongo replicas:

```
$ kubectl run -it --rm --image busybox busybox ping mongo-1.mongo
```

Next, we're going to manually set up Mongo replication using these per-Pod hostnames. We'll choose `mongo-0.mongo` to be our initial primary. Run the `mongo` tool in that Pod:

```
$ kubectl exec -it mongo-0 mongo
> rs.initiate( {
  _id: "rs0",
  members:[ { _id: 0, host: "mongo-0.mongo:27017" } ]
});
OK
```

This command tells `mongodb` to initiate the ReplicaSet `rs0` with `mongo-0.mongo` as the primary replica.

> The `rs0` name is arbitrary. You can use whatever you'd like, but you'll need to change it in the *mongo-simple.yaml* StatefulSet definition as well.

Once you have initiated the Mongo ReplicaSet, you can add the remaining replicas by running the following commands in the `mongo` tool on the `mongo-0.mongo` Pod:

```
> rs.add("mongo-1.mongo:27017");
> rs.add("mongo-2.mongo:27017");
```

As you can see, we are using the replica-specific DNS names to add them as replicas in our Mongo cluster. At this point, we're done. Our replicated MongoDB is up and running. But it's really not as automated as we'd like it to be—in the next section, we'll see how to use scripts to automate the setup.

Automating MongoDB Cluster Creation

To automate the deployment of our StatefulSet-based MongoDB cluster, we're going to add a container to our Pods to perform the initialization. To configure this Pod without having to build a new Docker image, we're going to use a ConfigMap to add a script into the existing MongoDB image.

We are going to run this script using an *initialization container*. Initialization containers (or "init" containers) are specialized containers that run once at the startup of a Pod. They are generally used for cases like this, where there is a small amount of setup work to do before the main application runs. In the Pod definition, there is a separate `initContainers` list where init containers can be defined. An example of this is given here:

```
    ...
        initContainers:
        - name: init-mongo
          image: mongo:3.4.24
          command:
          - bash
          - /config/init.sh
          volumeMounts:
          - name: config
            mountPath: /config
    ...
        volumes:
        - name: config
          configMap:
            name: "mongo-init"
```

Note that it is mounting a ConfigMap volume whose name is `mongo-init`. This ConfigMap holds a script that performs our initialization. First, the script determines whether it is running on `mongo-0` or not. If it is on `mongo-0`, it creates the ReplicaSet using the same command we ran imperatively previously. If it is on a different Mongo replica, it waits until the ReplicaSet exists, and then it registers itself as a member of that ReplicaSet.

Example 16-12 has the complete ConfigMap object.

Example 16-12. mongo-configmap.yaml

```
apiVersion: v1
kind: ConfigMap
metadata:
  name: mongo-init
data:
  init.sh: |
    #!/bin/bash
```

```
# Need to wait for the readiness health check to pass so that the
# Mongo names resolve. This is kind of wonky.
until ping -c 1 ${HOSTNAME}.mongo; do
  echo "waiting for DNS (${HOSTNAME}.mongo)..."
  sleep 2
done

until /usr/bin/mongo --eval 'printjson(db.serverStatus())'; do
  echo "connecting to local mongo..."
  sleep 2
done
echo "connected to local."

HOST=mongo-0.mongo:27017

until /usr/bin/mongo --host=${HOST} --eval 'printjson(db.serverStatus())'; do
  echo "connecting to remote mongo..."
  sleep 2
done
echo "connected to remote."

if [[ "${HOSTNAME}" != 'mongo-0' ]]; then
  until /usr/bin/mongo --host=${HOST} --eval="printjson(rs.status())" \
        | grep -v "no replset config has been received"; do
    echo "waiting for replication set initialization"
    sleep 2
  done
  echo "adding self to mongo-0"
  /usr/bin/mongo --host=${HOST} \
    --eval="printjson(rs.add('${HOSTNAME}.mongo'))"
fi

if [[ "${HOSTNAME}" == 'mongo-0' ]]; then
  echo "initializing replica set"
  /usr/bin/mongo --eval="printjson(rs.initiate(\
      {'_id': 'rs0', 'members': [{'_id': 0, \
       'host': 'mongo-0.mongo:27017'}]}))"
fi
echo "initialized"
```

You'll notice that this script immediately exits. This is important when using init Containers. Each initialization container waits until the previous container has finished, before running. The main application container waits until all of the initialization containers are done. If this script didn't exit, the main Mongo server would never start up.

Putting it all together, Example 16-13 is the complete StatefulSet that uses the ConfigMap.

Example 16-13. mongo.yaml

```yaml
apiVersion: apps/v1
kind: StatefulSet
metadata:
  name: mongo
spec:
  serviceName: "mongo"
  replicas: 3
  selector:
    matchLabels:
      app: mongo
  template:
    metadata:
      labels:
        app: mongo
    spec:
      containers:
      - name: mongodb
        image: mongo:3.4.24
        command:
        - mongod
        - --replSet
        - rs0
        ports:
        - containerPort: 27017
          name: web
      # This container initializes the MongoDB server, then sleeps.
      - name: init-mongo
        image: mongo:3.4.24
        command:
        - bash
        - /config/init.sh
        volumeMounts:
        - name: config
          mountPath: /config
      volumes:
      - name: config
        configMap:
          name: "mongo-init"
```

Given all of these files, you can create a Mongo cluster with:

```
$ kubectl apply -f mongo-config-map.yaml
$ kubectl apply -f mongo-service.yaml
$ kubectl apply -f mongo-simple.yaml
```

Or, if you want, you can combine them all into a single YAML file where the individual objects are separated by ---. Ensure that you keep the same ordering, since the StatefulSet definition relies on the ConfigMap definition existing.

Persistent Volumes and StatefulSets

For persistent storage, you need to mount a persistent volume into the */data/db*
directory. In the Pod template, you need to update it to mount a persistent volume
claim to that directory:

```
...
        volumeMounts:
        - name: database
          mountPath: /data/db
```

While this approach is similar to the one we saw with reliable singletons, because the
StatefulSet replicates more than one Pod, you cannot simply reference a persistent
volume claim. Instead, you need to add a *persistent volume claim template*. You can
think of the claim template as identical to the Pod template, but instead of creating
Pods, it creates volume claims. You need to add the following to the bottom of your
StatefulSet definition:

```
  volumeClaimTemplates:
  - metadata:
      name: database
      annotations:
        volume.alpha.kubernetes.io/storage-class: anything
    spec:
      accessModes: [ "ReadWriteOnce" ]
      resources:
        requests:
          storage: 100Gi
```

When you add a volume claim template to a StatefulSet definition, each time the
StatefulSet controller creates a Pod that is part of the StatefulSet, it will create a
persistent volume claim based on this template as part of that Pod.

> For these replicated persistent volumes to work correctly, you need
> to either set up autoprovisioning for persistent volumes or prepo-
> pulate a collection of persistent volume objects for the StatefulSet
> controller to draw from. If there are no claims that can be created,
> the StatefulSet controller will not be able to create the correspond-
> ing Pods.

One Final Thing: Readiness Probes

The final piece in productionizing our MongoDB cluster is to add liveness checks
to our Mongo-serving containers. As we learned in "Health Checks" on page 55, the
liveness probe is used to determine if a container is operating correctly.

For the liveness checks, we can use the `mongo` tool itself by adding the following to the Pod template in the StatefulSet object:

```
...
livenessProbe:
  exec:
    command:
    - /usr/bin/mongo
    - --eval
    - db.serverStatus()
  initialDelaySeconds: 10
  timeoutSeconds: 10
...
```

Summary

Once we have combined StatefulSets, persistent volume claims, and liveness probing, we have a hardened, scalable cloud native MongoDB installation running on Kubernetes. While this example dealt with MongoDB, the steps for creating StatefulSets to manage other storage solutions are quite similar and similar patterns can be followed.

## CHAPTER 17

Extending Kubernetes

From the beginning, it was clear that Kubernetes was going to be more than its core set of APIs; once an application is orchestrated within the cluster, there are countless other useful tools and utilities that can be represented and deployed as API objects in the Kubernetes cluster. The challenge was how to embrace this explosion of objects and use cases without having an API that sprawled without bound.

To resolve this tension between extended use cases and API sprawl, significant effort was put into making the Kubernetes API extensible. This extensibility meant that cluster operators could customize their clusters with the additional components that suited their needs. This extensibility enables people to augment their clusters themselves, consume community-developed cluster add-ons, and even develop extensions that are bundled and sold in an ecosystem of cluster plug-ins. Extensibility has also given rise to whole new patterns of managing systems, such as the operator pattern.

Regardless of whether you are building your own extensions or consuming operators from the ecosystem, understanding how the Kubernetes API server is extended and how extensions can be built and delivered is a key component to unlocking the complete power of Kubernetes and its ecosystem. As more and more advanced tools and platforms are built on top of Kubernetes using these extensibility mechanisms, a working knowledge of how they operate is critical to understanding how to build applications in a modern Kubernetes cluster.

What It Means to Extend Kubernetes

In general, extensions to the Kubernetes API server either add new functionality to a cluster or limit and tweak the ways that users can interact with their clusters. There is a rich ecosystem of plug-ins that cluster administrators can use to add services and capabilities to their clusters. It's worth noting that extending the cluster is a very high-privilege thing to do. It is not a capability that should be extended to arbitrary users or arbitrary code because cluster administrator privileges are required to extend a cluster. Even cluster administrators should be careful and use diligence when installing third-party tools. Some extensions, like admission controllers, can be used to view all objects being created in the cluster, and could easily be used as a vector to steal Secrets or run malicious code. Additionally, extending a cluster makes it different than stock Kubernetes. When running on multiple clusters, it is very valuable to build tooling to maintain consistency of experience across the clusters, and this includes the extensions that are installed.

Points of Extensibility

There are many ways to extend Kubernetes, from CustomResourceDefinitions to Container Network Interface plug-ins. This chapter is going to focus on extending the API server by adding new resource types or admission controllers to API requests. We will not cover CNI/CSI/CRI (Container Network Interface/Container Storage Interface/Container Runtime Interface) extensions, as they are more commonly used by Kubernetes cluster providers rather than by the Kubernetes end users, for whom this book was written.

In addition to admission controllers and API extensions, there are actually a number of ways to "extend" your cluster without ever modifying the API server at all. These include DaemonSets that install automatic logging and monitoring, tools that scan your services for cross-site scripting (XSS) vulnerabilities, and more. Before embarking on extending your cluster yourself, however, it's worth considering the landscape of things that are possible within the confines of the existing Kubernetes APIs.

To understand the role of admission controllers and CustomResourceDefinitions, it helps to review the flow of requests through the Kubernetes API server, shown in Figure 17-1.

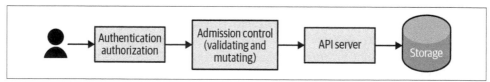

Figure 17-1. API server request flow

Admission controllers are called prior to the API object being written into the backing storage. Admission controllers can reject or modify API requests. Several admission controllers are built into the Kubernetes API server; for example, the limit range admission controller that sets default limits for Pods without them. Many other systems use custom admission controllers to auto-inject sidecar containers into all Pods created on the system to enable "auto-magic" experiences.

The other form of extension, which can also be used in conjunction with admission controllers, is *custom resources*. With custom resources, whole new API objects are added to the Kubernetes API surface area. These new API objects can be added to namespaces, are subject to RBAC, and can be accessed with existing tools like kubectl as well as via the Kubernetes API.

The following sections describe these Kubernetes extension points in greater detail and give both use cases and hands-on examples of how to extend your cluster.

The first thing to do to create a custom resource is to create a CustomResourceDefinition. This object is actually a meta-resource; that is, a resource that is the definition of another resource.

As a concrete example, consider defining a new resource to represent load tests in your cluster. When a new LoadTest resource is created, a load test is spun up in your Kubernetes cluster and drives traffic to a service.

The first step in creating this new resource is defining it through a CustomResource-Definition. An example definition looks as follows:

```
apiVersion: apiextensions.k8s.io/v1beta1
kind: CustomResourceDefinition
metadata:
  name: loadtests.beta.kuar.com
spec:
  group: beta.kuar.com
  versions:
    - name: v1
      served: true
      storage: true
  scope: Namespaced
  names:
    plural: loadtests
    singular: loadtest
    kind: LoadTest
    shortNames:
    - lt
```

You can see that this is a Kubernetes object like any other. It has a metadata sub-object, and within that sub-object, the resource is named. However, in the case of custom resources, the name is special. It has to be the format *<resource-plural>.<api-group>* to ensure that each resource definition is unique in the cluster, because the name of each CustomResourceDefinition has to match this pattern, and no two objects in the cluster can have the same name. We are thus guaranteed that no two CustomResourceDefinitions define the same resource.

In addition to metadata, the CustomResourceDefinition has a spec sub-object. This is where the resource itself is defined. In that spec object, there is an apigroup field that supplies the API group for the resource. As mentioned previously, it must match the suffix of the CustomResourceDefinition's name. Additionally, there is a list of versions for the resource, which includes the name of the version (e.g., v1, v2, etc.), as well as fields that indicate if that version is served by the API server and which version is used for storing data in the backing storage for the API server. The storage field must be true for only a single version for the resource. There is also a scope field to indicate whether the resource is namespaced (the default is namespaced), and a names field that allows for the definition of the singular, plural, and kind values for the resource. It also allows the definition of convenience "short names" for the resource for use in kubectl and elsewhere.

Given this definition, you can create the resource in the Kubernetes API server. But first, to show the true nature of dynamic resource types, try to list our loadtests resource using kubectl:

```
$ kubectl get loadtests
```

You'll see that there is no such resource currently defined. Now use *loadtest-resource.yaml* to create this resource:

```
$ kubectl create -f loadtest-resource.yaml
```

Then get the loadtests resource again:

```
$ kubectl get loadtests
```

This time you'll see that there is a LoadTest resource type defined, though there are still no instances of this resource type. Let's change that by creating a new LoadTest resource.

As with all built-in Kubernetes API objects, you can use YAML or JSON to define a custom resource (in this case our LoadTest). See the following definition:

```
apiVersion: beta.kuar.com/v1
kind: LoadTest
metadata:
  name: my-loadtest
spec:
  service: my-service
  scheme: https
  requestsPerSecond: 1000
  paths:
  - /index.html
  - /login.html
  - /shares/my-shares/
```

One thing you'll note is that we never defined the schema for the custom resource in the CustomResourceDefinition. It actually is possible to provide an OpenAPI specification (known previously as Swagger) for a custom resource, but this complexity is generally not worth it for simple resource types. If you do want to perform validation, you can register a validating admission controller, as described in the following sections.

You can now use this *loadtest.yaml* file to create a resource just like you would with any built-in type:

```
$ kubectl create -f loadtest.yaml
```

Now when you list the loadtests resource, you'll see your newly created resource:

```
$ kubectl get loadtests
```

This may be exciting, but it doesn't really do anything yet. Sure, you can use this simple CRUD (Create/Read/Update/Delete) API to manipulate the data for LoadTest objects, but no actual load tests are created in response to this new API we defined because there is no controller present in the cluster to react and take action when a LoadTest object is defined. The LoadTest custom resource is only half of the infrastructure needed to add LoadTests to our cluster. The other half is a piece of code that will continuously monitor the custom resources and create, modify, or delete LoadTests as necessary to implement the API.

Just like the user of the API, the controller interacts with the API server to list LoadTests and watches for any changes that might occur. This interaction between controller and API server is shown in Figure 17-2.

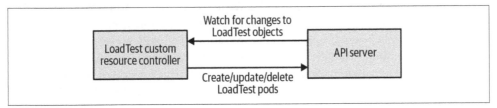

Figure 17-2. CustomResourceDefinition interactions

The code for such a controller can range from simple to complex. The simplest controllers run a for loop and repeatedly poll for new custom objects, and then take actions to create or delete the resources that implement those custom objects (e.g., the LoadTest worker Pods).

However, this polling-based approach is inefficient: the period of the polling loop adds unnecessary latency, and the overhead of polling may add unnecessary load on the API server. A more efficient approach is to use the watch API on the API server, which provides a stream of updates when they occur, eliminating both the latency and overhead of polling. However, using this API correctly in a bug-free way is complicated. As a result, if you want to use watches, it is highly recommended that you use a well-supported mechanism such as the Informer pattern exposed in the *client-go* library (*https://oreil.ly/L0QK2*).

Now that we have created a custom resource and implemented it via a controller, we have the basic functionality of a new resource in our cluster. However, many parts of what it means to be a well-functioning resource are missing. The two most important are validation and defaulting. *Validation* is the process of ensuring that LoadTest objects sent to the API server are well formed and can be used to create load tests, while *defaulting* makes it easier for people to use our resources by providing automatic, commonly used values by default. We'll now cover adding these capabilities to our custom resource.

As mentioned earlier, one option for adding validation is via an OpenAPI specification for our objects. This can be useful for basic validation of the presence of required fields or the absence of unknown fields. A complete OpenAPI tutorial is beyond the scope of this book, but there are lots of resources online, including the complete Kubernetes API specification (*https://oreil.ly/u3rRl*).

Generally speaking, an API schema is actually insufficient for validation of API objects. For example, in our `loadtests` example, we may want to validate that the LoadTest object has a valid scheme (e.g., *http* or *https*) or that `requestsPerSecond` is a nonzero positive number.

To accomplish this, we will use a validating admission controller. As discussed previously, admission controllers intercept requests to the API server before they are processed and can reject or modify the requests in flight. Admission controllers can be added to a cluster via the dynamic admission control system. A dynamic admission controller is a simple HTTP application. The API server connects to the admission controller via either a Kubernetes Service object or an arbitrary URL. This means that admission controllers can optionally run outside of the cluster—for example, in a cloud provider's Function-as-a-Service offering, like Azure Functions or AWS Lambda.

To install our validating admission controller, we need to specify it as a Kubernetes ValidatingWebhookConfiguration. This object specifies the endpoint where the admission controller runs, as well as the resource (in this case LoadTest) and the action (in this case `CREATE`) where the admission controller should be run. You can see the full definition for the validating admission controller in the following code:

```
apiVersion: admissionregistration.k8s.io/v1beta1
kind: ValidatingWebhookConfiguration
metadata:
  name: kuar-validator
webhooks:
- name: validator.kuar.com
  rules:
  - apiGroups:
    - "beta.kuar.com"
    apiVersions:
    - v1
```

```
        operations:
        - CREATE
        resources:
        - loadtests
    clientConfig:
        # Substitute the appropriate IP address for your webhook
        url: https://192.168.1.233:8080
        # This should be the base64-encoded CA certificate for your cluster,
        # you can find it in your ${KUBECONFIG} file
        caBundle: REPLACEME
```

Fortunately for security, but unfortunately for complexity, webhooks that are accessed by the Kubernetes API server can only be accessed via HTTPS. So we need to generate a certificate to serve the webhook. The easiest way to do this is to use the cluster's ability to generate new certificates using its own certificate authority (CA).

First, we need a private key and a certificate signing request (CSR). Here's a simple Go program that generates these:

```go
package main

import (
        "crypto/rand"
        "crypto/rsa"
        "crypto/x509"
        "crypto/x509/pkix"
        "encoding/asn1"
        "encoding/pem"
        "net/url"
        "os"
)

func main() {
        host := os.Args[1]
        name := "server"

        key, err := rsa.GenerateKey(rand.Reader, 1024)
        if err != nil {
                panic(err)
        }
        keyDer := x509.MarshalPKCS1PrivateKey(key)
        keyBlock := pem.Block{
                Type:  "RSA PRIVATE KEY",
                Bytes: keyDer,
        }
        keyFile, err := os.Create(name + ".key")
        if err != nil {
                panic(err)
        }
        pem.Encode(keyFile, &keyBlock)
        keyFile.Close()
```

```go
commonName := "myuser"
emailAddress := "someone@myco.com"

org := "My Co, Inc."
orgUnit := "Widget Farmers"
city := "Seattle"
state := "WA"
country := "US"

subject := pkix.Name{
        CommonName:         commonName,
        Country:            []string{country},
        Locality:           []string{city},
        Organization:       []string{org},
        OrganizationalUnit: []string{orgUnit},
        Province:           []string{state},
}

uri, err := url.ParseRequestURI(host)
if err != nil {
        panic(err)
}

asn1, err := asn1.Marshal(subject.ToRDNSequence())
if err != nil {
        panic(err)
}
csr := x509.CertificateRequest{
        RawSubject:         asn1,
        EmailAddresses:     []string{emailAddress},
        SignatureAlgorithm: x509.SHA256WithRSA,
        URIs:               []*url.URL{uri},
}

bytes, err := x509.CreateCertificateRequest(rand.Reader, &csr, key)
if err != nil {
        panic(err)
}
csrFile, err := os.Create(name + ".csr")
if err != nil {
        panic(err)
}

pem.Encode(csrFile, &pem.Block{Type: "CERTIFICATE REQUEST", Bytes: bytes})
csrFile.Close()
}
```

You can run this program with:

```
$ go run csr-gen.go <URL-for-webhook>
```

and it will generate two files, *server.csr* and *server-key.pem*.

You can then create a certificate signing request for the Kubernetes API server using the following YAML:

```
apiVersion: certificates.k8s.io/v1beta1
kind: CertificateSigningRequest
metadata:
  name: validating-controller.default
spec:
  groups:
  - system:authenticated
  request: REPLACEME
  usages:
  usages:
  - digital signature
  - key encipherment
  - key agreement
  - server auth
```

You will notice for the `request` field the value is `REPLACEME`; this needs to be replaced with the base64-encoded certificate signing request we produced in the preceding code:

```
$ perl -pi -e s/REPLACEME/$(base64 server.csr | tr -d '\n')/ \
admission-controller-csr.yaml
```

Now that your certificate signing request is ready, you can send it to the API server to get the certificate:

```
$ kubectl create -f admission-controller-csr.yaml
```

Next, you need to approve that request:

```
$ kubectl certificate approve validating-controller.default
```

Once approved, you can download the new certificate:

```
$ kubectl get csr validating-controller.default -o json | \
  jq -r .status.certificate | base64 -d > server.crt
```

With the certificate, you are finally ready to create an SSL-based admission controller (phew!). When the admission controller code receives a request, it contains an object of type `AdmissionReview`, which contains metadata about the request as well as the body of the request itself. In our validating admission controller, we have only registered for a single resource type and a single action (`CREATE`), so we don't need to examine the request metadata. Instead, we dive directly into the resource itself and validate that `requestsPerSecond` is positive and the URL scheme is valid. If they aren't, we return a JSON body disallowing the request.

Implementing an admission controller to provide defaulting is similar to the steps just described, but instead of using a ValidatingWebhookConfiguration, you use a MutatingWebhookConfiguration, and you need to provide a JSON Patch object to mutate the request object before it is stored.

Here's a TypeScript snippet that you can add to your validating admission controller to add defaulting. If the `paths` field in the `loadtest` is of length zero, add a single path for `/index.html`:

```
if (needsPatch(loadtest)) {
    const patch = [
        { 'op': 'add', 'path': '/spec/paths', 'value': ['/index.html'] },
    ]
    response['patch'] = Buffer.from(JSON.stringify(patch))
        .toString('base64');
    response['patchType'] = 'JSONPatch';
}
```

You can then register this webhook as a MutatingWebhookConfiguration by simply changing the `kind` field in the YAML object and saving the file as *mutating-controller.yaml*. Then create the controller by running:

```
$ kubectl create -f mutating-controller.yaml
```

At this point, you've seen a complete example of how to extend the Kubernetes API server using custom resources and admission controllers. The following section describes some general patterns for various extensions.

Patterns for Custom Resources

Not all custom resources are identical. There are a variety of reasons for extending the Kubernetes API surface area, and the following sections discuss some general patterns you may want to consider.

Just Data

The easiest pattern for API extension is the notion of "just data." In this pattern, you are simply using the API server for storage and retrieval of information for your application. It is important to note that you should *not* use the Kubernetes API server for application data storage. The Kubernetes API server is not designed to be a key/value store for your app; instead, API extensions should be control or configuration objects that help you manage the deployment or runtime of your application. An example use case for the "just data" pattern might be configuration for canary deployments of your application—for example, directing 10% of all traffic to an experimental backend. While in theory such configuration information could also be stored in a ConfigMap, ConfigMaps are essentially untyped, and sometimes using a more strongly typed API extension object provides clarity and ease of use.

Extensions that are just data don't need a corresponding controller to activate them, but they may have validating or mutating admission controllers to ensure that they are well formed. For example, in the canary use case, a validating controller might ensure that all percentages in the canary object sum to 100%.

Compilers

A slightly more complicated pattern is the "compiler" or "abstraction" pattern. In this pattern, the API extension object represents a higher-level abstraction that is "compiled" into a combination of lower-level Kubernetes objects. The LoadTest extension in the previous example is an example of this compiler abstraction pattern. A user consumes the extension as a high-level concept, in this case a loadtest, but it comes into being by being deployed as a collection of Kubernetes Pods and services. To achieve this, a compiled abstraction requires an API controller to be running somewhere in the cluster to watch the current LoadTests and create the "compiled" representation (and likewise delete representations that no longer exist). In contrast to the operator pattern described next, however, there is no online health maintenance for compiled abstractions; it is delegated down to the lower-level objects (e.g., Pods).

Operators

While compiler extensions provide easy-to-use abstractions, extensions that use the "operator" pattern provide online, proactive management of the resources created by the extensions. These extensions likely provide a higher-level abstraction (for example, a database) that is compiled down to a lower-level representation, but they also provide online functionality, such as snapshot backups of the database or upgrade notifications when a new version of the software is available. To achieve this, the controller not only monitors the extension API to add or remove things as necessary, but also monitors the running state of the application supplied by the extension (e.g., a database) and takes actions to remediate unhealthy databases, take snapshots, or restore from a snapshot if a failure occurs.

Operators are the most complicated pattern for API extension of Kubernetes, but they are also the most powerful, enabling users to get easy access to "self-driving" abstractions that are responsible not just for deployment, but also health checking and repair.

Getting Started

Getting started extending the Kubernetes API can be a daunting and exhausting experience. Fortunately, there is a great deal of code to help you out. The Kubebuilder project (*https://kubebuilder.io*) contains a library of code intended to help you easily build reliable Kubernetes API extensions. It's a great resource to help you bootstrap your extension.

Summary

One of the great "superpowers" of Kubernetes is its ecosystem, and one of the most significant things powering this ecosystem is the extensibility of the Kubernetes API. Whether you're designing your own extensions to customize your cluster or consuming off-the-shelf extensions as utilities, cluster services, or operators, API extensions are the key to making your cluster your own and building the right environment for the rapid development of reliable applications.

## CHAPTER 18

Accessing Kubernetes from Common Programming Languages

Though most of this book is dedicated to using declarative YAML configurations, either directly via kubectl or through tools like Helm, there are situations when it is necessary to interact with the Kubernetes API directly from a programming language. For example, the authors of the Helm tool (*https://helm.sh*) itself needed to write that application in a programming language. More generally, this is common if you need to write some additional tool, like a kubectl plug-in, or a more complex piece of code, like a Kubernetes operator.

Much of the Kubernetes ecosystem is written in the Go programming language. As a result, the Go language has the richest and most extensive client. However, there are a high-quality clients for most common programming languages (and even some uncommon ones as well). Because there is already so much documentation and so many examples of how to use the Go client, this chapter will cover the basics of interacting with the Kubernetes API server with examples in Python, Java, and .NET.

The Kubernetes API: A Client's Perspective

At the end of the day, the Kubernetes API server is just an HTTP(S) server and that is exactly how each client library perceives it, though each client has a lot of additional logic that implements the various API calls and serializes to and from JSON. Given this, you might be tempted to simply use a plain HTTP client to work with the Kubernetes APIs, but the client libraries wrap these various HTTP calls into meaningful APIs that make your code more readable (e.g., readNamespacedPod(...)), and meaningful typed object-models that facilitate static type checking and therefore result in fewer bugs (e.g., Deployment). Perhaps more importantly, the client libraries also implement Kubernetes-specific capabilities, like loading authorization information from a *kubeconfig* file or from a Pod's environment. The clients also provide implementations of the non-RESTful parts of the Kubernetes API surface area like port-forward, logs, and watches. We'll describe these advanced capabilities in later sections.

OpenAPI and Generated Client Libraries

The set of resources and functions in the Kubernetes API is huge. There are many different resources in different API groups and many different operations on each of these resources. Keeping up with all of these different resources and resource versions would be a massive (and unmistakably boring) undertaking if developers had to hand-author all of these API calls. Especially when considering that clients have to be handwritten across each of the programming languages. Instead, the clients take a different approach, and the basics of interacting with the Kubernetes API server are all generated by a computer program that is sort of like a compiler in reverse. The code generator for the API clients takes a data specification for the Kubernetes API and uses this specification to generate a client for a specific language.

The Kubernetes API is expressed in a format known as OpenAPI, which is the most common schema for representing RESTful APIs. To give you a sense of the size of the Kubernetes API, the OpenAPI specification (*https://oreil.ly/3gRIW*) found on GitHub is over four megabytes in size. That's a pretty big text file! The official Kubernetes client libraries are all generated using the same core code generation logic, which can be found on GitHub (*https://oreil.ly/F39uK*). It is unlikely that you will actually have to generate the client libraries yourself, but nonetheless, it is useful to understand the process by which these libraries are created. In particular, because most of the client code is generated, updates and fixes can't be made directly in the generated client code, since it would be overwritten the next time the API was generated. Instead, when an error in a client is found, fixes need to be made to either the OpenAPI specification (if the error is in the specification itself) or the code generator (if the error is in the generated code). Although this process can seem excessively complex, it is the only way that a small number of Kubernetes client authors can keep up with the breadth of the Kubernetes API.

But What About kubectl x?

When you start implementing your own logic for interacting with the Kubernetes API, it probably won't be long before you find yourself asking how to do kubectl x. Most people start with the kubectl tool when they learn Kubernetes and consequently expect that there is a 1-1 mapping between the capabilities in kubectl and the Kubernetes API. While some commands are directly represented in the Kubernetes API (e.g., kubectl get pods), most of the more sophisticated features are actually a larger number of API calls with complex logic in the kubectl tool.

This balance between client-side and server-side features has been a design trade-off since the beginning of Kubernetes. Many features that are now present in the API server began as client-side implementations in kubectl. For example, the rollout capabilities now implemented on the server by the Deployment resource were previously implemented in the client. Likewise, until recently, kubectl apply ... was only available within the command-line tool, but was migrated to the server as the server-side apply capabilities that will be discussed later in this chapter.

Despite the general trajectory toward server-side implementations, there are still significant capabilities that remain in the client. Each of these capabilities must be reimplemented in each client library. Parity with the kubectl command line tool varies between languages. The Java client in particular has built a thick client that emulates much of the kubectl functionality.

If you can't find the functionality that you are looking for in your client library, a useful trick is to add the --v=10 flag to your kubectl command. That will turn on verbose logging, including all of the HTTP requests and responses sent to the Kubernetes API server. You can use this logging to reconstruct much of what kubectl is doing. If you still need to dig deeper, the kubectl source code is also available within the Kubernetes repository.

Programming the Kubernetes API

Now you have a deeper perspective about how the Kubernetes API works and how the client and server interact. In the following sections, we'll go through how to authenticate to the Kubernetes API server and interact with resources. We'll close with advanced topics from writing operators to interacting with Pods for interactive operations.

Installing the Client Libraries

Before you can start programming with the Kubernetes API, you need to find the client libraries. We will be using the official client libraries produced by the Kubernetes project itself, though there are also a number of high-quality clients developed as independent projects. The client libraries are all hosted under the kubernetes-client repository on GitHub:

- Python (*https://oreil.ly/ku6mT*)
- Java (*https://oreil.ly/aUSkD*)
- .NET (*https://oreil.ly/9J8iy*)

Each of these projects features a compatibility matrix to show which versions of the client work with which versions of the Kubernetes API and also give instructions for installing the libraries using the package managers (e.g., npm) associated with a particular programming language.[1]

Authenticating to the Kubernetes API

The Kubernetes API server wouldn't be very safe if it allowed anyone in the world to access it and read or write the resources that it orchestrates. Consequently, the first step in programming the Kubernetes API is connecting to it and identifying yourself for authentication. Because the API server is an HTTP server at its core, these methods of authentication are core HTTP authentication methods. The very first implementations of Kubernetes used basic HTTP authentication via a user and password combination, but this approach has been deprecated in favor of more modern authentication infrastructure.

If you have been using the kubectl command-line tool for your interactions with Kubernetes, you may not have considered the implementation details of authentication. Fortunately, the client libraries generally make it easy to connect to the API. However, a basic understanding of how Kubernetes authentication works is still useful for debugging when things go wrong.

There are two basic ways that the kubectl tool and clients obtain authentication information: from a kubeconfig file and from the context of a Pod within the Kubernetes cluster.

Code that is not running inside a Kubernetes cluster requires a kubeconfig file to provide the necessary information for authentication. By default, the client searches for this file in *${HOME}/.kube/config* or the $KUBECONFIG environment variables. If the KUBECONFIG variable is present, it takes precedence over any config file located in the default home location. The kubeconfig file contains all of the information necessary to access the Kubernetes API server. The clients all have easy-to-use calls to create a client either from the default locations or from a kubeconfig file supplied in the code itself:

Python

```
config.load_kube_config()
```

Java

```
ApiClient client = Config.defaultClient();
Configuration.setDefaultApiClient(client);
```

---

[1] We did not include JavaScript (*https://oreil.ly/8mw5F*) examples for brevity, but it is also actively developed.

.NET

```
var config = KubernetesClientConfiguration.BuildDefaultConfig();
var client = new Kubernetes(config);
```

Authentication for many cloud providers occurs via an external executable that knows how to generate a token for the Kubernetes cluster. This executable is often installed as part of the cloud provider's command-line tooling. When you write code to interact with the Kubernetes API, you need to make sure that this executable is also available in the context where the code is running so that it can be executed to obtain the token.

Within the context of a Pod in a Kubernetes cluster, the code running in the Pod has access to a Kubernetes service account that is associated with that Pod. The files containing the relevant token and certificate authority are placed into the Pod by Kubernetes as a volume when the Pod is created. Within a Kubernetes cluster, the API server is always available at a fixed DNS name, generally kubernetes. Because all of the necessary data is present in the Pod, a kubeconfig file is unnecessary and the client can synthesize its configuration from its context. The clients all have easy-to-use calls to create such an "in cluster" client:

Python

```
config.load_incluster_config()
```

Java

```
ApiClient client = ClientBuilder.cluster().build();
Configuration.setDefaultApiClient(client);
```

.NET

```
var config = KubernetesClientConfiguration.InClusterConfig()
var client = new Kubernetes(config);
```

The default service account associated with Pods has minimal roles (RBAC) granted to it. This means that by default, the code running in a Pod can't do much with the Kubernetes API. If you are getting authorization errors, you may need to adjust the service account to one that is specific to your code and has access to the necessary roles in the cluster.

Accessing the Kubernetes API

The most common ways that people interact with the Kubernetes API is via basic operations like creating, listing, and deleting resources. Because all of the clients are generated from the same OpenAPI specification, they all follow the same rough pattern. Before diving into the code, there are a couple more details of the Kubernetes API that are necessary to understand.

In Kubernetes, there is a distinction between namespaced and cluster-level resources. *Namespaced* resources exist within a Kubernetes namespace; for example, a Pod or Deployment may exist in the kube-system namespace. *Cluster-level* resources exist only once throughout the entire cluster. The most obvious example of such a resource is a Namespace, but other cluster-level resources include CustomResourceDefinitions and ClusterRoleBindings. This distinction is important because it is preserved in the function calls that you use to access the resources. For example, to list Pods in the default namespace in Python, you would write api.list_namespaced_pods('default'). To list Namespaces, you would write api.list_namespaces().

The second concept you need to understand is an *API group*. In Kubernetes, all of the resources are grouped into different sets of APIs. This is largely hidden from users of the kubectl tool, though you may have seen it within the apiVersion field in a YAML specification of a Kubernetes object. When programming against the Kubernetes API, this grouping becomes important, because often each API group has its own client for interacting with that set of resources. For example, to create a client to interact with a Deployment resource (which exists in the apps/v1 API group and version) you create a new AppsV1Api() object that knows how to interact with all resources in the apps/v1 API group and version. An example of how to create a client for an API group is shown in the following section.

Putting It All Together: Listing and Creating Pods in Python, Java, and .NET

We're now ready to actually write some code. Begin by creating a client object, then use that to list the Pods in the "default" namespace; here is code to do that in Python, Java, and .NET:

Python

```
config.load_kube_config()
api = client.CoreV1Api()
pod_list = api.list_namespaced_pod('default')
```

Java

```
ApiClient client = Config.defaultClient();
Configuration.setDefaultApiClient(client);
```

```
CoreV1Api api = new CoreV1Api();
V1PodList list = api.listNamespacedPod("default");
```

.NET

```
var config = KubernetesClientConfiguration.BuildDefaultConfig();
var client = new Kubernetes(config);
var list = client.ListNamespacedPod("default");
```

Once you have figured out how to list, read, and delete objects, the next common
task is creating new objects. The API call to create the object is easy enough to figure
out (e.g., `create_namespaced_pod` in Python), but actually defining the new Pod
resources can be more complicated.

Here's how you create a Pod in Python, Java, and .NET:

Python

```
container = client.V1Container(
    name="myapp",
    image="my_cool_image:v1",
 )


pod = client.V1Pod(
    metadata = client.V1ObjectMeta(
      name="myapp",
    ),
    spec=client.V1PodSpec(containers=[container]),
 )
```

Java

```
V1Pod pod =
    new V1PodBuilder()
        .withNewMetadata().withName("myapp").endMetadata()
        .withNewSpec()
          .addNewContainer()
            .withName("myapp")
            .withImage("my_cool_image:v1")
          .endContainer()
        .endSpec()
        .build();
```

.NET

```
var pod = new V1Pod()
{
    Metadata = new V1ObjectMeta{ Name = "myapp", },
    Spec = new V1PodSpec
    {
        Containers = new[] {
          new V1Container() {
            Name = "myapp", Image = "my_cool_image:v1",
```

```
        },
      },
    }
  };
```

Creating and Patching Objects

When you explore the client API for Kubernetes, you will notice that there are seemingly three different ways to manipulate resources, namely `create`, `replace`, and `patch`. These three verbs represent slightly different semantics for interacting with resources:

Create

As you can tell from the name, this creates a new resource. However, it will fail if the resource already exists.

Replace

This replaces an existing resource completely, without looking at the existing resource. When you use `replace`, you have to specify a complete resource.

Patch

This modifies an existing resource, leaving untouched the parts of the resource that did not change. When using `patch`, you use a special Patch resource rather than sending the resource (e.g., the Pod) that you are modifying.

 Patching a resource can be complicated. In many cases, it is easier to just replace it. However, in some cases, especially with large resources, patching the resource can be much more efficient in terms of network bandwidth and API server processing. Additionally, multiple actors can patch different parts of the resource simultaneously without worrying about write conflicts, which reduces overhead.

To patch a Kubernetes resource, you have to create a Patch object representing the change that you want to make to the resource. There are three formats for this patch supported by Kubernetes: JSON Patch, JSON Merge Patch, and strategic merge patch. The first two patch formats are RFC standards used in other places, and the third is a Kubernetes-developed patch format. Each of the patch formats has advantages and disadvantages. In these examples, we will use JSON Patch because it is the simplest to understand.

Here's how you patch a Deployment to increase the replicas to three:

Python

```
deployment.spec.replicas = 3
```

```
api_response = api_instance.patch_namespaced_deployment(
    name="my-deployment",
    namespace="some-namespace",
    body=deployment)
```

Java

```
// JSON-patch format
static String jsonPatch =
  "[{\"op\":\"replace\",\"path\":\"/spec/replicas\",\"value\":3}]";

V1Deployment patched =
        PatchUtils.patch(
            V1Deployment.class,
            () ->
                api.patchNamespacedDeploymentCall(
                    "my-deployment",
                    "some-namespace",
                    new V1Patch(jsonPatchStr),
                    null,
                    null,
                    null,
                    null,
                    null),
            V1Patch.PATCH_FORMAT_JSON_PATCH,
            api.getApiClient());
```

.NET

```
var jsonPatch = @"
[{
    ""op"": ""replace"",
    ""path"": ""/spec/replicas"",
    ""value"": 3
}]";

client.PatchNamespacedPod(
  new V1Patch(patchStr, V1Patch.PatchType.JsonPatch),
  "my-deployment",
  "some-namespace");
```

In each of these code samples, the Deployment resource has been patched to set the number of replicas in the deployment to three.

Watching Kubernetes APIs for Changes

Resources in Kubernetes are declarative. They represent the desired state of the system. To make that desired state a reality, a program must watch the desired state for changes and take action to make the current state of the world match the desired state.

Because of this pattern, one of the most common tasks when programming against the Kubernetes API is to watch for changes to a resource and then take some action based on those changes. The easiest way to do this is through polling. *Polling* simply calls the list function described above at a constant interval (such as every 60 seconds) and enumerates all of the resources that the code is interested in. While this code is easy to write, it has numerous drawbacks for both the client code and the API server. Polling introduces unnecessary latency, since waiting for the polling cycle to come around introduces delays for changes that occur just after the previous poll completed. Additionally, polling causes heavier load on the API server because it repeatedly returns resources that haven't changed. While many simple clients begin by using polling, too many clients polling the API server can overload it and add latency.

To solve this problem, the Kuberentes API also provides *watch*, or event-based, semantics. Using a watch call, you can register interest in specific changes with the API server and, instead of repeatedly polling, the API server will send notifications whenever a change occurs. In practical terms, the client performs a hanging GET to the HTTP API server. The TCP connection that underlies this HTTP request stays open for the duration of the watch, and the server writes a response to that stream (but does not close the stream) whenever a change occurs.

From a programmatic perspective, watch semantics enable event-based programming, changing a while loop that repeatedly polls into a collection of callbacks. Here are examples of watching Pods for changes:

Python

```
config.load_kube_config()
api = client.CoreV1Api()
w = watch.Watch()

for event in w.stream(v1.list_namespaced_pods, "some-namespace"):
  print(event)
```

Java

```
ApiClient client = Config.defaultClient();
CoreV1Api api = new CoreV1Api();

Watch<V1Namespace> watch =
    Watch.createWatch(
        client,
        api.listNamespacedPodCall(
            "some-namespace",
            null,
            null,
            null,
            null,
            null,
```

```
                  Integer.MAX_VALUE,
                  null,
                  null,
                  60,
                  Boolean.TRUE);
          new TypeToken<Watch.Response<V1Pod>>() {}.getType());

      try {
        for (Watch.Response<V1Pod> item : watch) {
          System.out.printf(
            "%s : %s%n", item.type, item.object.getMetadata().getName());
        }
      } finally {
        watch.close();
      }
```

.NET

```
var config = KubernetesClientConfiguration.BuildConfigFromConfigFile();
var client = new Kubernetes(config);

var watch =
  client.ListNamespacedPodWithHttpMessagesAsync("default", watch: true);
using (watch.Watch<V1Pod, V1PodList>((type, item) =>
{
  Console.WriteLine(item);
}
```

In each of these examples, rather than a repetitive polling loop, the watch API call delivers each change to a resource to a callback provided by the user. This both reduces latency and load on the Kubernetes API server.

Interacting with Pods

The Kubernetes API also provides functions for directly interacting with the applications running in a Kubernetes Pod. The kubectl tool provides a number of commands for interacting with Pods, namely logs, exec, and port-forward, and it is possible to use each of these from within custom code as well.

 Because the logs, exec, and port-forward APIs are nonstandard in a RESTful sense, they require custom logic in the client libraries and are thus somewhat less consistent between the different clients. Unfortunately, there is no option other than learning the implementation for each language.

When getting the logs for a Pod, you have to decide if you are going to read the Pod logs to get a snapshot of their current state or if you are going to stream them to receive new logs as they happen. If you stream the logs (the equivalent of kubectl logs -f ...), you create an open connection to the API server, and new log lines are written to this stream as they are written to the Pod. If not, you simply receive the current contents of the logs.

Here's how you both read and stream the logs:

Python

```
config.load_kube_config()
api = client.CoreV1Api()
log = api_instance.read_namespaced_pod_log(
  name="my-pod", namespace="some-namespace")
```

Java

```
V1Pod pod = ...; // some code to define or get a Pod here
PodLogs logs = new PodLogs();
InputStream is = logs.streamNamespacedPodLog(pod);
```

.NET

```
IKubernetes client = new Kubernetes(config);
var response = await client.ReadNamespacedPodLogWithHttpMessagesAsync(
    "my-pod", "my-namespace", follow: true);
var stream = response.Body;
```

Another common task is to execute some command within a Pod and get the output of running that task. You can use the kubectl exec ... command on the command line. Under the hood, the API that implements this is creating a WebSocket connection to the API server. WebSockets enable multiple streams of data (in this case, stdin, stdout, and stderr) to coexist on the same HTTP connection. If you've never had experience with WebSockets, don't worry; the details of interacting with WebSockets are handled by the client libraries.

Here's how you execute the ls /foo command in a Pod:

Python

```
cmd = [ 'ls', '/foo' ]
response = stream(
    api_instance.connect_get_namespaced_pod_exec,
    "my-pod",
    "some-namespace",
    command=cmd,
    stderr=True,
    stdin=False,
    stdout=True,
    tty=False)
```

Java

```
ApiClient client = Config.defaultClient();
Configuration.setDefaultApiClient(client);
Exec exec = new Exec();
final Process proc =
```

```
exec.exec("some-namespace",
          "my-pod",
          new String[] {"ls", "/foo"},
          true,
          true /*tty*/);
```

.NET

```
var config = KubernetesClientConfiguration.BuildConfigFromConfigFile();
IKubernetes client = new Kubernetes(config);
var webSocket =
    await client.WebSocketNamespacedPodExecAsync(
      "my-pod", "some-namespace", "ls /foo", "my-container-name");
var demux = new StreamDemuxer(webSocket);
demux.Start();
var stream = demux.GetStream(1, 1);
```

In addition to running commands in a Pod, you can also port-forward network connections from a Pod to code running on the local machine. Like exec, the port-forwarded traffic goes over a WebSocket. It is up to your code what it does with this port-forwarded socket. You could simply send a single request and receive a response as a string of bytes, or you could build a complete proxy server (like what kubectl port-forward does) to serve arbitrary requests through this proxy.

Regardless of what you intend to do with the connection, here's how you set up port-forwarding:

Python

```
pf = portforward(
    api_instance.connect_get_namespaced_pod_portforward,
    'my-pod', 'some-namespace',
    ports='8080',
)
```

Java

```
PortForward fwd = new PortForward();

List<Integer> ports = new ArrayList<>();
int localPort = 8080;
int targetPort = 8080;
ports.add(targetPort);
final PortForward.PortForwardResult result =
    fwd.forward("some-namespace", "my-pod", ports);
```

.NET

```
var config = KubernetesClientConfiguration.BuildConfigFromConfigFile();
IKubernetes client = new Kubernetes(config);
var webSocket = await client.WebSocketNamespacedPodPortForwardAsync(
  "some-namespace", "my-pod", new int[] {8080}, "v4.channel.k8s.io");
var demux = new StreamDemuxer(webSocket, StreamType.PortForward);
```

```
demux.Start();
var stream = demux.GetStream((byte?)0, (byte?)0);
```

Each of these examples creates a connection from port 8080 in a Pod to port 8080 in your program. The code returns the byte streams necessary, communicating across this port-forwarding channel. You can use these streams for sending and receiving messages.

Summary

The Kubernetes API provides rich and powerful functionality for you to write custom code. Writing your applications in the language that best suits a task or a persona shares the power of the orchestration API with as many Kubernetes users as possible. When you're ready to move beyond scripting calls to the kubectl executable, the Kubernetes client libraries provide a way to dive deep into the API to build an operator, a monitoring agent, a new user interface, or whatever your imagination can dream up.

## CHAPTER 19

Securing Applications in Kubernetes

Providing a secure platform to run your workloads is critical for Kubernetes to be broadly used in production. Thankfully, Kubernetes ships with many different security-focused APIs that allow you to construct a secure operating environment. The challenge is that there are many different security APIs, and you have to declaratively opt-in to use them. Using these security-focused APIs can be cumbersome and convoluted, which makes it difficult to achieve your desired security goals.

It's important to understand the following two concepts when securing Pods in Kubernetes: defense in depth and principle of least privilege. *Defense in depth* is a concept where you use multiple layers of security controls across your computing systems that include Kubernetes. The *principle of least privilege* means giving your workloads access only to resources that are required for them to operate. Both these concepts are not destinations, but constantly applied to the ever-changing computing system landscape.

In this chapter, we will take a look at security-focused Kubernetes APIs that can be incrementally applied to help secure your workloads at the Pod level.

Understanding SecurityContext

At the core of securing Pods is SecurityContext, which is an aggregation of all security-focused fields that may be applied at both the Pod and container specification level. Here are some example security controls covered by SecurityContext:

- User permissions and access control (e.g., setting User ID and Group ID)
- Read-only root filesystem
- Allow privilege escalation
- Seccomp, AppArmor, and SELinux profile and label assignments

- Run as privileged or unprivileged

Let's take a look at an example Pod with a SecurityContext defined in Example 19-1.

Example 19-1. kuard-pod-securitycontext.yaml

```yaml
apiVersion: v1
kind: Pod
metadata:
  name: kuard
spec:
  securityContext:
    runAsNonRoot: true
    runAsUser: 1000
    runAsGroup: 3000
    fsGroup: 2000
  containers:
    - image: gcr.io/kuar-demo/kuard-amd64:blue
      name: kuard
      securityContext:
          allowPrivilegeEscalation: false
          readOnlyRootFilesystem: true
          privileged: false
      ports:
        - containerPort: 8080
          name: http
          protocol: TCP
```

You can see in this example that there is a SecurityContext at both the Pod and the container level. Many of the security controls can be applied at both of these levels. In the case that they are applied in both, the container level configuration takes precedence. Let's take a look at fields we have defined in the Pod specification in this example and the impact they have on securing your workload:

runAsNonRoot

The Pod or container must run as a nonroot user. The container will fail to start if it is running as a root user. Running as a nonroot user is considered best practice as many misconfigurations and exploits happen via the container runtime conflating the container process running as the root user with the host root user. This can be set at both the PodSecurityContext and the SecurityContext. The kuard container image is configured to run as user "nobody" as defined in the Dockerfile (*https://oreil.ly/4IZI7*). It's always best practice to run your container as a nonroot user; however, if you are running a container downloaded from another source that doesn't explicitly set the container user, you may have to extend the original Dockerfile to do so. This method doesn't always work, as the application may have other requirements that needs to be considered.

runAsUser/runAsGroup

This setting overrides the user and group that the container process is run as. Container images may have this configured as part of the Dockerfile.

fsgroup

Configures Kubernetes to change the group of all files in a volume when they are mounted into a Pod. An additional field, fsGroupChangePolicy, may be used to configure the exact behavior.

allowPrivilegeEscalation

Configures whether a process in a container can gain more privileges than its parent. This is a common vector for attack, and it's important to explicitly set this to false. It's also important to understand that this will be set to true if privileged: true is set.

privileged

Runs the container as privileged, which elevates the container to the same permissions as the host.

readOnlyRootFilesystem

Mounts the container root filesystem to read-only. This is a common attack vector and is best practice to enable. Any data or logs that the workloads need write access to can be mounted via a volume.

The fields in this example aren't a complete list of all the security controls available; however, they represent a good starting point when working with SecurityContext. We will cover some more in context later in this chapter.

Let's now create the Pod by saving this example to a file called *kuard-pod-securitycontext.yaml*. We will demonstrate how the SecurityContext configuration is being applied to a running Pod. Create the Pod using the following command:

```
$ kubectl create -f kuard-pod-securitycontext.yaml
pod/kuard created
```

Now we'll start a shell inside the kuard container and check which user ID and group ID the processes are running as:

```
$ kubectl exec -it kuard -- ash
/ $ id
uid=1000 gid=3000 groups=2000
/ $ ps
PID   USER     TIME  COMMAND
    1 1000     0:00  /kuard
   30 1000     0:00  ash
   37 1000     0:00  ps
/ $ touch file
touch: file: Read-only file system
```

We can see that the shell that we started, `ash`, is running as user ID (uid) 1000, group ID (gid) 3000, and is in group 2000. We can also see that the kuard process is running as user 1000 as defined by the SecurityContext in the Pod specification. We also confirmed that we aren't able to create any new files because the container is read-only. If you only apply the following changes to you workloads, you're already off to a great start.

We will now introduce several other security controls covered by SecurityContext, which enable even more fine-grained control over what access and privileges your workloads have. First, we will introduce the operating system level security controls and then how to configure them via SecurityContext. It's important to note that many of these controls are host operating system dependent. This means that they may only apply to containers running on Linux operating systems as opposed to other supported Kubernetes operating systems like Windows. Here are a list of the core set of operating system controls that are covered by SecurityContext:

Capabilities

> Allow either the addition or removal of groups of privilege that may be required for a workload to operate. For example, your workload may configure the host's network configuration. Rather than configuring the Pod to be privileged, which is effectively host root access, you could add the specific capability to configure the host networking configuration (NET_ADMIN is the specific capability name). This follows the principal of least privilege.

AppArmor

> Controls which files processes can access. AppArmor profiles can be applied to containers via the addition of an annotation of `container.apparmor.secu rity.beta.kubernetes.io/<container_name>: <profile_ref>` to the Pod specification. Acceptable values for `<profile ref>` include `runtime/default`, `localhost/<path to profile>`, and `unconfined`. The default is `unconfined`, which explicitly sets no profile to be applied.

Seccomp

> Seccomp (secure computing) profiles allow the creation of syscall filters. These filters allow specific syscalls to be allowed or blocked, which limits the surface area of the Linux kernel that is exposed to the processes in the Pods.

SELinux

> Defines access controls for files and processes. SELinux operators use labels that are grouped together to create a security context (not to be mistaken with a Kubernetes SecurityContext), which is used to limit access to a process. By default, Kubernetes allocates a random SELinux context for each container; however, you may choose to set one via SecurityContext.

Both AppArmor and seccomp have the ability to set the runtime default profile to be used. Each container runtime ships with default AppArmor and seccomp profiles that have been carefully curated to reduce the attack surface area by removing syscalls and file access that are known to be attack vectors or aren't commonly used by applications. These defaults are rarely workload impacting and offer a great starting point.

To demonstrate how these security controls are applied to a Pod, we will use a tool called amicontained (*https://oreil.ly/6ubkU*) ("Am I contained") written by Jess Frazelle. Save the Pod specification in Example 19-2 to a file called *amicontained-pod.yaml*. The first Pod has no SecurityContext applied and will be used to show which security controls are applied to a Pod by default. Note that your output may look different because different Kubernetes distributions and managed services provide different defaults.

Example 19-2. amicontained-pod.yaml

```
apiVersion: v1
kind: Pod
metadata:
  name: amicontained
spec:
  containers:
    - image: r.j3ss.co/amicontained:v0.4.9
      name: amicontained
      command: [ "/bin/sh", "-c", "--" ]
      args: [ "amicontained" ]
```

Create the amicontainer Pod:

```
$ kubectl apply -f amicontained-pod.yaml
pod/amicontained created
```

Let's review the Pod logs to examine the output of the amicontained tool:

```
$ kubectl logs amicontained
Container Runtime: kube
Has Namespaces:
        pid: true
        user: false
AppArmor Profile: docker-default (enforce)
Capabilities:
        BOUNDING -> chown dac_override fowner fsetid kill setgid setuid
        setpcap net_bind_service net_raw sys_chroot mknod audit_write
        setfcap
Seccomp: disabled
Blocked Syscalls (21):
        SYSLOG SETPGID SETSID VHANGUP PIVOT_ROOT ACCT SETTIMEOFDAY UMOUNT2
```

```
     SWAPON SWAPOFF REBOOT SETHOSTNAME SETDOMAINNAME INIT_MODULE
     DELETE_MODULE LOOKUP_DCOOKIE KEXEC_LOAD FANOTIFY_INIT
     OPEN_BY_HANDLE_AT FINIT_MODULE KEXEC_FILE_LOAD
 Looking for Docker.sock
```

From the output above we see that the AppArmor runtime default is being applied. We also see the capabilities that are allowed by default along with seccomp being disabled. Finally, we see that a total of 21 syscalls are being blocked by default. Now that we have a baseline, let's apply seccomp, AppArmor, and Capabilities security controls to the Pod specification. Create a file called *amicontained-pod-securitycontext.yaml* with the contents of Example 19-3.

Example 19-3. amicontained-pod-securitycontext.yaml

```
apiVersion: v1
kind: Pod
metadata:
  name: amicontained
  annotations:
    container.apparmor.security.beta.kubernetes.io/amicontained: "runtime/default"
spec:
  securityContext:
    runAsNonRoot: true
    runAsUser: 1000
    runAsGroup: 3000
    fsGroup: 2000
    seccompProfile:
      type: RuntimeDefault
  containers:
  - image: r.j3ss.co/amicontained:v0.4.9
    name: amicontained
    command: [ "/bin/sh", "-c", "--" ]
    args: [ "amicontained" ]
    securityContext:
      capabilities:
        add: ["SYS_TIME"]
        drop: ["NET_BIND_SERVICE"]
      allowPrivilegeEscalation: false
      readOnlyRootFilesystem: true
      privileged: false
```

First, we need to delete the existing amicontained Pod:

```
$ kubectl delete pod amicontained
pod "amicontained" deleted
```

Now we can create the new Pod with the SecurityContext applied. We are specifically declaring that the runtime default AppArmor and seccomp profiles be applied. In addition, we have added and dropped a Capability:

```
$ kubectl apply -f amicontained-pod-securitycontext.yaml
pod/amicontained created
```

Let's again review the Pod logs to examine the output of the amicontained tool:

```
$ kubectl logs amicontained
Container Runtime: kube
Has Namespaces:
        pid: true
        user: false
AppArmor Profile: docker-default (enforce)
Capabilities:
        BOUNDING -> chown dac_override fowner fsetid kill setgid setuid setpcap
        net_raw sys_chroot sys_time mknod audit_write setfcap
Seccomp: filtering
Blocked Syscalls (67):
        SYSLOG SETUID SETGID SETPGID SETSID SETREUID SETREGID SETGROUPS
        SETRESUID SETRESGID USELIB USTAT SYSFS VHANGUP PIVOT_ROOT_SYSCTL ACCT
        SETTIMEOFDAY MOUNT UMOUNT2 SWAPON SWAPOFF REBOOT SETHOSTNAME
        SETDOMAINNAME IOPL IOPERM CREATE_MODULE INIT_MODULE DELETE_MODULE
        GET_KERNEL_SYMS QUERY_MODULE QUOTACTL NFSSERVCTL GETPMSG PUTPMSG
        AFS_SYSCALL TUXCALL SECURITY LOOKUP_DCOOKIE VSERVER MBIND SET_MEMPOLICY
        GET_MEMPOLICY KEXEC_LOAD ADD_KEY REQUEST_KEY KEYCTL MIGRATE_PAGES
        FUTIMESAT UNSHARE MOVE_PAGES PERF_EVENT_OPEN FANOTIFY_INIT
        NAME_TO_HANDLE_AT OPEN_BY_HANDLE_AT SETNS PROCESS_VM_READV
        PROCESS_VM_WRITEV KCMP FINIT_MODULE KEXEC_FILE_LOAD BPF USERFAULTFD
        PKEY_MPROTECT PKEY_ALLOC PKEY_FREE
Looking for Docker.sock
```

SecurityContext Challenges

As you can see, there is a lot to understand to use a SecurityContext, and it is not easy to apply a baseline set of security controls by directly configuring all fields of every Pod. The creation and management of AppArmor, seccomp, and SELinux profiles and contexts is not easy and is error prone. The cost of an error is breaking the ability for an application to perform its function. There are several tools out there that create a way to generate a seccomp profile from a running Pod, which can then be applied using SecurityContext. One such project is the Security Profiles Operator (*https://oreil.ly/grPCN*), which makes it easy to generate and manage Seccomp profiles. We will now take a look at other security APIs that make the management of how SecurityContext is applied consistent across a cluster.

Pod Security

Now that we've taken a look at SecurityContext as a way to manage security controls applied to Pods and containers, we will cover how to make sure that a set of Security Context values are applied at scale. Kubernetes has a now-deprecated PodSecurity-Policy (PSP) API, which enabled both validation and mutation. *Validation* will not allow the creation of Kubernetes resources unless they have a specific SecurityContext applied. *Mutation*, on the other hand, will change Kubernetes resources and apply a specific SecurityContext based on criteria applied via the PSP. Given that PSP is deprecated and will be removed in Kubernetes v1.25, we will not cover it in depth but will instead cover its successor, Pod Security. One of the main differences between Pod Security and its predecessor is that Pod Security only performs validation and not mutation. If you want to learn more about mutation, we encourage you to take a look at Chapter 20.

What Is Pod Security?

Pod Security allows you to declare different security profiles for Pods. These security profiles are known as Pod Security Standards and are applied at the namespace level. Pod Security Standards are a collection of security-sensitive fields in a Pod specification (including, but not limited to, SecurityContext) and their associated values. There are three different standards that range from restricted to permissive. The idea is that you can apply a general security posture to all Pods in a given namespace. The three Pod Security Standards are as follows:

Baseline
> Most common privilege escalation while enabling easier onboarding.

Restricted
> Highly restricted, covering security best practices. May cause workloads to break.

Privileged
> Open and unrestricted.

 Pod Security is currently a beta feature as of Kubernetes v1.23 and may be subject to change.

Each Pod Security Standard defines a list of fields in the Pod specification and their allowed values. Here are some fields that are covered by these standards:

- `spec.securityContext`
- `spec.containers[*].securityContext`
- `spec.containers[*].ports`
- `spec.volumes[*].hostPath`

You can view the complete list of fields covered by each of the Pod Security Standards in the offical documentation (*https://oreil.ly/xPK2p*).

Each standard is applied to a namespace using a given mode. There are three modes a policy may be applied to. They are as follows:

Enforce
Any Pods that violate the policy will be denied.

Warn
Any Pods that violate the policy will be allowed, and a warning message will be displayed to the user.

Audit
Any Pods that violate the policy will generate an audit message in the audit log.

Applying Pod Security Standards

Pod Security Standards are applied to a namespace using labels as follows:

- Required: `pod-security.kubernetes.io/<MODE>: <LEVEL>`
- Optional: `pod-security.kubernetes.io/<MODE>-version: <VERSION>` (defaults to latest)

The namespace in Example 19-4 illustrates how you may use multiple modes to enforce at one standard (baseline in this example) and audit and warn at another (restricted). Using multiple modes allows you to deploy a policy with a lower security posture and audit which workloads violate a standard with a more restricted policy. You can then remediate the policy violations before enforcing the more restricted standard. You can also pin a mode to a specific version, e.g., v1.22. This allows the policy standards to change with each Kubernetes release and allows you to pin a specific version. In Example 19-4, we are enforcing the baseline standard and both warning and auditing the restricted standard. All modes are pinned to v1.22 of the standard.

Example 19-4. baseline-ns.yaml

```
apiVersion: v1
kind: Namespace
metadata:
  name: baseline-ns
  labels:
    pod-security.kubernetes.io/enforce: baseline
    pod-security.kubernetes.io/enforce-version: v1.22
    pod-security.kubernetes.io/audit: restricted
    pod-security.kubernetes.io/audit-version: v1.22
    pod-security.kubernetes.io/warn: restricted
    pod-security.kubernetes.io/warn-version: v1.22
```

Deploying a policy for the first time can be a daunting task. Thankfully, Pod Security has made it easy to see which existing workloads violate a Pod Security Standard with a single dry-run command:

```
$ kubectl label --dry-run=server --overwrite ns \
  --all pod-security.kubernetes.io/enforce=baseline
Warning: kuard: privileged
namespace/default labeled
namespace/kube-node-lease labeled
namespace/kube-public labeled
Warning: kube-proxy-vxjwb: host namespaces, hostPath volumes, privileged
Warning: kube-proxy-zxqzz: host namespaces, hostPath volumes, privileged
Warning: kube-apiserver-kind-control-plane: host namespaces, hostPath volumes
Warning: etcd-kind-control-plane: host namespaces, hostPath volumes
Warning: kube-controller-manager-kind-control-plane: host namespaces, ...
Warning: kube-scheduler-kind-control-plane: host namespaces, hostPath volumes
namespace/kube-system labeled
namespace/local-path-storage labeled
```

This command evaluates all Pods on a Kubernetes cluster against the baseline Pod Security Standard and reports violations as warning messages in the output.

Let's see Pod Security in action. Create a file called *baseline-ns.yaml* with the content in Example 19-5.

Example 19-5. baseline-ns.yaml

```
apiVersion: v1
kind: Namespace
metadata:
  name: baseline-ns
  labels:
    pod-security.kubernetes.io/enforce: baseline
    pod-security.kubernetes.io/enforce-version: v1.22
    pod-security.kubernetes.io/audit: restricted
    pod-security.kubernetes.io/audit-version: v1.22
    pod-security.kubernetes.io/warn: restricted
    pod-security.kubernetes.io/warn-version: v1.22
```

```
$ kubectl apply -f baseline-ns.yaml
namespace/baseline-ns created
```

Create a file called *kuard-pod.yaml* with the content in Example 19-6.

Example 19-6. kuard-pod.yaml

```
apiVersion: v1
kind: Pod
metadata:
  name: kuard
  labels:
```

```
    app: kuard
spec:
  containers:
    - image: gcr.io/kuar-demo/kuard-amd64:blue
      name: kuard
      ports:
        - containerPort: 8080
          name: http
          protocol: TCP
```

Create the Pod and review the output with the following command:

```
$ kubectl apply -f kuard-pod.yaml --namespace baseline-ns
Warning: would violate "v1.22" version of "restricted" PodSecurity profile:
allowPrivilegeEscalation != false (container "kuard" must set
securityContext.allowPrivilegeEscalation=false), unrestricted capabilities
(container "kuard" must set securityContext.capabilities.drop=["ALL"]),
runAsNonRoot != true (pod or container "kuard" must set securityContext.
runAsNonRoot=true), seccompProfile (pod or container "kuard" must set
securityContext.seccompProfile.type to "RuntimeDefault" or "Localhost")
pod/kuard created
```

In this output, you can see that the Pod was successfully created; however, it violated the restricted Pod Security Standard, and the details of the violations are provided in the output so that you can remediate. We can also see the message in the API server audit log because we configured the audit mode:

```
{"kind":"Event","apiVersion":"audit.k8s.io/v1","level":"Metadata","auditID":"...
```

Pod Security is a great way to manage the security posture of your workloads by applying policy at the namespace level and allowing Pods to be created only if they don't violate the policy. It's flexible and offers different prebuilt policies from permissive to restricted along with tooling to easily roll out policy changes without the risk of breaking workloads.

Service Account Management

Service accounts are Kubernetes resources that provide an identity to workloads that run inside Pods. RBAC can be applied to service accounts to control what resources, via the Kubernetes API, the identity has access to. Please see Chapter 14 to learn more. If your application doesn't require access to the Kubernetes API, you should disable access following the least privilege principal. By default, Kubernetes creates a default service account in each namespace, which is automatically set as the service account for all Pods. This service account contains a token that is automounted in each Pod and is used to access the Kubernetes API. To disable this behavior, you must add `automountServiceAccountToken: false` to the service account configuration. Example 19-7 demonstrates how this can be done for the default service account. This must be done in each namespace.

Example 19-7. service-account.yaml

```
apiVersion: v1
kind: ServiceAccount
metadata:
  name: default
automountServiceAccountToken: false
```

Service accounts are often overlooked when considering Pod security; however, they allow direct access to the Kubernetes API and, without adequate RBAC, could allow an attacker access to Kubernetes. It's important to understand how to limit access by making a simple change to how service account tokens are handled.

Role-Based Access Control

We would be remiss not to mention Kubernetes role-based access control (RBAC) in a chapter about securing Pods. Everything you need to know about RBAC can be found in Chapter 14 and can be applied to complement you workload's security posture.

RuntimeClass

Kubernetes interacts with the container runtime on the node's operating system via the Container Runtime Interface (CRI). The creation and standardization of this interface has allowed for an ecosystem of container runtimes to exist. These container runtimes may offer different levels of isolation, which include stronger security guarantees based on how they are implemented. Projects like Kata Containers, Firecracker, and gVisor are based on different isolation mechanisms from nested virtualization to more sophisticated syscall filtering. These security and isolation guarantees provide a Kubernetes administrator the flexibility to allow users to select a container runtime based on their workload type. For example, if your workload needs stronger security guarantees, then you can choose to run in a Pod that uses a different container runtime.

The RuntimeClass API was introduced to allow container runtime selection. It allows users to select one of a supported list of container runtimes in the cluster. Figure 19-1 depicts how RuntimeClass functions.

> Different RuntimeClasses must be configured by a cluster administrator and may required specific `nodeSelectors` or `tolerations` on your workload to be scheduled to the correct node.

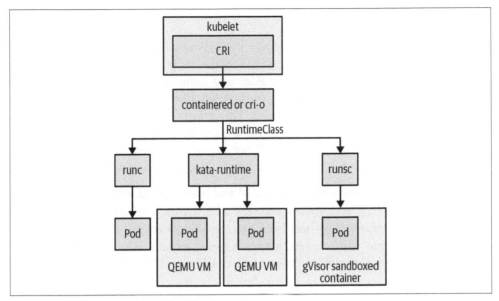

Figure 19-1. RuntimeClass flow diagram

You can use a RuntimeClass by specifying `runtimeClassName` in the Pod specification. Example 19-8 is an example Pod that specifies a RuntimeClass.

Example 19-8. kuard-pod-runtimeclass.yaml

```
apiVersion: v1
kind: Pod
metadata:
  name: kuard
  labels:
    app: kuard
spec:
  runtimeClassName: firecracker
  containers:
    - image: gcr.io/kuar-demo/kuard-amd64:blue
      name: kuard
      ports:
        - containerPort: 8080
          name: http
          protocol: TCP
```

RuntimeClass allows users to select different container runtimes that may have different security isolation. Using RuntimeClass can help complement the overall security of your workloads, especially if workloads are processing sensitive information or running untrusted code.

Network Policy

Kubernetes also has a Network Policy API that allows you to create both ingress and egress network policies for your workload. Network policies are configured using labels that allow you to select specific Pods and define how they can communicate with other Pods and endpoints. A Network Policy like Ingress doesn't actually ship with an associated Kubernetes controller. This means that you can create Network Policy resources but if you haven't installed a controller that acts upon the creation of Network Policy resources, then they will not be enforced. Network Policy resources are implemented by network plug-ins, such as Calico, Cilium, and Weave Net.

The Network Policy resource is namespaced and is structured with the `podSelector`, `policyTypes`, `ingress`, and `egress` sections with the only required field being pod Selector. If the `podSelector` field is empty, the policy matches all Pods in a namespace. This field may also contain a `matchLabels` section, which functions in the same way as a Service resource, allowing you to add a set of labels to match a specific set of Pods.

There are several idiosyncrasies when using Network Policy that you need to be aware of. If a Pod is matched by any Network Policy resource, then any ingress or egress communication must be explicitly defined, otherwise it will be blocked. If a Pod matches multiple Network Policy resources, then the policies are additive. If a Pod isn't matched by any Network Policy, then traffic is allowed. This decision was intentionally made to ease onboarding of new workloads. If you do, however, want all traffic to be blocked by default, you can create a default deny rule per namespace. Example 19-9 shows a default deny rule that can be applied per namespace.

Example 19-9. networkpolicy-default-deny.yaml

```
apiVersion: networking.k8s.io/v1
kind: NetworkPolicy
metadata:
  name: default-deny-ingress
spec:
  podSelector: {}
  policyTypes:
  - Ingress
```

Let's walk through an example set of network policies to demonstrate how you can use them to secure your workloads. First, create a namespace to test using the following command:

```
$ kubectl create ns kuard-networkpolicy
namespace/kuard-networkpolicy created
```

Create a file named *kuard-pod.yaml* with the contents of Example 19-10.

Example 19-10. kuard-pod.yaml

```
apiVersion: v1
kind: Pod
metadata:
  name: kuard
  labels:
    app: kuard
spec:
  containers:
    - image: gcr.io/kuar-demo/kuard-amd64:blue
      name: kuard
      ports:
        - containerPort: 8080
          name: http
          protocol: TCP
```

Create the kuard Pod in the kuard-networkpolicy namespace:

```
$ kubectl apply -f kuard-pod.yaml \
  --namespace kuard-networkpolicy
pod/kuard created
```

Expose the kuard Pod as a service:

```
$ kubectl expose pod kuard --port=80 --target-port=8080 \
  --namespace kuard-networkpolicy
pod/kuard created
```

Now we can use kubectl run to spin up a Pod to test as our source and test access to the kuard Pod without applying any Network Policy:

```
$ kubectl run test-source --rm -ti --image busybox /bin/sh \
  --namespace kuard-networkpolicy
If you don't see a command prompt, try pressing enter.
/ # wget -q kuard -O -
<!doctype html>

<html lang="en">
<head>
  <meta charset="utf-8">

  <title><KUAR Demo></title>
 ...
```

We can successfully connect to the kuard Pod from our test-source Pod. Now let's apply a default deny policy and test again. Create a file called *networkpolicy-default-deny.yaml* with the contents of Example 19-11.

Example 19-11. networkpolicy-default-deny.yaml

```
apiVersion: networking.k8s.io/v1
kind: NetworkPolicy
metadata:
  name: default-deny-ingress
spec:
  podSelector: {}
  policyTypes:
  - Ingress
```

Now apply the default deny network policy:

```
$ kubectl apply -f networkpolicy-default-deny.yaml \
  --namespace kuard-networkpolicy
networkpolicy.networking.k8s.io/default-deny-ingress created
```

Now let's test access to the kuard Pod from the test-source Pod:

```
$ kubectl run test-source --rm -ti --image busybox /bin/sh \
  --namespace kuard-networkpolicy
If you don't see a command prompt, try pressing enter.
/ # wget -q --timeout=5 kuard -O -
wget: download timed out
```

We can no longer access the kuard Pod from the test-source Pod due to the default deny Network Policy. Create a Network Policy that allows access from the test-source to the kuard Pod. Create a file called *networkpolicy-kuard-allow-test-source.yaml* with the contents of Example 19-12.

Example 19-12. networkpolicy-kuard-allow-test-source.yaml

```
kind: NetworkPolicy
apiVersion: networking.k8s.io/v1
metadata:
  name: access-kuard
spec:
  podSelector:
    matchLabels:
      app: kuard
  ingress:
    - from:
      - podSelector:
          matchLabels:
            run: test-source
```

Apply the Network Policy:

```
$ kubectl apply \
  -f code/chapter-security/networkpolicy-kuard-allow-test-source.yaml \
  --namespace kuard-networkpolicy
networkpolicy.networking.k8s.io/access-kuard created
```

Again, verify that the test-source Pod can indeed access the kuard Pod:

```
$ kubectl run test-source --rm -ti --image busybox /bin/sh \
  --namespace kuard-networkpolicy
If you don't see a command prompt, try pressing enter.
/ # wget -q kuard -O -
<!doctype html>

<html lang="en">
<head>
  <meta charset="utf-8">

  <title><KUAR Demo></title>
...
```

Clean up the namespace by running the following command:

```
$ kubectl delete namespace kuard-networkpolicy
namespace "kuard-networkpolicy" deleted
```

Applying Network Policy provides an extra layer of security for your workloads and continues to build on the defense in depth and principle of least privilege concepts.

Service Mesh

Service mesh can also be used to increase your workload's security posture. Service meshes offer access policies, which allow the configuration of protocol-aware policies based on services. For example, your access policy might declare that ServiceA connects to ServiceB via HTTPS on port 443. In addition, service meshes typically implement mutual TLS on all service-to-service communication, which means that not only is the communication encrypted but the service identities are also verified. If you would like to learn more about service meshes and how they can be used to secure your workloads, check out Chapter 15.

Security Benchmark Tools

There are several open source tools that allow you to run a suite of security benchmarks against your Kubernetes cluster to determine if your configuration meets a predefined set of security baselines. Once such tool is called kube-bench (*https://oreil.ly/TnUlm*). kube-bench can be used to run the CIS Benchmarks (*https://oreil.ly/VvUe5*) for Kubernetes. Tools like kube-bench running the CIS Benchmarks aren't specifically focused on Pod security; however, they can certainly expose any cluster misconfigurations and help identify remediations. kube-bench can be run using the following command:

```
$ kubectl apply -f https://raw.githubusercontent.com/aquasecurity/kube-bench...
job.batch/kube-bench created
```

You can then review the benchmark output and remediations via the Pod logs:

```
$ kubectl logs job/kube-bench
[INFO] 4 Worker Node Security Configuration
[INFO] 4.1 Worker Node Configuration Files
[PASS] 4.1.1 Ensure that the kubelet service file permissions are set to 644...
[PASS] 4.1.2 Ensure that the kubelet service file ownership is set to root  ...
[PASS] 4.1.3 If proxy kubeconfig file exists ensure permissions are set to  ...
[PASS] 4.1.4 Ensure that the proxy kubeconfig file ownership is set to root ...
[PASS] 4.1.5 Ensure that the --kubeconfig kubelet.conf file permissions are ...
[PASS] 4.1.6 Ensure that the --kubeconfig kubelet.conf file ownership is set...
[PASS] 4.1.7 Ensure that the certificate authorities file permissions are   ...
[PASS] 4.1.8 Ensure that the client certificate authorities file ownership  ...
[PASS] 4.1.9 Ensure that the kubelet --config configuration file has permiss...
[PASS] 4.1.10 Ensure that the kubelet --config configuration file ownership ...
[INFO] 4.2 Kubelet
[PASS] 4.2.1 Ensure that the anonymous-auth argument is set to false (Automated)
[PASS] 4.2.2 Ensure that the --authorization-mode argument is not set to     ...
[PASS] 4.2.3 Ensure that the --client-ca-file argument is set as appropriate...
[PASS] 4.2.4 Ensure that the --read-only-port argument is set to 0 (Manual)
[PASS] 4.2.5 Ensure that the --streaming-connection-idle-timeout argument is...
[FAIL] 4.2.6 Ensure that the --protect-kernel-defaults argument is set to    ...
[PASS] 4.2.7 Ensure that the --make-iptables-util-chains argument is set to ...
[PASS] 4.2.8 Ensure that the --hostname-override argument is not set (Manual)
[WARN] 4.2.9 Ensure that the --event-qps argument is set to 0 or a level     ...
[WARN] 4.2.10 Ensure that the --tls-cert-file and --tls-private-key-file arg...
[PASS] 4.2.11 Ensure that the --rotate-certificates argument is not set to  ...
[PASS] 4.2.12 Verify that the RotateKubeletServerCertificate argument is set...
[WARN] 4.2.13 Ensure that the Kubelet only makes use of Strong Cryptographic...


== Remediations node ==
4.2.6 If using a Kubelet config file, edit the file to set protectKernel...
If using command line arguments, edit the kubelet service file
/etc/systemd/system/kubelet.service.d/10-kubeadm.conf on each worker node and
set the below parameter in KUBELET_SYSTEM_PODS_ARGS variable.
--protect-kernel-defaults=true
Based on your system, restart the kubelet service. For example:
systemctl daemon-reload
systemctl restart kubelet.service

4.2.9 If using a Kubelet config file, edit the file to set eventRecordQPS...
If using command line arguments, edit the kubelet service file
/etc/systemd/system/kubelet.service.d/10-kubeadm.conf on each worker node and
set the below parameter in KUBELET_SYSTEM_PODS_ARGS variable.
Based on your system, restart the kubelet service. For example:
systemctl daemon-reload
systemctl restart kubelet.service
...
```

Using tools like kube-bench with the CIS benchmarks can help identify whether your Kubernetes cluster meets a security baseline and provide remediations if needed.

Image Security

Another important part of Pod security is keeping the code and application within the Pod secure. Securing an application's code is a complex topic beyond the scope of this chapter; however, the basics for container image security include making sure that your container image registry is doing *static scanning* for known code vulnerabilities. Additionally, you should have a tool for doing *runtime scanning* that identifies vulnerabilities that have been discovered after an image started running and also looks for potentially malicious activity like intrusions. There are many scanning tools provided by both open source and proprietary companies. In addition to security scanning, focusing on minimizing the contents of your container image to remove unnecessary dependencies minimizes the noise from this scanning. Finally, image security is another great reason to invest in continuous delivery so that you can rapidly patch and redeploy an image when vulnerabilities are found.

Summary

In this chapter, we covered many different security-focused APIs and resources that can be used to improve the security posture of your workloads. By practicing defense in depth and principle of least privilege, you can incrementally improve the baseline security of your Kubernetes cluster. It's never too late to start practicing better security, and this chapter provides everything you need to be confident that you have an understanding of the security controls Kubernetes offers.

## CHAPTER 20

Policy and Governance for Kubernetes Clusters

Throughout this book we have introduced many different Kubernetes resource types, each with a specific purpose. It doesn't take long before the resources on a Kubernetes cluster go from several, for a single microservice application, to hundreds and thousands, for a complete distributed application. In the context of a production cluster it isn't hard to imagine the challenges associated with managing thousands of resources.

In this chapter, we introduce the concepts of policy and governance. *Policy* is a set of constraints and conditions for how Kubernetes resources can be configured. *Governance* provides the ability to verify and enforce organizational policies for all resources deployed to a Kubernetes cluster, such as ensuring all resources use current best practices, comply with security policy, or adhere to company conventions. Whatever your case may be, your tooling needs to be flexible and scalable so that all resources defined on a cluster comply with your organization's defined policies.

Why Policy and Governance Matter

There are many different types of policies in Kubernetes. For example, NetworkPolicy allows you to specify what network services and endpoints a Pod can connect to. PodSecurityPolicy enables fine-grained control over the security elements of a Pod. Both can be used to configure network or container runtimes.

However, you might want to enforce a policy before Kubernetes resources are even created. This is the problem that policy and governance solve. At this point, you might be thinking, "Isn't this what role-based access control does?" However, as you'll see in this chapter, RBAC isn't granular enough to restrict specific fields within resources from being set.

Here are some common examples of policies that cluster administrators often configure:

- All containers *must* only come from a specific container registry.
- All Pods *must* be labeled with the department name and contact information.
- All Pods *must* have both CPU and memory resource limits set.
- All Ingress hostnames *must* be unique across a cluster.
- A certain service *must* not be made available on the internet.
- Containers *must* not listen on privileged ports.

Cluster administrators may also want to audit existing resources on a cluster, perform dry-run policy evaluations, or even mutate a resource based on a set of conditions—for example, applying labels to a Pod if they aren't present.

It's very important for cluster administrators to be able to define policy and perform compliance audits without interfering with the developers' ability to deploy applications to Kubernetes. If developers are creating noncompliant resources, you need a system to make sure they get the feedback and remediation they need to bring their work into compliance.

Let's take a look at how to achieve policy and governance by leveraging core extensibility components of Kubernetes.

Admission Flow

To understand how policy and governance ensures resources are compliant before they are created in your Kubernetes cluster, you must first understand the request flow through the Kubernetes API server. Figure 20-1 depicts the flow of an API request through the API server. Here, we'll focus on mutating admission, validating admission, and webhooks.

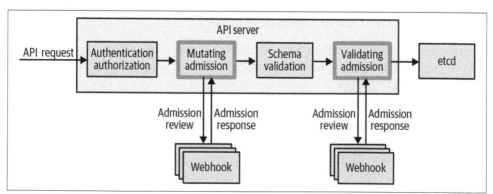

Figure 20-1. API request flow through the Kubernetes API server

Admission controllers operate inline as an API request flows through the Kubernetes API server and are used to either mutate or validate the API request resource before it's saved to storage. Mutating admission controllers allow the resource to be modified; validating admission controllers do not. There are many different types of admission controllers; this chapter focuses on admission webhooks, which are dynamically configurable. They allow a cluster administrator to configure an endpoint to which the API server can send requests for evaluation by creating either a MutatingWebhookConfiguration or a ValidatingWebhookConfiguration resource. The admission webhook will respond with an "admit" or "deny" directive to let the API server know whether to save the resource to storage.

Policy and Governance with Gatekeeper

Let's dive into how to configure policies and ensure that Kubernetes resources are compliant. The Kubernetes project doesn't provide any controllers that enable policy and governance, but there are open source solutions. Here, we will focus on an open source ecosystem project called Gatekeeper (*https://oreil.ly/u0deR*).

Gatekeeper is a Kubernetes-native policy controller that evaluates resources based on defined policy and determines whether to allow a Kubernetes resource to be created or modified. These evaluations happen server-side as the API request flows through the Kubernetes API server, which means each cluster has a single point of processing. Processing the policy evaluations server-side means that you can install Gatekeeper on existing Kubernetes clusters without changing developer tooling, workflows, or continuous delivery pipelines.

Gatekeeper uses *custom resource definitions* (CRDs) to define a new set of Kubernetes resources specific to configuring it, which allows cluster administrators to use familiar tools like kubectl to operate Gatekeeper. In addition, it provides real-time, meaningful feedback to the user on why a resource was denied and how to remediate the problem. These Gatekeeper-specific custom resources can be stored in source control and managed using GitOps workflows.

Gatekeeper also performs *resource mutation* (resource modification based on defined conditions) and auditing. It is highly configurable and offers fine-grained control over what resources to evaluate and in which namespaces.

What Is Open Policy Agent?

At the core of Gatekeeper is Open Policy Agent (*https://oreil.ly/nbR5d*), a cloud native open source policy engine that is extensible and allows policy to be portable across different applications. Open Policy Agent (OPA) is responsible for performing all policy evaluations and returning either an admit or deny. This gives Gatekeeper access to an ecosystem of policy tooling, such as, Conftest (*https://oreil.ly/ElWYE*), which enables you to write policy tests and implement them in continuous integration pipelines before deployment.

Open Policy Agent exclusively uses a native query language called Rego (*https:// oreil.ly/Ar55f*) for all policies. One of the core tenets of Gatekeeper is to abstract the inner workings of Rego from the cluster administrator and present a structured API in the form of a Kubernetes CRD to create and apply policy. This lets you share parameterized policies across organizations and the community. The Gatekeeper project maintains a policy library solely for this purpose (discussed later in this chapter).

Installing Gatekeeper

Before you start configuring policies, you'll need to install Gatekeeper. Gatekeeper components run as Pods in the `gatekeeper-system` namespace and configure a webhook admission controller.

> Do not install Gatekeeper on a Kubernetes cluster without first understanding how to safely create and disable policy. You should also review the installation YAML before installing Gatekeeper to ensure that you are comfortable with the resources it creates.

You can install Gatekeeper using the Helm package manager:

```
$ helm repo add gatekeeper https://open-policy-agent.github.io/gatekeeper/charts
$ helm install gatekeeper/gatekeeper --name-template=gatekeeper \
  --namespace gatekeeper-system --create-
```

> Gatekeeper installation requires cluster-admin permissions and is version specific. Please refer to the official documentation for the latest release of Gatekeeper (*https://oreil.ly/GvLHc*).

Once the installation is complete, confirm that Gatekeeper is up and running:

```
$ kubectl get pods -n gatekeeper-system
NAME                                                READY  STATUS   RESTARTS  AGE
gatekeeper-audit-54c9759898-ljwp8                   1/1    Running  0         1m
gatekeeper-controller-manager-6bcc7f8fb5-4nbkt      1/1    Running  0         1m
gatekeeper-controller-manager-6bcc7f8fb5-d85rn      1/1    Running  0         1m
gatekeeper-controller-manager-6bcc7f8fb5-f8m8j      1/1    Running  0         1m
```

You can also review how the webhook is configured using this command:

```
$ kubectl get validatingwebhookconfiguration -o yaml
apiVersion: admissionregistration.k8s.io/v1
kind: ValidatingWebhookConfiguration
metadata:
```

```
    labels:
      gatekeeper.sh/system: "yes"
    name: gatekeeper-validating-webhook-configuration
webhooks:
- admissionReviewVersions:
  - v1
  - v1beta1
  clientConfig:
    service:
      name: gatekeeper-webhook-service
      namespace: gatekeeper-system
      path: /v1/admit
  failurePolicy: Ignore
  matchPolicy: Exact
  name: validation.gatekeeper.sh
  namespaceSelector:
    matchExpressions:
    - key: admission.gatekeeper.sh/ignore
      operator: DoesNotExist
  rules:
  - apiGroups:
    - '*'
    apiVersions:
    - '*'
    operations:
    - CREATE
    - UPDATE
    resources:
    - '*'
  sideEffects: None
  timeoutSeconds: 3
      ...
```

Under the `rules` section of the output above, we see that all resources are being
sent to the webhook admission controller, running as a service named `gatekeeper-`
`webhook-service` in the `gatekeeper-system` namespace. Only resources from namespaces that aren't labeled `admission.gatekeeper.sh/ignore` will be considered for
policy evaluation. Finally, the `failurePolicy` is set to `Ignore`, which means that
this is a *fail open configuration*: if the Gatekeeper service doesn't respond within the
configured timeout of three seconds, the request will be admitted.

Configuring Policies

Now that you have Gatekeeper installed, you can start configuring policies. We will
first go through a canonical example and demonstrate how the cluster administrator
creates policies. Then we'll look at the developer experience when creating compliant
and noncompliant resources. We will then expand on each step to gain a deeper
understanding, and walk you through the process of creating a sample policy stating

that container images can only come from one specific registry. This example is based on the Gatekeeper policy library (*https://oreil.ly/ikfZk*).

First, you'll need to configure the policy we need to create a custom resource called a *constraint template*. This is usually done by a cluster administrator. The constraint template in Example 20-1 requires you to provide a list of container repositories as parameters that Kubernetes resources are allowed to use.

Example 20-1. allowedrepos-constraint-template.yaml

```
apiVersion: templates.gatekeeper.sh/v1beta1
kind: ConstraintTemplate
metadata:
  name: k8sallowedrepos
  annotations:
    description: Requires container images to begin with a repo string from a
      specified list.
spec:
  crd:
    spec:
      names:
        kind: K8sAllowedRepos
      validation:
        # Schema for the `parameters` field
        openAPIV3Schema:
          properties:
            repos:
              type: array
              items:
                type: string
  targets:
    - target: admission.k8s.gatekeeper.sh
      rego: |
        package k8sallowedrepos

        violation[{"msg": msg}] {
          container := input.review.object.spec.containers[_]
          satisfied := [good | repo = input.parameters.repos[_] ; good = starts...
          not any(satisfied)
          msg := sprintf("container <%v> has an invalid image repo <%v>, allowed...
        }

        violation[{"msg": msg}] {
          container := input.review.object.spec.initContainers[_]
          satisfied := [good | repo = input.parameters.repos[_] ; good = starts...
          not any(satisfied)
          msg := sprintf("container <%v> has an invalid image repo <%v>, allowed...)
        }
```

Create the constraint template using the following command:

```
$ kubectl apply -f allowedrepos-constraint-template.yaml
constrainttemplate.templates.gatekeeper.sh/k8sallowedrepos created
```

Now you can create a constraint resource to put the policy into effect (again, playing the role of the cluster administrator). The constraint in Example 20-2 allows all containers with the prefix of gcr.io/kuar-demo/ in the default namespace. The enforcementAction is set to "deny": any noncompliant resources will be denied.

Example 20-2. allowedrepos-constraint.yaml

```
apiVersion: constraints.gatekeeper.sh/v1beta1
kind: K8sAllowedRepos
metadata:
  name: repo-is-kuar-demo
spec:
  enforcementAction: deny
  match:
    kinds:
      - apiGroups: [""]
        kinds: ["Pod"]
    namespaces:
      - "default"
  parameters:
    repos:
      - "gcr.io/kuar-demo/"
```

```
$ kubectl create -f allowedrepos-constraint.yaml
k8sallowedrepos.constraints.gatekeeper.sh/repo-is-kuar-demo created
```

The next step is to create some Pods to test that the policy is indeed working. Example 20-3 creates a Pod using a container image, gcr.io/kuar-demo/kuard-amd64:blue, that complies with the constraint we defined in the previous step. Workload resource creation is typically performed by the developer responsible for operating the service or a continuous delivery pipeline.

Example 20-3. compliant-pod.yaml

```
apiVersion: v1
kind: Pod
metadata:
  name: kuard
spec:
  containers:
    - image: gcr.io/kuar-demo/kuard-amd64:blue
      name: kuard
      ports:
        - containerPort: 8080
          name: http
          protocol: TCP
```

```
$ kubectl apply -f compliant-pod.yaml
pod/kuard created
```

What happens if we create a noncompliant Pod? Example 20-4 creates a Pod using a container image, nginx, that is *not* compliant with the constraint we defined in the previous step. Workload resource creation would typically be performed by the developer or continuous delivery pipeline responsible for operating the service. Note the output in Example 20-4.

Example 20-4. noncompliant-pod.yaml

```
apiVersion: v1
kind: Pod
metadata:
  name: nginx-noncompliant
spec:
  containers:
    - name: nginx
      image: nginx
```

```
$ kubectl apply -f noncompliant-pod.yaml
Error from server ([repo-is-kuar-demo] container <nginx> has an invalid image
repo <nginx>, allowed repos are ["gcr.io/kuar-demo/"]): error when creating
"noncompliant-pod.yaml": admission webhook "validation.gatekeeper.sh" denied
the request: [repo-is-kuar-demo] container <nginx> has an invalid image
repo <nginx>, allowed repos are ["gcr.io/kuar-demo/"]
```

Example 20-4 shows that an error is returned to the user with details on why the resource was not created and how to remediate the issue. Cluster administrators can configure the error message in the constraint template.

 If your constraint's scope is Pods and you create a resource that generates Pods, such as ReplicaSets, Gatekeeper will return an error. However, it won't be returned to you, the user, but to the controller trying to create the Pod. To see these error messages, look in the event log for the relevant resource.

Understanding Constraint Templates

Now that we have walked through a canonical example, take a closer look at the constraint template in Example 20-1, which takes a list of container repositories that are allowed in Kubernetes resources.

This constraint template has an apiVersion and kind that are part of the custom resources used only by Gatekeeper. Under the spec section, you'll see the name K8sAllowedRepos: remember that name, because you'll use it as the constraint kind when creating constraints. You'll also see a schema that defines an array of strings for the cluster administrator to configure. This is done by providing a list of allowed container registries. It also contains the raw Rego policy definition (under the `target` section). This policy evaluates containers and initContainers to ensure that the container repository name starts with the values provided by the constraint. The `msg` section defines the message that is sent back to the user if the policy is violated.

Creating Constraints

To instantiate a policy, you must create a constraint that provides the template's required parameters. There may be many constraints that match the kind of a specific constraint template. Let's take a closer look at the constraint we used in Example 20-2, which allows only container images that originate from *gcr.io/kuar-demo/*.

You may notice that the constraint is of the kind "K8sAllowedRepos," which was defined as part of the constraint template. It also defines an `enforcementAction` of "deny," meaning that noncompliant resources will be denied. `enforcementAction` also accepts "dryrun" and "warn": "dryrun" uses the audit feature to test policies and verify their impact; "warn" sends a warning back to the user with the associated message, but allows them to create or update. The `match` portion defines the scope of this constraint, all Pods in the default namespace. Finally, the `parameters` section is required to satisfy the constraint template (an array of strings). The following demonstrates the user experience when the `enforcementAction` is set to "warn":

```
$ kubectl apply -f noncompliant-pod.yaml
Warning: [repo-is-kuar-demo] container <nginx> has an invalid image repo...
pod/nginx-noncompliant created
```

Constraints are only enforced on resource CREATE and UPDATE events. If you already have workloads running on a cluster, Gatekeeper will not reevaluate them until a CREATE or UPDATE event takes place.

Here is a real-world example to demonstrate: say you create a policy that only allows containers from a specific registry. All workloads that are already running on the cluster will continue to do so. If you scale the workload Deployment from 1 to 2, the ReplicaSet will attempt to create another Pod. If that Pod doesn't have a container from an allowed repository, then it will be denied. It's important to set the `enforcementAction` to "dryrun" and audit to confirm that any policy violations are known before setting the `enforcementAction` to "deny."

Audit

Being able to enforce policy on new resources is only one piece of the policy and governance story. Policies often change over time, and you can also use Gatekeeper to confirm that everything currently deployed is still compliant. Additionally, you may already have a cluster full of services and wish to install Gatekeeper to bring these resources into compliance. Gatekeeper's audit capabilities allow cluster administrators to get a list of current, noncompliant resources on a cluster.

To demonstrate how auditing works, let's look at an example. We're going to update the `repo-is-kuar-demo` constraint to have an `enforcementAction` action of "dryrun" (as shown in Example 20-5). This will allow users to create noncompliant resources. We will then determine which resources are noncompliant using audit.

Example 20-5. allowedrepos-constraint-dryrun.yaml

```
apiVersion: constraints.gatekeeper.sh/v1beta1
kind: K8sAllowedRepos
metadata:
  name: repo-is-kuar-demo
spec:
  enforcementAction: dryrun
  match:
    kinds:
      - apiGroups: [""]
        kinds: ["Pod"]
    namespaces:
      - "default"
  parameters:
    repos:
      - "gcr.io/kuar-demo/"
```

Update the constraint by running the following command:

```
$ kubectl apply -f allowedrepos-constraint-dryrun.yaml
k8sallowedrepos.constraints.gatekeeper.sh/repo-is-kuar-demo configured
```

Create a noncompliant Pod using the following command:

```
$ kubectl apply -f noncompliant-pod.yaml
pod/nginx-noncompliant created
```

To audit the list of noncompliant resources for a given constraint, run a `kubectl get constraint` on that constraint and specify that you want the output in YAML format as follows:

```
$ kubectl get constraint repo-is-kuar-demo -o yaml
apiVersion: constraints.gatekeeper.sh/v1beta1
kind: K8sAllowedRepos
...
```

```
spec:
  enforcementAction: dryrun
  match:
    kinds:
    - apiGroups:
      - ""
      kinds:
      - Pod
    namespaces:
    - default
  parameters:
    repos:
    - gcr.io/kuar-demo/
status:
  auditTimestamp: "2021-07-14T20:05:38Z"
      ...
  totalViolations: 1
  violations:
  - enforcementAction: dryrun
    kind: Pod
    message: container <nginx> has an invalid image repo <nginx>, allowed repos
      are ["gcr.io/kuar-demo/"]
    name: nginx-noncompliant
    namespace: default
```

Under the `status` section, you can see the `auditTimestamp`, which is the last time
the audit was run. `totalViolations` lists the number of resources that violate this
constraint. The `violations` section lists the violations. We can see that the nginx-
noncompliant Pod is in violation and the message with the details why.

> Using a constraint `enforcementAction` of "dryrun" along with
> audit is a powerful way to confirm that your policy is having the
> desired impact. It also creates a workflow to bring resources into
> compliance.

Mutation

So far we have covered how you can use constraints to validate if a resource is compliant. What about modifying resources to make them compliant? This is handled via
the mutation feature in Gatekeeper. Earlier in this chapter, we discussed two different
type of admission webhooks, mutating and validating. By default, Gatekeeper is only
deployed as a validating admission webhook, but it can be configured to operate as a
mutating admission webhook.

Mutation features in Gatekeeper are in beta state and may change. We share them to demonstrate Gatekeeper's upcoming capabilities. The installation steps in this chapter do not cover enabling mutation. Please refer to the Gatekeeper project for more information on enabling mutation (*https://oreil.ly/DQKhl*).

Let's walk through an example to demonstrate the power of mutation. In this example, we will set the `imagePullPolicy` to "Always" on all Pods. We will assume that Gatekeeper is configured correctly to support mutation. Example 20-6 defines a mutation assignment that matches all Pods except those in the "system" namespace, and assigns a value of "Always" to `imagePullPolicy`.

Example 20-6. imagepullpolicyalways-mutation.yaml

```
apiVersion: mutations.gatekeeper.sh/v1alpha1
kind: Assign
metadata:
  name: demo-image-pull-policy
spec:
  applyTo:
  - groups: [""]
    kinds: ["Pod"]
    versions: ["v1"]
  match:
    scope: Namespaced
    kinds:
    - apiGroups: ["*"]
      kinds: ["Pod"]
    excludedNamespaces: ["system"]
  location: "spec.containers[name:*].imagePullPolicy"
  parameters:
    assign:
      value: Always
```

Create the mutation assignment:

```
$ kubectl apply -f imagepullpolicyalways-mutation.yaml
assign.mutations.gatekeeper.sh/demo-image-pull-policy created
```

Now create a Pod. This Pod doesn't have `imagePullPolicy` explicitly set, so by default this field is set to "IfNotPresent." However, we expect Gatekeeper to mutate this field to "Always":

```
$ kubectl apply -f compliant-pod.yaml
pod/kuard created
```

Validate that the `imagePullPolicy` has been successfully mutated to "Always" by running the following:

```
$ kubectl get pods kuard -o=jsonpath="{.spec.containers[0].imagePullPolicy}"
```

Always

 Mutating admission happens before validating admission, so create constraints that validate the mutations you expect to apply to the specific resource.

Delete the Pod using the following command:

```
$ kubectl delete -f compliant-pod.yaml
pod/kuard deleted
```

Delete the mutation assignment using the following command:

```
$ kubectl delete -f imagepullpolicyalways-mutation.yaml
assign.mutations.gatekeeper.sh/demo-image-pull-policy deleted
```

Unlike validation, mutation provides a way to remediate noncompliant resources automatically on behalf of the cluster administrator.

Data Replication

When writing constraints you may want to compare the value of one field to the value of a field in another resource. A specific example of when you might need to do this is making sure that ingress hostnames are unique across a cluster. By default, Gatekeeper can only evaluate fields within the current resource: if comparisons across resources are required to fulfill a policy, it must be configured. Gatekeeper can be configured to cache specific resources into Open Policy Agent to allow comparisons across resources. The resource in Example 20-7 configures Gatekeeper to cache Namespace and Pod resources.

Example 20-7. config-sync.yaml

```
apiVersion: config.gatekeeper.sh/v1alpha1
kind: Config
metadata:
  name: config
  namespace: "gatekeeper-system"
spec:
  sync:
    syncOnly:
      - group: ""
        version: "v1"
        kind: "Namespace"
      - group: ""
```

```
version: "v1"
kind: "Pod"
```

 You should only cache the specific resources needed to perform a policy evaluation. Having hundreds or thousands of resources cached in OPA will require more memory and may also have security implications.

The constraint template in Example 20-8 demonstrates how to compare something in the Rego section (in this case, unique ingress hostnames). Specifically, "data.inventory" refers to the cache resources, as opposed to "input," which is the resource sent for evaluation from the Kubernetes API server as part of the admission flow. This example is based on the Gatekeeper policy library (*https://oreil.ly/gGrts*).

Example 20-8. uniqueingresshost-constraint-template.yaml

```
apiVersion: templates.gatekeeper.sh/v1beta1
kind: ConstraintTemplate
metadata:
  name: k8suniqueingresshost
  annotations:
    description: Requires all Ingress hosts to be unique.
spec:
  crd:
    spec:
      names:
        kind: K8sUniqueIngressHost
  targets:
    - target: admission.k8s.gatekeeper.sh
      rego: |
        package k8suniqueingresshost

        identical(obj, review) {
          obj.metadata.namespace == review.object.metadata.namespace
          obj.metadata.name == review.object.metadata.name
        }

        violation[{"msg": msg}] {
          input.review.kind.kind == "Ingress"
          re_match("^(extensions|networking.k8s.io)$", input.review.kind.group)
          host := input.review.object.spec.rules[_].host
          other := data.inventory.namespace[ns][otherapiversion]["Ingress"][name]
          re_match("^(extensions|networking.k8s.io)/.+$", otherapiversion)
          other.spec.rules[_].host == host
          not identical(other, input.review)
          msg := sprintf("ingress host conflicts with an existing ingress <%v>"...
        }
```

Data replication is a powerful tool that allows you to make comparisons across Kubernetes resources. We recommend only configuring it if you have policies that require it to function. If you use it, scope it only to the relevant resources.

Metrics

Gatekeeper emits metrics in Prometheus format to enable continuous resource compliance monitoring. You can view simple metrics regarding Gatekeeper's overall health, such as the numbers of constraints, constraint templates, and requests being set to Gatekeeper.

In addition, details on policy compliance and governance are also available:

- The total number of audit violations
- Number of constraints by enforcementAction
- Audit duration

 Completely automating the policy and governance process is the ideal goal, so we strongly recommended that you monitor Gatekeeper from an external monitoring system and set alerts based on resource compliance.

Policy Library

One of the core tenets of the Gatekeeper project is to create reusable policy libraries that can be shared between organizations. Being able to share policies reduces boilerplate policy work and allows cluster administrators to focus on applying policy rather than writing it. The Gatekeeper project has a great policy library (*https://oreil.ly/uBY2h*). It contains a general library with the most common policies as well as a *pod-security-policy* library that models the capabilities of the PodSecurityPolicy API as Gatekeeper policy. The great thing about this library is that it is always expanding and is open source, so feel free to contribute any policies that you write.

Summary

In this chapter, you've learned about policy and governance and why they are important as more and more resources are deployed to Kubernetes. We covered the Gatekeeper project, a Kubernetes-native policy controller built on Open Policy Agent, and showed you to use it to meet your policy and governance requirements. From writing policies to auditing, you are now equipped with the know-how to meet your compliance needs.

## CHAPTER 21

Multicluster Application Deployments

Twenty chapters into this book, it should be clear that Kubernetes can be a complex topic, though of course we hope that if you have made it this far, it is less murky than it was. Given the complexities of building and running an application in a single Kubernetes cluster, why would you incur the added complexity of designing and deploying your application into multiple clusters?

The truth is that the demands of the real world mean that multicluster application deployment is a reality for most applications. There are many reasons for this, and it is likely that your application fits under at least one of these requirements.

The first requirement is one of redundancy and resiliency. Whether in the cloud or on-premise, a single datacenter is generally a single failure domain. Whether it is a hunter using a fiber-optic cable for target practice, a power outage from an ice storm, or simply a botched software rollout, any application deployed to a single location can fail completely and leave your users without recourse. In many cases, a single Kubernetes cluster is tied to a single location and thus is a single failure domain.

In some cases, especially in cloud environments, the Kubernetes cluster is designed to be *regional*. Regional clusters span across multiple independent zones and are thus resilient to the problems in the underlying infrastructure previously described. It would be tempting then to assume that such regional clusters are sufficient for resiliency and they might be except for the fact that Kubernetes itself can be a single point of failure. Any single Kubernetes cluster is tied to a specific version of Kubernetes (e.g., 1.21.3), and it is very possible for an upgrade of the cluster to break your application. From time to time Kubernetes deprecates APIs or changes the behavior of those APIs. These changes are infrequent, and the Kubernetes community takes care to make sure that they are communicated ahead of time. Additionally, despite a great deal of testing, bugs do creep into a release from time to time. Though it is unlikely for any one issue to affect your application, viewed over the lifespan of most applications (years), it's probable that your application will be affected at some point. For most applications, that's not aa\n acceptable risk.

In addition to resiliency requirements, another strong driver of multicluster deployments is some business or application need for regional affinity. For example, game servers have a strong need to be near the players to reduce network latency and improve the playing experience. Other applications may be subject to legal or regulatory requirements that demand that data be located within specific geographic regions. Since any Kubernetes cluster is tied to a specific place, these needs for application deployment to specific geographies mean that applications must span multiple clusters.

Finally, though there are numerous ways to isolate users within a single cluster (e.g., namespaces, RBAC, node pools—collections of Kubernetes nodes that are organized for different capabilities or workloads), a Kubernetes cluster is still largely a single cooperative space. For some teams and some products, the risks of a different team impacting their application, even by accident, are not worth it, and they would rather take on the complexity of managing multiple clusters.

At this point, you can see that regardless of your application, it's very likely that either now or sometime in the near future, your application will need to span multiple clusters. The rest of this chapter will help you understand how to accomplish that.

Before You Even Begin

It is critical that you have the right foundations in place in a single cluster deployment before you consider moving to multiple clusters. There is inevitably a list of to-do items that everyone has for their setup, but such shortcuts and problems are magnified in a multicluster deployment. Similarly, fixing foundational problems in your infrastructure is 10 times harder when you have 10 clusters. Furthermore, if adding an additional cluster incurs significant extra work, you will resist adding additional clusters, when (for all of the reasons already given) it is the right thing to do for your application.

When we say "foundations," what do we mean? The most important part to get right is automation. Importantly, this includes both automation to deploy your application(s), but also automation to create and manage the clusters themselves. When you have a single cluster, it is consistent with itself by definition. However, when you add clusters, you add the possibility of version skew between all of the pieces of your cluster. You could have clusters with different Kubernetes versions, different versions of your monitoring and logging agents, or even something as basic as the container runtime. All of this variance should be viewed as something that makes your life harder. Differences in your infrastructure make your system "weirder." Knowledge gained in one cluster does not transfer over to other clusters, and problems sometimes occur seemingly at random in certain places because of this variability. One of the most important parts of maintaining a stable foundation is maintaining consistency across all of your clusters.

The only way to achieve this consistency is automation. You may think, "I always create clusters this way," but experience has taught us that this is simply not true. The next chapter discusses at length the value of infrastructure as code for managing your applications, but the same things apply to managing your clusters. Don't use a GUI or CLI tool to create your cluster. It may seem cumbersome at first to push all changes through source control and CI/CD, but the stable foundation pays significant dividends.

The same is true of the foundational components that you deploy into your clusters. These components include monitoring, logging, and security scanners, which need to be present before any application is deployed. These tools also need to be managed using infrastructure as code tools like Helm and deployed using automation.

Moving beyond the shape of your clusters, there are other aspects of consistency that are necessary. The first is using a single identity system for all of your clusters. Though Kubernetes supports simple certificate-based authentication, we strongly suggest using integrations with a global identity provider, such as Azure Active Directory or any other OpenID Connect–compatible identity provider. Ensuring that everyone uses the same identity when accessing all of the clusters is a critical part of maintaining security best practices and avoiding dangerous behaviors like sharing certificates. Additionally, most of these identity providers make available additional security controls like two-factor authentication, which enhance the security of your clusters.

Just like identity, it is also critical to ensure consistent access control to your clusters. In most clouds, this means using a cloud-based RBAC, where the RBAC roles and bindings are stored in a central cloud location rather than in the clusters themselves. Defining RBAC in a single location prevents mistakes like leaving permissions behind in one of your clusters or failing to add permissions to some single cluster. Unfortunately, if you are defining RBAC for on-premise clusters, the situation is somewhat more complicated than it is for identity. There are some solutions (e.g., Azure Arc for Kubernetes) that can provide RBAC for on-premise clusters, but if such a service is not available in your environment, defining RBAC in source control and using infrastructure as code to apply the rules to all of your clusters can ensure consistent privileges are applied across your fleet.

Similarly, when you think about defining policy for your clusters, it's critical to define those policies in a single place and have a single dashboard for viewing the compliance state of all clusters. As with RBAC, such global services are often available via your cloud provider, but for on-premise there are limited options. Using infrastructure as code for policies as well can help close this gap and ensure that you can define your policies in a single place.

Just like setting up the right unit testing and build infrastructure is critical to your application development, setting up the right foundation for managing multiple Kubernetes clusters sets the stage for stable application deployments across a broad fleet of infrastructure. In the coming sections, we'll talk about how to build your application to operate successfully in a multicluster environment.

Starting at the Top with a Load-Balancing Approach

Once you begin to think about deploying your application into multiple locations, it becomes essential to think about how users get access to it. Typically this is through a domain name (e.g., my.company.com). Though we will spend a great deal of time discussing how to construct your application for operation in multiple locations, a more important place to start is how access is implemented. This is both because obviously enabling people to use your application is essential, but also because the design of how people access your application can improve your ability to quickly respond and reroute traffic in the case of unexpected load or failures.

Access to your application starts with a domain name. This means that the start of your multicluster load-balancing strategy starts with a DNS lookup. This DNS lookup is the first choice in your load-balancing strategy. In many traditional load-balancing approaches, this DNS lookup was used for routing traffic to specific locations. This is generally referred to as "GeoDNS." In GeoDNS, the IP address returned by the DNS lookup is tied to the physical location of the client. The IP address is generally the regional cluster that is closest to the client.

Though GeoDNS is still prevalent in many applications and may be the only possible approach for on-premise applications, it has a number of drawbacks. The first is that DNS is cached in various places throughout the internet and though you can set the time-to-live (TTL) for a DNS lookup, there are many places where this TTL is ignored in pursuit of higher performance. In a steady state operation, this caching isn't a big deal since DNS is generally pretty stable regardless of the TTL. However, it becomes a very big deal when you need to move traffic from one cluster to another; for example, in response to an outage in a particular datacenter. In such urgent cases, the fact that DNS lookups are cached can significantly extend the duration and impact of the outage. Additionally, since GeoDNS is guessing your physical location based on your client's IP address, it is frequently confused and guesses the wrong locations when many different clients egress their traffic from the same firewall's IP address despite being in many different geographic locations.

The other alternative to using DNS to select your cluster is a load-balancing technique known as *anycast*. With anycast networking, a single static IP address is advertised from multiple locations around the internet using core routing protocols. While traditionally we think of an IP address mapping to a single machine, with anycast networking the IP address is actually a virtual IP address that is routed to a different location depending on your network location. Your traffic is routed to the "closest" location based on the distance in terms of network performance rather than geographic distance. Anycast networking generally produces better results, but it is not always available in all environments.

One final consideration as you design your load balancing is whether the load balancing happens at the TCP or HTTP level. So far we have only discussed TCP-level balancing, but for web-based applications there are significant benefits for load-balancing at the HTTP layer. If you are writing an HTTP-based application (as most applications these days are), then using a global HTTP-aware load balancer enables you to be aware of more details of the client communication. For example, you can make load-balancing decisions based on cookies that have been set in the browser. Additionally, a load balancer that is aware of the protocol can make smarter routing decisions since it sees each HTTP request instead of just a stream of bytes across a TCP connection.

Regardless of which approach you choose, ultimately the location of your service is mapped from a global DNS endpoint to a collection of regional IP addresses representing the entry point to your service. These IP addresses are generally the IP address of a Kubernetes Service or Ingress resource that you have learned about in previous chapters of the book. Once the user traffic hits that endpoint, it will flow through your cluster based on the design of your application.

Building Applications for Multiple Clusters

Once you have load balancing sorted out, the next challenge for designing a multi-cluster application is thinking about state. Ideally, your application doesn't require state, or all of the state is read-only. In such circumstances, there is little that you need to do to support multiple cluster deployments. Your application can be deployed individually to each of your clusters, a load balancer added to the top, and your multicluster deployment is complete. Unfortunately, for most applications there is state that must be managed in a consistent way across the replicas of your application. If you don't handle state correctly, your users will end up with a confusing, flawed experience.

To understand how replicated state impacts user experience, let's use a simple retail shop as an example. It's obvious to see that if you only store a customer's order in one of your multiple clusters, the customer may have the unsettling experience of being unable to see their order when their requests move to a different region, either because of load balancing, or because they physically move geographies. So it is clear that a user's state needs to be replicated across regions. It may be somewhat less clear that the approach to replication also can impact the customer experience. The challenges of replicated data and customer experience is succinctly captured by this question: "Can I read my own write?" It may seem obvious that the answer should be "Yes," but achieving this is harder than it seems. Consider for example a customer who places an order on their computer, but then immediately tries to view it on their phone. They may be coming at your application from two entirely different networks and consequently landing on two completly different clusters. A user's expectation around their ability to see an order that they just placed is an example of data *consistency*.

Consistency governs how you think about replicating data. We assume that we want our data to be consistent; that is, that we will be able to read the same data regardless of where we read it from. But the complicating factor is time: how quickly must our data be consistent? And do we get any sort of error indication when it is not consistent? There are two basic models of consistency: *strong consistency*, which guarantees that a write doesn't succeed until it has been successfully replicated, and *eventual consistency*, where a write always succeeds immediately and is only guaranteed to be successfully replicated at some later point in time. Some systems also provide the ability for the client to choose their consistency needs per request. For example, Azure Cosmos DB implements *bounded consistency*, where there are some assurances about how stale data may be in an eventually consistent system. Google Cloud Spanner enables clients to specify that they are willing to tolerate stale reads in exchange for better performance.

It might seem that everyone would choose strong consistency, as it is clearly an easier model to reason about because the data is always the same everywhere. But strong consistency comes at a price. It takes much more effort to guarantee the replication at the time of the write, and many more writes will fail when replication isn't possible. Strong consistency is more expensive and can support many fewer simultaneous transactions relative to eventual consistency. Eventual consistency is cheaper and can support a much higher write load, but it is more complicated for the application developer and may expose some edge conditions to the end user. Many storage systems support only a single concurrency model. Those that support multiple concurrency models require that it be specified when the storage system is created. Your choice of concurrency model also has significant implications for your application's design and is difficult to change. Consequently, choosing your consistency model is an important first step before designing your application for multiple environments.

Deploying and managing replicated stateful storage is a complicated task that requires a dedicated team with domain expertise to set up, maintain, and monitor. You should strongly consider using cloud-based storage for a replicated data store so that this burden is carried by the depth of a large team at the cloud provider rather than your own teams. In an on-premise environment, you can also offload support of storage to a company that has focused expertise on running the storage solution that you choose. Only when you are at large scale does it make sense to invest in building your own team to manage storage.

Once you have determined your storage layer, the next step is to build up your application design.

Replicated Silos: The Simplest Cross-Regional Model

The simplest way to replicate your application across multiple clusters and multiple regions is simply to copy your application into every region. Each instance of your application is an exact clone and looks exactly alike no matter which cluster it is running in. Because there is a load balancer at the top spreading customer requests, and you have implemented data replication in the places where you need state, your application doesn't need to change much to support this model. Depending on the consistency model that you choose for your data, you will need to deal with the fact that data may not be replicated quickly between regions, but, especially if you opt for strong consistency, this won't require major application refactoring.

When you design your application this way, each region is its own silo. All of the data that it needs is present within the region, and once a request enters that region, it is served entirely by the containers running in that one cluster. This has significant benefits in terms of reduced complexity, but as is always the case, this comes at the cost of efficiency.

To understand how the silo approach impacts efficiency, consider an application that is distributed to a large number of geographic regions around the world in order to deliver very low latency to their users. The reality of the world is that some geographic regions have large populations and some regions have small populations. If every silo in each cluster of the application is exactly the same, then every silo has to be sized to meet the needs of the largest geographic region. The result of this is that most replicas of the application in regional clusters are massively overprovisioned and thus cost efficiency for the application is low. The obvious solution to this excess cost is to reduce the size of the resources used by the application in the smaller geographic regions. While it might seem easy to resize your application, it's not always feasible due to bottlenecks or other requirements (e.g., maintaining at least three replicas).

Especially when taking an existing application from single cluster to multicluster, a replicated silos design is the easiest approach to use, but it is worth understanding that it comes with costs that may be sustainable initially but eventually will require your application to be refactored.

Sharding: Regional Data

As your application scales, one of the pain points that you are likely to encounter with a regional silo approach is that globally replicating all of your data becomes increasingly expensive and also increasingly wasteful. While replicating data for reliability is a good thing, it is unlikely that all of the data for your application needs to be colocated in every cluster where you deploy your application. Most users will only access your application from a small number of geographic regions.

Additionally, as your application grows around the world you may encounter regulatory and other legal requirements around data locality. There may be external restrictions on where you can store a user's data depending on their nationality or other considerations. The combination of these requirements means that eventually you will need to think about regional data sharding. Sharding your data across regions means that not all data is present in all of the clusters where your application is present and this (obviously) impacts the design of your application.

As an example of what this looks like, imagine that our application is deployed into six regional clusters (A, B, C, D, E, F). We take the dataset for our application and break the data into three subsets or *shards* (1, 2, 3).

Our data shard deployment then might look as follows:

```
   A   B   C   D   E   F
1  ✓   -   -   ✓   -   -
2  -   ✓   -   -   ✓   -
3  -   -   ✓   -   -   ✓
```

Each shard is present in two regions for redundancy, but each regional cluster can only serve one-third of the data. This means that you have to add an additional routing layer to your service whenever you need to access the data. The routing layer is responsible for determining whether the request needs to go to a local or cross-regional data shard.

While it might be tempting to simply implement this data routing as part of a client library that is linked into your main application, we strongly recommend that the data routing be built as a separate microservice. Introducing a new microservice might seem to introduce complexity, but it actually introduces an abstraction that simplifies things. Instead of every service in your application worrying about data routing, you have a single service that encapsulates those concerns and all other services simply access the data service. Applications that are separated into independent microservices provide significant flexibility in multicluster environments.

Better Flexibility: Microservice Routing

When we discussed the regional silo approach to multicluster application development, we gave an example of how it might reduce the cost-efficiency of your deployed multicluster application. But there are other impacts to flexibility as well. In creating the silo, you are creating at a larger scale the same sort of monoliths that containers and Kubernetes seek to break up. Furthermore, you are forcing every microservice within an application to scale at the same time to the same number of regions.

If your application is small and contained, this may make sense, but as your services become larger, and especially when they may start being shared between multiple applications, the monolithic approach to multicluster begins to significantly impact your flexibility. If a cluster is the unit of deployment and all of your CI/CD is tied to that cluster, you will force every team to adhere to the same rollout process and schedule even if it is a bad fit.

For a concrete example of this, suppose you have one very large application that is deployed to thirty clusters, and a small new application under development. It doesn't make sense to force the small team developing a new application to immediately reach the scale of your larger application, but if you are too rigid in your application design, this can be exactly what happens.

A better approach is to treat each microservice within your application as a public-facing service in terms of its application design. It may never be expected to actually be public facing, but it should have its own global load balancer as described in the previous sections, and it should manage its own data replication service. For all intents and purposes, the different microservices should be independent of each other. When a service calls into a different service, its load is balanced in the same way that an external load would be. With this abstraction in place, each team can scale and deploy their multicluster service independently, just like they do within a single cluster.

Of course, doing this for every single microservice within an application can become a significant burden on your teams and can also increase costs via the maintenance of a load balancer for each service and also possibly cross-regional network traffic. Like everything in software design, there is a trade-off between complexity and performance, and you will need to determine for your application the right places to add the isolation of a service boundary, and where it makes sense to group services into a replicated silo. Just like microservices in the single cluster context, this design is likely to change and adapt as your application changes and grows. Expecting (and designing) with this fluidity in mind will help ensure that your application can adapt without requiring massive refactoring.

Summary

Though deploying your application to multiple clusters adds complexity, the requirements and user expectations in the real world make this complexity necessary for most applications that you build. Designing your application and your infrastructure from the ground up to support multicluster application deployments will greatly increase the reliability of your application and significantly reduce the probability of a costly refactor as your application grows. One of the most important pieces of a multicluster deployment is managing the configuration and deployment of the application to the cluster. Whether your application is regional or multicluster, the following chapter will help ensure that you can quickly and reliably deploy it.

## CHAPTER 22

Organizing Your Application

Throughout this book we have described various components of an application built on top of Kubernetes. We have described how to wrap programs up as containers, place those containers in Pods, replicate those Pods with ReplicaSets, and roll them out with Deployments. We have even described how to deploy stateful and real-world applications that collect these objects into a single distributed system. But we have not covered how to actually work with such an application in a practical way. How can you lay out, share, manage, and update the various configurations that make up your application? That is the topic of this chapter.

Principles to Guide Us

Before digging into the concrete details of how to structure your application, it's worth considering the goals that drive this structure. Obviously, reliability and agility are the general goals of developing a cloud native application in Kubernetes, but how does this relate to how you design your application's maintenance and deployment? The following sections describe three principles that can guide you in designing a structure that best suits these goals. The principles are:

- Treat filesystems as the source of truth
- Conduct code review to ensure the quality of changes
- Use feature flags to stage rollouts and rollbacks

Filesystems as the Source of Truth

When you first begin to explore Kubernetes, as we did in the beginning of this book, you generally interact with it imperatively. You run commands like kubectl run or `kubectl edit` to create and modify Pods or other objects running in your cluster. Even when we started exploring how to write and use YAML files, this was presented in an ad-hoc manner, as if the file itself is just a way station on the road to modifying the state of the cluster. In reality, in a true productionized application the opposite should be true.

Rather than viewing the state of the cluster—the data in `etcd`—as the source of truth, it is optimal to view the filesystem of YAML objects as the source of truth for your application. The API objects deployed into your Kubernetes cluster(s) are then a reflection of the truth stored in the filesystem.

There are numerous reasons why this is the right point of view. The first and foremost is that it largely enables you to treat your cluster as if it is immutable infrastructure. As we have moved into cloud native architectures, we have become increasingly comfortable with the notion that our applications and their containers are immutable infrastructure, but treating a cluster as such is less common. And yet, the same reasons for moving our applications to immutable infrastructure apply to our clusters. If your cluster is a snowflake you made by applying random YAML files downloaded from the internet ad hoc, it is as dangerous as a virtual machine built from imperative bash scripts.

Additionally, managing the cluster state via the filesystem makes it very easy to collaborate with multiple team members. Source-control systems are well understood and can easily enable multiple people to edit the state of the cluster simultaneously, while making conflicts (and the resolution of those conflicts) clear to everyone.

 It is absolutely a first principle that *all applications deployed to Kubernetes should first be described in files stored in a filesystem*. The actual API objects are then just a projection of this filesystem into a particular cluster.

The Role of Code Review

It wasn't long ago that code review for application source code was a novel idea. But it is clear now that multiple people looking at a piece of code before it is committed to an application is a best practice for producing high-quality, reliable code.

It is therefore surprising that the same is somewhat less true for the configurations used to deploy those applications. All of the same reasons for reviewing code apply directly to application configurations. But when you think about it, it is also obvious that code review of these configurations is critical to the reliable deployment of services. In our experience, most service outages are self-inflicted via unexpected consequences, typos, or other simple mistakes. Ensuring that at least two people look at any configuration change significantly decreases the probability of such errors.

The second principle of our application layout is that it must facilitate the review of every change merged into the set of files that represents the source of truth for our cluster.

Feature Gates

Once your application source code and your deployment configuration files are in source control, one of the most common questions is how these repositories relate to one another. Should you use the same repository for application source code and configuration? This can work for small projects, but in larger projects it often makes sense to separate the two. Even if the same people are responsible for both building and deploying the application, the perspectives of the builder versus those of the deployer are different enough that this separation of concerns makes sense.

If that is the case, then how do you bridge the development of new features in source control with the deployment of those features into a production environment? This is where feature gates play an important role.

The idea is that when some new feature is developed, that development takes place entirely behind a feature flag or *gate*. This gate looks something like:

```
if (featureFlags.myFlag) {
    // Feature implementation goes here
}
```

There are a variety of benefits to this approach. First, it lets the team commit to the production branch long before the feature is ready to ship. This enables feature development to stay much more closely aligned with the HEAD of a repository, and thus you avoid the horrendous merge conflicts of a long-lived branch.

Working behind a feature flag also means that enabling a feature simply involves making a configuration change to activate the flag. This makes it very clear what changed in the production environment, and very simple to roll back the feature activation if it causes problems.

Using feature flags thus both simplifies debugging and ensures that disabling a feature doesn't require a binary rollback to an older version of the code that would remove all of the bug fixes and other improvements made by the newer version.

The third principle of application layout is that code lands in source control, by default off, behind a feature flag, and is only activated through a code-reviewed change to configuration files.

Managing Your Application in Source Control

Now that we have determined that the filesystem should represent the source of truth for your cluster, the next important question is how to actually lay out the files in the filesystem. Obviously, filesystems contain hierarchical directories, and a source-control system adds concepts like tags and branches, so this section describes how to put these together to represent and manage your application.

Filesystem Layout

This section describes how to lay out an instance of your application for a single cluster. In later sections, we will describe how to parameterize this layout for multiple instances. It's worth getting this organization right when you begin. Much like modifying the layout of packages in source control, modifying your deployment configurations after the fact is a complicated and expensive refactor that you'll probably never get around to.

The first cardinality on which you want to organize your application is the semantic component or layer (for instance, *frontend* or *batch work queue*). Though early on this might seem like overkill, since a single team manages all of these components, it sets the stage for team scaling—eventually, different teams (or subteams) may be responsible for each of these components.

Thus, for an application with a frontend that uses two services, the filesystem might look like this:

```
frontend/
service-1/
service-2/
```

Within each of these directories, the configurations for each application are stored. These are the YAML files that directly represent the current state of the cluster. It's generally useful to include both the service name and the object type within the same file.

 While Kubernetes allows you to create YAML files with multiple objects in the same file, this is generally an antipattern. The only good reason to group several objects in the same file is if they are conceptually identical. When deciding what to include in a single YAML file, consider design principles similar to those for defining a class or struct. If grouping the objects together doesn't form a single concept, they probably shouldn't be in a single file.

Thus, extending our previous example, the filesystem might look like:

```
frontend/
    frontend-deployment.yaml
    frontend-service.yaml
    frontend-ingress.yaml
service-1/
    service-1-deployment.yaml
    service-1-service.yaml
    service-1-configmap.yaml
...
```

Managing Periodic Versions

What about managing releases? It is very useful to be able to look back and see what your application deployment previously looked like. Similarly, it is very useful to be able to iterate a configuration forward while still deploying a stable release configuration.

Consequently, it's handy to be able to simultaneously store and maintain multiple revisions of your configuration. There are two different approaches that you can use with the file and version control systems we've outlined here. The first is to use tags, branches, and source-control features. This is convenient because it maps to the way people manage revisions in source control, and leads to a more simplified directory structure. The other option is to clone the configuration within the filesystem and use directories for different revisions. This makes viewing the configurations simultaneously very straightforward.

These approaches have the same capabilities in terms of managing different release versions, so it is ultimately an aesthetic choice between the two. We will discuss both approaches and let you or your team decide which you prefer.

Versioning with branches and tags

When you use branches and tags to manage configuration revisions, the directory structure does not change from the example in the previous section. When you are ready for a release, you place a source-control tag (such as git tag v1.0) in the configuration source-control system. The tag represents the configuration used for that version, and the HEAD of source control continues to iterate forward.

Updating the release configuration is somewhat more complicated, but the approach models what you would do in source control. First, you commit the change to the HEAD of the repository. Then you create a new branch named v1 at the v1.0 tag. You cherry-pick the desired change onto the release branch (git cherry-pick *<edit>*), and finally, you tag this branch with the v1.1 tag to indicate a new point release. This approach is illustrated in Figure 22-1.

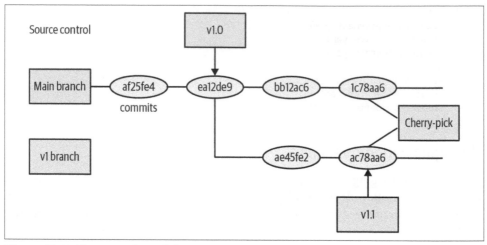

Figure 22-1. Cherry-pick workflow

One common error when cherry-picking fixes into a release branch is to only pick the change into the latest release. It's a good idea to cherry-pick it into all active releases, in case you need to roll back versions but the fix is still needed.

Versioning with directories

An alternative to using source-control features is to use filesystem features. In this approach, each versioned deployment exists within its own directory. For example, the filesystem for your application might look like this:

```
frontend/
  v1/
    frontend-deployment.yaml
    frontend-service.yaml
  current/
    frontend-deployment.yaml
    frontend-service.yaml
service-1/
  v1/
    service-1-deployment.yaml
    service-1-service.yaml
  v2/
    service-1-deployment.yaml
    service-1-service.yaml
  current/
    service-1-deployment.yaml
    service-1-service.yaml
...
```

Thus, each revision exists in a parallel directory structure within a directory associated with the release. All deployments occur from HEAD instead of from specific revisions or tags. You would add a new configuration to the files in the *current* directory.

When creating a new release, you copy the *current* directory to create a new directory associated with the new release.

When you're performing a bug-fix change to a release, your pull request must modify the YAML file in all the relevant release directories. This is a slightly better experience than the cherry-picking approach described earlier, since it is clear in a single change request that all of the relevant versions are being updated with the same change, instead of requiring a cherry-pick per version.

Structuring Your Application for Development, Testing, and Deployment

In addition to structuring your application for a periodic release cadence, you also want to structure your application to enable Agile development, quality testing, and safe deployment. This allows developers to make and test changes to the distributed application rapidly and roll those changes out to customers safely.

Goals

There are two goals for your application with regard to development and testing. The first is that each developer should be able to easily develop new features for the application. In most cases, the developer is only working on a single component, yet that component is interconnected to all of the other microservices within the cluster. Thus, to facilitate development, it is essential that developers be able to work in their own environment with all services available.

The other goal is to structure your application for easy and accurate testing prior to deployment. This is essential for rolling out features quickly while maintaining high reliability.

Progression of a Release

To achieve both of these goals, it is important to relate the stages of development to the release versions described earlier. The stages of a release are:

HEAD
    The bleeding edge of the configuration; the latest changes.

Development

Largely stable, but not ready for deployment. Suitable for developers to use for building features.

Staging

The beginnings of testing, unlikely to change unless problems are found.

Canary

The first real release to users, used to test for problems with real-world traffic and likewise give users a chance to test what is coming next.

Release

The current production release.

Introducing a development tag

Regardless of whether you structure releases using the filesystem or version control, the right way to model the development stage is via a source-control tag. This is because development is necessarily fast moving as it tracks stability only slightly behind HEAD.

To introduce a development stage, you add a new development tag to the source-control system and use an automated process to move this tag forward. On a periodic cadence, you'll test HEAD via automated integration testing. If these tests pass, you move the development tag forward to HEAD. Thus, developers can track reasonably close to the latest changes when deploying their own environments, but also be assured that the deployed configurations have at least passed a limited smoke test. This approach is illustrated in Figure 22-2.

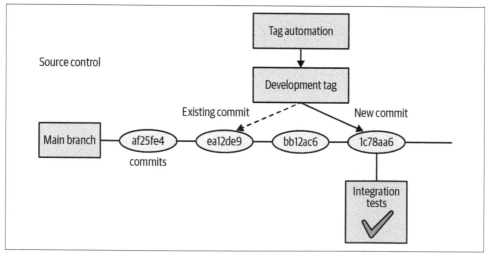

Figure 22-2. Development tag workflow

Mapping stages to revisions

It might be tempting to introduce a new set of configurations for each of these stages, but in reality, every combination of versions and stages would create a mess that would be very difficult to reason about. Instead, the right practice is to introduce a mapping between revisions and stages.

Regardless of whether you are using the filesystem or source-control revisions to represent different configuration versions, it is easy to implement a map from stage to revision. In the filesystem case, you can use symbolic links to map a stage name to a revision:

```
frontend/
   canary/ -> v2/
   release/ -> v1/
   v1/
      frontend-deployment.yaml
...
```

For version control, it is simply an additional tag at the same revision as the appropriate version.

In either case, versioning proceeds using the processes described previously, and the stages are moved forward to new versions separately as appropriate. In effect, this means that there are two simultaneous processes: the first for cutting new release versions and the second for qualifying a release version for a particular stage in the application life cycle.

Parameterizing Your Application with Templates

Once you have a Cartesian product of environments and stages, it becomes impractical or impossible to keep them all entirely identical. And yet, it is important to strive for the environments to be as identical as possible. Variance and drift between different environments produces snowflakes and systems that are hard to reason about. If your staging environment is different than your release environment, can you really trust the load tests that you ran in the staging environment to qualify a release? To ensure that your environments stay as similar as possible, it is useful to use parameterized environments. Parameterized environments use *templates* for the bulk of their configuration, but they mix in a limited set of *parameters* to produce the final configuration. In this way, most of the configuration is contained within a shared template, while the parameterization is limited in scope and maintained in a small parameters file for easy visualization of differences between environments.

Parameterizing with Helm and Templates

There are a variety of different languages for creating parameterized configurations. In general they all divide the files into a *template* file, which contains the bulk of the configuration, and a *parameters* file, which can be combined with the template to produce a complete configuration. In addition to parameters, most templating languages allow parameters to have default values if no value is specified.

The following gives examples of how to parameterize configurations using Helm (*https://helm.sh*), a package manager for Kubernetes. Despite what devotees of various languages may say, all parameterization languages are largely equivalent, and as with programming languages, which one you prefer is largely a matter of personal or team style. Thus, the patterns described here for Helm apply regardless of the templating language you choose.

The Helm template language uses "mustache" syntax:

```
metadata:
  name: {{ .Release.Name }}-deployment
```

This indicates that `Release.Name` should be substituted with the name of a deployment.

To pass a parameter for this value, you use a *values.yaml* file with contents like:

```
Release:
  Name: my-release
```

After parameter substitution, this results in:

```
metadata:
  name: my-release-deployment
```

Filesystem Layout for Parameterization

Now that you understand how to parameterize your configurations, how do you apply that to the filesystem layouts? Instead of treating each deployment life cycle stage as a pointer to a version, think of each deployment life cycle as the combination of a parameters file and a pointer to a specific version. For example, in a directory-based layout, it might look like this:

```
frontend/
  staging/
    templates -> ../v2
    staging-parameters.yaml
  production/
    templates -> ../v1
    production-parameters.yaml
  v1/
    frontend-deployment.yaml
    frontend-service.yaml
  v2/
    frontend-deployment.yaml
    frontend-service.yaml
  ...
```

Doing this with version control looks similar, except that the parameters for each life cycle stage are kept at the root of the configuration directory tree:

```
frontend/
  staging-parameters.yaml
  templates/
    frontend-deployment.YAML
...
```

Deploying Your Application Around the World

Now that you have multiple versions of your application moving through multiple stages of deployment, the final step in structuring your configurations is to deploy your application around the world. But don't think that these approaches are only for large-scale applications. You can use them to scale from two different regions to tens or hundreds around the world. In the cloud, where an entire region can fail, deploying to multiple regions (and managing that deployment) is the only way to achieve sufficient uptime for demanding users.

Architectures for Worldwide Deployment

Generally speaking, each Kubernetes cluster is intended to live in a single region and to contain a single, complete deployment of your application. Consequently, worldwide deployment of an application consists of multiple different Kubernetes clusters, each with its own application configuration. Describing how to actually build a worldwide application, especially with complex subjects like data replication, is beyond the scope of this chapter, but we will describe how to arrange the application configurations in the filesystem.

A particular region's configuration is conceptually the same as a stage in the deployment life cycle. Thus, adding multiple regions to your configuration is identical to adding new life cycle stages. For example, instead of:

- Development
- Staging
- Canary
- Production

You might have:

- Development
- Staging
- Canary

- EastUS
- WestUS
- Europe
- Asia

Modeling this in the filesystem for configuration looks like:

```
frontend/
  staging/
    templates -> ../v3/
    parameters.yaml
  eastus/
    templates -> ../v1/
    parameters.yaml
  westus/
    templates -> ../v2/
    parameters.yaml
  ...
```

If you instead are using version control and tags, the filesystem would look like:

```
frontend/
  staging-parameters.yaml
  eastus-parameters.yaml
  westus-parameters.yaml
  templates/
    frontend-deployment.yaml
  ...
```

Using this structure, you would introduce a new tag for each region and use the file contents at that tag to deploy to that region.

Implementing Worldwide Deployment

Now that you have configurations for each region around the world, the question becomes how to update those various regions. One of the primary goals of using multiple regions is to ensure very high reliability and uptime. While it would be tempting to assume that cloud and datacenter outages are the primary causes of downtime, the truth is that outages are generally caused by new versions of software rolling out. Because of this, the key to a highly available system is limiting the effect, or "blast radius," of any change that you might make. Thus, as you roll out a version across a variety of regions, it makes sense to move carefully from region to region, and to validate and gain confidence in one region before moving on to the next.

Rolling out software across the world generally looks more like a workflow than a single declarative update: you begin by updating the version in staging to the latest version and then proceed through all regions until it is rolled out everywhere. But how should you structure the various regions, and how long should you wait to validate between regions?

 You can use tools such as GitHub Actions (*https://oreil.ly/BhWxi*) to automate the deployment workflow. They provide a declarative syntax to define your workflow and are also stored in source control.

To determine the length of time between rollouts to regions, consider the "mean time to smoke" for your software. This is the time it takes on average after a new release is rolled out to a region for a problem (if it exists) to be discovered. Obviously, each problem is unique and can take a varying amount of time to make itself known, and that is why you want to understand the *average* time. Managing software at scale is a business of probability, not certainty, so you want to wait for a time that makes the probability of an error low enough that you are comfortable moving on to the next region. Something like two to three times the mean time to smoke is probably a reasonable place to start, but it is highly variable depending on your application.

To determine the order of regions, it is important to consider the characteristics of various regions. For example, you are likely to have high-traffic regions and low-traffic regions. Depending on your application, you may have features that are more popular in one geographic area than another. All of these characteristics should be considered when putting together a release schedule. You likely want to begin by rolling out to a low-traffic region. This ensures that any early problems you catch are limited to an area of little impact. Though it is not a hard-and-fast rule, early problems are often the most severe, since they manifest quickly enough to be caught in the first region you roll out to. Thus, minimizing the impact of such problems on your customers makes sense. Next, roll out to a high-traffic region. Once you have successfully validated that your release works correctly via the low-traffic region, validate that it works correctly at scale. The only way to do this is to roll it out to a single high-traffic region. When you have successfully rolled out to both a low- and a high-traffic region, you may have confidence that your application can safely roll out everywhere. However, if there are regional variations, you may want to also test slowly across a variety of geographies before pushing your release more broadly.

When you put your release schedule together, it is important to follow it completely for every release, no matter how big or how small. Many outages have been caused by people accelerating releases, either to fix some other problem or because they believed it to be "safe."

Dashboards and Monitoring for Worldwide Deployments

It may seem an odd concept when you are developing at a small scale, but one significant problem that you will likely run into at a medium or large scale is having different versions of your application deployed to different regions. This can happen for a variety of reasons (such as, because a release has failed, been aborted, or had problems in a particular region), and if you don't track things carefully you can rapidly end up with an unmanageable snowflake of different versions deployed around the world. Furthermore, as customers inquire about fixes to bugs they are experiencing, a common question will become: "Is it deployed yet?"

Thus, it is essential to develop dashboards, which can tell you at a glance which version is running in which region, as well as alerting, which will fire when too many versions of your application are deployed. A best practice is to limit the number of active versions to no more than three: one testing, one rolling out, and one being replaced by the rollout. Any more active versions than this is asking for trouble.

Summary

This chapter provides guidance on how to manage a Kubernetes application through software versions, deployment stages, and regions around the world. It highlights the principles at the foundation of organizing your application: relying on the filesystem for organization, using code review to ensure quality changes, and relying on feature flags, or gates, to make it easy to incrementally add and remove functionality.

As with everything, the recipes in this chapter should be taken as inspiration, rather than absolute truth. Read the guidance, and find the mix of approaches that works best for the particular circumstances of your application. But keep in mind that in laying out your application for deployment, you are setting a process that you will likely have to live with for years.

Building Your Own Kubernetes Cluster

While Kubernetes is often experienced through the virtual world of public cloud computing, where the closest you get to your cluster is a web browser or a terminal, it can be a very rewarding experience to physically build a Kubernetes cluster on bare metal. Likewise, nothing compares to physically pulling the power or network on a node and watching how Kubernetes reacts to heal your application to convince you of its utility.

Building your own cluster might seem like both a challenging and an expensive effort, but fortunately it is neither. The ability to purchase low-cost, system-on-chip computer boards, as well as a great deal of work by the community to make Kubernetes easier to install, means that it is possible to build a small Kubernetes cluster in a few hours.

In the following instructions, we focus on building a cluster of Raspberry Pi machines, but with slight adaptations, the same instructions could be made to work with a variety of different single-board machines or any other computers you may have around.

Parts List

The first thing you need to do is assemble the pieces for your cluster. In all the examples here, we assume a four-node cluster. You could build a cluster of three nodes, or even a cluster of a hundred nodes if you wanted to, but four is a pretty good number. To start, you'll need to purchase (or scrounge) the various pieces needed to build the cluster.

Here is the shopping list, with some approximate prices as of the time of writing:

1. Four Raspberry Pi 4 machines with at least 2 GB of memory—$180
2. Four SDHC memory cards, at least 8 GB (buy high-quality ones!)—$30–50
3. Four 12-inch Cat. 6 Ethernet cables—$10
4. Four 12-inch USB-A to USB-C cables—$10
5. One 5-port 10/100 fast Ethernet switch—$10
6. One 5-port USB charger—$25
7. One Raspberry Pi stackable case capable of holding four Pis—$40 (or build your own)
8. One USB-to-barrel plug for powering the Ethernet switch (optional)—$5

The total for the cluster comes to about $300, which you can drop down to $200 by building a three-node cluster and skipping the case and the USB power cable for the switch (though the case and the cable really clean up the whole cluster).

One other note on memory cards: do not scrimp here. Low-end memory cards behave unpredictably and make your cluster really unstable. If you want to save some money, buy a smaller, high-quality card. High-quality 8 GB cards can be had for around $7 each online.

Once you have your parts, you're ready to move on to building the cluster.

 These instructions also assume that you have a device capable of flashing an SDHC card. If you do not, you will need to purchase a USB memory card reader/writer.

Flashing Images

The default Ubuntu 20.04 image supports Raspberry Pi 4 and also is a common operating system used by many Kubernetes clusters. The easiest way to install that is using the Raspberry Pi Imager provided by the Raspberry Pi project (*https://oreil.ly/4s8Wa*):

- macOS (*https://oreil.ly/g7Lzw*)
- Windows (*https://oreil.ly/Y7CD3*)
- Linux (*https://oreil.ly/u4YvC*)

Use the imager to write the Ubuntu 20.04 image onto each of your memory cards. Ubuntu may not be the default image choice in the imager, but you can select it as an option.

First Boot

The first thing to do is to boot just your API server node. Assemble your cluster, and decide which is going to be the API server node. Insert the memory card, plug the board into an HDMI output, and plug a keyboard into the USB port.

Next, attach the power to boot the board.

Log in at the prompt using the username **ubuntu** and the password **ubuntu**.

 The very first thing you should do with your Raspberry Pi (or any new device) is to change the default password. The default password for every type of install everywhere is well known by people who will misbehave given a default login to a system. This makes the internet less safe for everyone. Please change your default passwords!

Repeat these steps for each of the nodes in your cluster.

Setting Up Networking

The next step is to set up networking on the API server. Setting up networking for a Kubernetes cluster can be complicated. In the following example, we are setting up a network where a single machine is attached to the internet using wireless networking; this machine is also connected to a cluster network over wired Ethernet and provides a DHCP (Dynamic Host Configuration Protocol) server to provide a network address to the remaining nodes in the cluster. An illustration of this network is shown here:

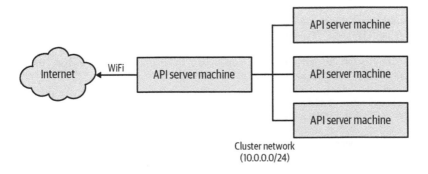

Decide which of your boards will host the API server and etcd. It's often easiest to remember which one this is by making it the top or bottom node in your stack, but some sort of label also works.

To do this, edit the file */etc/netplan/50-cloud-init.yaml*. If this file doesn't exist, you can create it. The contents of the file should look like:

```
network:
    version: 2
    ethernets:
        eth0:
            dhcp4: false
            dhcp6: false
            addresses:
            - '10.0.0.1/24'
            optional: true
    wifis:
        wlan0:
            access-points:
                <your-ssid-here>:
                    password: '<your-password-here>'
            dhcp4: true
            optional: true
```

This sets the main Ethernet interface to have the statically allocated address 10.0.0.1 and sets up the WiFi interface to connect to your local WiFi. You should then run `sudo netplan apply` to pick up these new changes.

Reboot the machine to claim the 10.0.0.1 address. You can validate that this is set correctly by running `ip addr` and looking at the address for the `eth0` interface. Also validate that the connection to the internet works correctly.

Next, we're going to install DHCP on this API server so it will allocate addresses to the worker nodes. Run:

```
$ apt-get install isc-dhcp-server
```

Then configure the DHCP server as follows (*/etc/dhcp/dhcpd.conf*):

```
# Set a domain name, can basically be anything
option domain-name "cluster.home";

# Use Google DNS by default, you can substitute ISP-supplied values here
option domain-name-servers 8.8.8.8, 8.8.4.4;

# We'll use 10.0.0.X for our subnet
subnet 10.0.0.0 netmask 255.255.255.0 {
    range 10.0.0.1 10.0.0.10;
    option subnet-mask 255.255.255.0;
    option broadcast-address 10.0.0.255;
    option routers 10.0.0.1;
}
```

```
default-lease-time 600;
max-lease-time 7200;
authoritative;
```

You may also need to edit */etc/default/isc-dhcp-server* to set the INTERFACES environment variable to eth0. Restart the DHCP server with `sudo systemctl restart isc-dhcp-server`. Now your machine should be handing out IP addresses. You can test this by hooking up a second machine to the switch via Ethernet. This second machine should get the address 10.0.0.2 from the DHCP server.

Remember to edit the */etc/hostname* file to rename this machine to node-1. To help Kubernetes do its networking, you also need to set up `iptables` so that it can see bridged network traffic. Create a file at */etc/modules-load.d/k8s.conf* that just contains `br_netfilter`. This will load the `br_netfilter` module into your kernel.

Next you need to enable some `systemctl` settings for network bridging and address translation (NAT) so that Kubernetes networking will work, and your nodes can reach the public internet. Create a file named */etc/sysctl.d/k8s.conf* and add:

```
net.ipv4.ip_forward=1
net.bridge.bridge-nf-call-ip6tables=1
net.bridge.bridge-nf-call-iptables=1
```

Then edit */etc/rc.local* (or the equivalent) and add `iptables` rules for forwarding from eth0 to wlan0 (and back):

```
iptables -t nat -A POSTROUTING -o wlan0 -j MASQUERADE
iptables -A FORWARD -i wlan0 -o eth0 -m state \
  --state RELATED,ESTABLISHED -j ACCEPT
iptables -A FORWARD -i eth0 -o wlan0 -j ACCEPT
```

At this point, the basic networking setup should be complete. Plug in and power up the remaining two boards (you should see them assigned the addresses 10.0.0.3 and 10.0.0.4). Edit the */etc/hostname* file on each machine to name them node-2 and node-3, respectively.

Validate this by first looking at */var/lib/dhcp/dhcpd.leases*, and then SSH to the nodes (remember again to change the default password first thing). Validate that the nodes can connect to the external internet.

Extra Credit

There are a couple of extra steps you can take that will make it easier to manage your cluster. The first is to edit */etc/hosts* on each machine to map the names to the right addresses. On each machine, add:

```
...
10.0.0.1 kubernetes
10.0.0.2 node-1
```

```
10.0.0.3 node-2
10.0.0.4 node-3
...
```

Now you can use those names when connecting to those machines.

The second is to set up passwordless SSH access. To do this, run `ssh-keygen` and then copy the *$HOME/.ssh/id_rsa.pub* file into */home/ubuntu/.ssh/authorized_keys* on node-1, node-2, and node-3.

Installing a Container Runtime

Before you can install Kubernetes, you need to install a container runtime. There are several possible runtimes you can use, but the most broadly adopted is `containerd` from Docker. `containerd` is provided by the standard Ubuntu package manager, but its version tends to lag a little bit. It's a little more work, but we recommend installing it from the Docker project itself.

The first step is to set up Docker as a repository for installing packages on your system:

```
# Add some prerequisites
sudo apt-get install ca-certificates curl gnupg lsb-release

# Install Docker's signing key
curl -fsSL https://download.docker.com/linux/ubuntu/gpg | sudo gpg --dearmor \
-o /usr/share/keyrings/docker-archive-keyring.gpg
```

As a final step, create the file */etc/apt/sources.list.d/docker.list* with the following contents:

```
deb [arch=arm64 signed-by=/usr/share/keyrings/docker-archive-keyring.gpg] \
https://download.docker.com/linux/ubuntu    focal stable
```

Now that you have installed the Docker package repository, you can install `contain erd.io` by running the following command. It is important to install `containerd.io`, not `containerd`, to get the Docker package instead of the default Ubuntu package:

```
sudo apt-get update; sudo apt-get install containerd.io
```

At this point, `containerd` is installed, but you need to configure it since the configuration supplied by the package won't work with Kubernetes:

```
containerd config default > config.toml
sudo mv config.toml /etc/containerd/config.toml

# Restart to pick up the config
sudo systemctl restart containerd
```

Now that you have a container runtime installed, you can move on to installing Kubernetes itself.

Installing Kubernetes

At this point you should have all nodes up with IP addresses and capable of accessing the internet. Now it's time to install Kubernetes on all of the nodes. Using SSH, run the following commands on all nodes to install the `kubelet` and `kubeadm` tools.

First, add the encryption key for the packages:

```
# curl -s https://packages.cloud.google.com/apt/doc/apt-key.gpg \
| sudo apt-key add -
```

Then add the repository to your list of repositories:

```
# echo "deb http://apt.kubernetes.io/ kubernetes-xenial main" \
  | sudo tee /etc/apt/sources.list.d/kubernetes.list
```

Finally, update and install the Kubernetes tools. This will also update all packages on your system for good measure:

```
# sudo apt-get update
$ sudo apt-get upgrade
$ sudo apt-get install -y kubelet kubeadm kubectl kubernetes-cni
```

Setting Up the Cluster

On the API server node (the one running DHCP and connected to the internet), run:

```
$ sudo kubeadm init --pod-network-cidr 10.244.0.0/16 \
        --apiserver-advertise-address 10.0.0.1 \
        --apiserver-cert-extra-sans kubernetes.cluster.home
```

Note that you are advertising your internal-facing IP address, not your external address.

Eventually, this will print out a command for joining nodes to your cluster. It will look something like:

```
$ kubeadm join --token=<token> 10.0.0.1
```

SSH onto each of the worker nodes in your cluster and run that command.

When all of that is done, you should be able to run this command and see your working cluster:

```
$ kubectl get nodes
```

Setting Up Cluster Networking

You have your node-level networking set up, but you still need to set up the Pod-to-Pod networking. Since all of the nodes in your cluster are running on the same physical Ethernet network, you can simply set up the correct routing rules in the host kernels.

The easiest way to manage this is to use the Flannel tool (*https://oreil.ly/ltaOv*) created by CoreOS and now supported by the Flannel project (*https://oreil.ly/RHfMH*). Flannel supports a number of different routing modes; we will use the `host-gw` mode. You can download an example configuration from the Flannel project page (*https://github.com/coreos/flannel*):

```
$ curl https://oreil.ly/kube-flannelyml \
  > kube-flannel.yaml
```

The default configuration that Flannel supplies uses `vxlan` mode instead. To fix this, open up that configuration file in your favorite editor; replace `vxlan` with `host-gw`.

You can also do this with the `sed` tool in place:

```
$ curl https://oreil.ly/kube-flannelyml \
  | sed "s/vxlan/host-gw/g" \
  > kube-flannel.yaml
```

Once you have your updated *kube-flannel.yaml* file, you can create the Flannel networking setup with:

```
$ kubectl apply -f kube-flannel.yaml
```

This will create two objects, a ConfigMap used to configure Flannel and a DaemonSet that runs the actual Flannel daemon. You can inspect these with:

```
$ kubectl describe --namespace=kube-system configmaps/kube-flannel-cfg
$ kubectl describe --namespace=kube-system daemonsets/kube-flannel-ds
```

Summary

At this point, you should have a working Kubernetes cluster operating on your Raspberry Pis. This can be great for exploring Kubernetes. Schedule some jobs, open up the UI, and try breaking your cluster by rebooting machines or disconnecting the network.

Index

startup probes, 57
state, 179
  benefits of reconciliation loop approach to,
    104
  desired state versus observed or current
    state, 104
  maintaining desired state in self-healing, 5
  managing cluster state via the filesystem,
    270
  viewing cluster state as source of truth, 270
StatefulSets, 188-196
  automating MongoDB cluster creation,
    192-194
  manually replicated MongoDB with State-
    fulSets, 189-191
  persistent volumes and, 195
  properties of, 189
static scanning, 241
storage
  cloud-based storage for replicated data
    store, 265
  consistency models, 264
  persistent data, 62
  storage field for CustomResourceDefinition,
    200
storage solutions, integrating with Kubernetes,
  179-196
  importing external services, 180-183
    limitation of external services, no health
      checking, 183
    services without selectors, 181
  Kubernetes-native storage with StatefulSets,
    188-196
    automating MongoDB cluster creation,
      192-194
    manually replicated MongoDB with
      StatefulSets, 189-191
    persistent volumes and StatefulSets, 195
    properties of StatefulSets, 189
  running reliable singletons, 183-187
    dynamic volume provisioning, 187
    MySQL singleton, 183-187
StorageClass objects, 187
strategies
  deployment, 117, 123-128
    slowing rollouts to ensure service health,
      126
  RollingUpdate, configuring for Daemon-
    Sets, 135

strong consistency, 264
subresources, testing authorization for, 168
synchronization, using volumes, 62
system containers, 18
system:unauthenticated group, 164, 167

T
tags
  deleting container images by tag name, 27
  introducing a development tag, 276
  kuard application example with target
    Docker registry, 25
  source control, 273
TCP, load balancing on, 263
tcpSocket health checks, 57
templates, parameterizing your application
  with, 277-279
Terminating state (Pods), 53
test environment, efficient creation with Kubernetes, 11
timeout for deployments, 127
TLS (Transport Layer Security)
  key and certificate for kuard application,
    154
  Mutual TLS (mTLS), 174
  serving in Ingress system, 99
tmpfs volumes, Secrets stored in, 155
traffic shaping, 175

U
UI (user interface) for Kubernetes, 37
unit testing, 262
Unix pipes, combining kubectl with, 40
user accounts, 164
utilization metric (resources), 58

V
validating admission controller, 202-206
  full definition, 202
  implementing to provide defaulting, 205
ValidatingWebhookConfiguration, 202, 246
validation, 202
valueFrom member, 152
velocity in software development, 2
version skew in multicluster deployments, 260
versioning
  in Kubernetes, 33
  managing periodic versions, 273

About the Authors

Brendan Burns began his career with a brief stint in the software industry followed by a PhD in robotics focused on motion planning for human-like robot arms. This was followed by a brief stint as a professor of computer science. Eventually, he returned to Seattle and joined Google, where he worked on web search infrastructure with a special focus on low-latency indexing. While at Google, he created the Kubernetes project with Joe Beda and Craig McLuckie. Brendan is currently a director of engineering at Microsoft Azure.

Joe Beda started his career at Microsoft working on Internet Explorer (he was young and naive). Throughout 7 years at Microsoft and 10 at Google, Joe has worked on GUI frameworks, real-time voice and chat, telephony, machine learning for ads, and cloud computing. Most notably, while at Google, Joe started the Google Compute Engine and, along with Brendan Burns and Craig McLuckie, created Kubernetes. Along with Craig, Joe founded and sold a startup (Heptio) to VMware, where he is now a principal engineer. Joe proudly calls Seattle home.

Kelsey Hightower is a principal developer advocate at Google working on Google's Cloud Platform. He has helped develop and refine many Google Cloud products including Google's Kubernetes Engine, Cloud Functions, and Apigee's API Gateway. Kelsey spends most of his time with executives and developers spanning the global Fortune 1000, helping them understand and leverage Google technologies and platforms to grow their businesses. Kelsey is a huge open source contributor, maintaining projects that aid software developers and operations professionals in building and shipping cloud native applications. He is an accomplished author and keynote speaker, and was the inaugural winner of the CNCF Top Ambassador award for helping bootstrap the Kubernetes community. He is a mentor and technical advisor, helping founders turn their visions into reality.

Lachlan Evenson is a principal program manager on the open source team at Azure. He is an active member of the Kubernetes community and has served on the steering committee and as a release lead. Lachlan has deep operational knowledge of many cloud native projects and spends his days building and contributing to open source projects in the cloud native ecosystem.

Colophon

The animal on the cover of *Kubernetes: Up and Running* is an Atlantic white-sided dolphin (*Lagenorhynchus acutus*). As its name suggests, the white-sided dolphin has light patches on its sides and a light gray stripe that runs from above the eye to below the dorsal fin. It is among the largest species of oceanic dolphins, and ranges throughout the North Atlantic Ocean. It prefers open water, so it is not often seen from the shore, but will readily approach boats and perform various acrobatic feats.

White-sided dolphins are social animals commonly found in large groups (known as pods) of about 60 individuals, though the size will vary depending on location and the availability of food. Dolphins often work as a team to harvest schools of fish, but they also hunt individually. They primarily search for prey using echolocation, which is similar to sonar. The bulk of this marine mammal's diet consists of herring, mackerel, and squid.

The average lifespan of the white-sided dolphin is between 22–27 years. Females only mate every 2–3 years, and the gestation period is 11 months. Calves are typically born in June or July, and are weaned after 18 months. Dolphins have very great intelligence and display complex social behaviors like grieving, cooperation, and problem solving, due to their high brain-to-body ratio (the highest among aquatic mammals).

Many of the animals on O'Reilly covers are endangered; all of them are important to the world.

The cover illustration is by Karen Montgomery, based on a black and white engraving from *British Quadrupeds*. The cover fonts are Gilroy Semibold and Guardian Sans. The text font is Adobe Minion Pro; the heading font is Adobe Myriad Condensed; and the code font is Dalton Maag's Ubuntu Mono.

Milton Keynes UK
Ingram Content Group UK Ltd.
UKHW050435041024
449169UK00002B/5

9 781098 110208